Emergency Planning and Response for Libraries, Archives and Museums

Emma Dadson

THE SCARECROW PRESS, INC.
Lanham, Maryland • Toronto • Plymouth UK
2012

SCARECROW PRESS, INC.

Published in the United States of America
by Scarecrow Press, Inc.
A wholly owned subsidiary of
The Rowman & Littlfield Publishing Group, Inc.
4501 Forbes Boulevard, Suite 200, Lanham, Maryland 20706
www.scarecrowpress.com

Estover Road
Plymouth PL6 7PY
United Kingdom

ISBN 978-0-81088-756-5

First published in the United Kingdom by Facet Publishing, 2012.
This simultaneous US edition published by Scarecrow Press, Inc.

The paper used in this publication meets the minimum requirements of
American National Standard for Information Sciences—Permanence of Paper for
Printed Library Materials, ANSI Z39.48-1992.

Typeset from author's files in 10/13 pt Palatino Linotype and Myriad Pro by
Flagholme Publishing Services.
Manufactured in the United States of America.

Contents

Foreword

Disasters make us acutely aware of just how vulnerable our cultural heritage can be. Natural or man-made, disasters remind us, as cultural stewards, of the importance of an up-to-date emergency plan. When a disaster has not directly affected our library, our museum, our archives, we breathe a sigh of relief, and the urgency to create a plan is superseded by more pressing day-to-day responsibilities. But events don't have to be catastrophic to have a profound impact on our institutions. Emergencies such as a roof leak or burst pipe can easily spiral out of control and turn into a large-scale disaster if we do not know how to respond properly – if we do not have a plan.

Heritage Preservation is a national nonprofit in Washington, DC, that has identified threats to collections and has responded with practical and pioneering solutions since 1973. While Heritage Preservation's focus is on preserving the cultural heritage of the United States, its initiatives resonate around the world. In 2005, Heritage Preservation published *A Public Trust at Risk: the Heritage Health Index Report on the State of America's Collections*, the first comprehensive survey to assess the condition and preservation needs of US collections. The Heritage Health Index found that 80% of US collecting institutions do not have a written emergency plan with staff trained to carry it out, putting 2.6 billion items at risk. The global news stories about cultural heritage institutions that falter and fail in the wake of a disaster suggest that this distressing trend is not unique to the USA.

When cultural stewards are asked why they do not have an emergency plan, they often reply, 'It won't happen here.' This response is often followed by the false notion that if something catastrophic were to happen, there is nothing that can be done to lessen damage. *Emergency Planning and Response for Libraries, Archives and Museums* refutes those assumptions and provides you with the tools you need to create an effective institutional emergency plan. We can lessen the effects of disaster by ensuring the safety of people, by protecting our records and collections, and by taking care of our facilities.

And when, not if, disaster strikes, knowing how to respond can spell the difference between success and failure.

Large or small, natural or man-made, emergencies remind us of the importance of protecting collections from disaster. Taking that first step – deciding to create a disaster plan – is empowering. While the ultimate goal is to produce a written document, the greatest benefit of emergency planning is the discussion and collaboration amongst staff and with emergency services personnel. By creating your plan, you will be working together to protect and preserve the cultural heritage that defines your institution, your community, and your nation.

Lori Foley
Vice President, Emergency Programs
Heritage Preservation
Washington, DC

Preface

This book aims to help those working in libraries, archives and museums to fast-track the composition of emergency plans, or, for those with existing plans, to provide a new perspective and insight into real disaster recovery situations, which can be used to refresh and improve current procedures. The principal aim is that any plan will operate as effectively as possible if ever put into action in a real emergency situation.

Emergency plans serve to preserve collections, reduce damage to buildings and in turn minimize the disruption to service provision if there is an incident, all while safeguarding staff and visitors. Through looking at real experiences of plan activation, the book will examine what content is really necessary, based on the author's professional experience in disaster recovery over 14 years in the UK and Ireland. In this role, hundreds of emergency response operations have been observed, providing a unique perspective on the elements of successful plans and common pitfalls.

This book will convey these critical plan elements, suggest how they can be succinctly and effectively presented, and explain the rationale behind the recommendations. The book will help those writing and implementing plans to consider tactics that might be necessary in different types and scales of incident. The details of emergency procedures aspire to be straightforward, sensible and safe, and should work effectively in the challenging circumstances of fire and flood recovery situations. The content should be flexible, and adaptive to the demands of minor and major incidents. Those who may benefit from reading this book range from staff in high-profile institutions of international renown through to those in volunteer-run independent institutions. The aim is to show how effective emergency planning is accessible and achievable for all.

Acknowledgements

I would first like to thank Sarah Busby for bringing the concept to me and for her support at the beginning of this project. Jennifer Hall at Facet Publishing has also been extremely helpful in the final phases of writing, as has Lin Franklin. Additionally I would like to thank all those who have contributed case studies and comments to the book, particularly Lori Foley, Debbie Lane, Lucy Waitt, Grant Collins, Linda Barron, Rory McLeod, Tokuda Seiko, Lynn Campbell, Deborah Shorley, Susan Maddock, Dianne Van der Reyden, Diane Vogt-O'Connor, Dr Richard Heseltine, Kathryn Riddington, Tanya Pollard and Sharon Robinson. Thank you also to Susie Bioletti, Kristie Short-Traxler and Gillian Boal for putting me in touch with some of the international contributors. I am very grateful to my employer Harwell Document Restoration Services, most particularly Kathryn Rodgers and Ken McKenzie, for their support and also to Harwell's Priority Users who have provided such an insight over the years to disaster recovery projects. Finally I would like to thank Patricia, Simon, Sophie and Thomas for their patience and encouragement throughout the last year.

CHAPTER 1

Introduction

A medical records store with unique, irreplaceable patient information in hard copy; a national museum whose galleries and stores are brimming with items of cultural significance; a public record office, home to a unique historical archive; a law firm, with wills and property deeds in its strongroom; a university library, an essential tool for students and academic staff in their studies and research: these institutions include library, archive and museum services, together with historic houses, but also encompass those engaged in the information services field such as records management services. All differ in scale, their core mission, staffing and client-base, but are linked by the potential impact of an emergency incident such as a fire or flood affecting the collections they store. Objects may either be unique, culturally significant or extremely financially valuable, and therefore impossible or extremely costly to replace. In the case of records and modern library collections, damage or destruction of these items may significantly disrupt service provision, threaten significant reputational damage or breach regulatory requirements.

Emergency response must be prompt, well organized and competent in order to protect collections, facilitating salvage and restoration at the earliest opportunity. The question is whether it is necessary to have a *plan* for such an emergency to ensure an adequate response. Can professional, capable individuals source the solutions required dynamically on the day to minimize damage without preparation? In an age where an internet search will list a dozen plumbers who would be able to repair a leaking pipe, or find websites detailing procedures for dealing with wet microfiche, is an emergency plan redundant? Surely common sense, a phone and internet access is all that is needed to resolve problems as they emerge on the day?

Why is a plan important?
More effective response through pre-incident planning
Experiences from countless emergency salvage operations in such institutions

indicate that disaster recovery is anything but straightforward. Pre-incident preparation is critical to maximize the success of salvage if the limited time after the incident before which existing damage will rapidly deteriorate can be used to greatest effect. Failure to respond quickly to an incident involving leaking of water, and organize staff and equipment to control and isolate the source of the damage, will potentially result in a leak of a longer duration, resulting in a much larger overall quantity of damaged material, which could have been avoided through quicker action. Simply knowing where stop-valves are so that the flow of water through to burst pipes can be halted could potentially prevent thousands of litres of water discharging, thus avoiding damage to the building fabric, environment, collections within and interruption to the public service.

A plan will avoid such situations as it can provide information that will be critical to successful incident control, which will ultimately save time, and thus avoid the quantity and severity of damage from increasing. The minimization of secondary damage such as mould growth can also be achieved through effective emergency planning. Secondary damage does not appear immediately but worsens over time if interventive action is not taken. This is explained further in Chapter 6. Time is limited and a plan will ensure available time is used as effectively as possible.

Figure 1.1 shows severe mould growth after water-damaged records had been left untreated for three weeks.

Figure 1.1 *Severe mould growth after water-damaged records had been left untreated for three weeks* © *Harwell Document Restoration Services*

Without a plan, the information, resources and external support you may require become apparent quickly, but institutions may find that they are one step behind other people in the same situation locally who are better prepared. This is particularly apparent in catastrophic incidents or claims surges, affecting multiple buildings in an area, all of which will require pumps, emergency lighting, security and safety equipment. The best prepared get those resources first, whereas those without preparation have to wait.

Without a plan, there is also an assumption that all key personnel will be available to assist and function as normal. Emergency situations can be extremely stressful and a plan provides a crutch, prompting individuals who may feel very overwhelmed with an action list, a starting point. Jim Duff, a conservator from the University of Manchester, recalls 'having an established in-house disaster plan was a great benefit and provided clear guidelines at a time of stress'. Additionally, without a plan, there is an assumption that catalogues, vital records and reference tools will be accessible. This may not necessarily be the case. Emergencies have a knack of happening at the least convenient time, when key staff are on holiday or new in post, as demonstrated in two of the case studies in Chapter 2.

Failure to plan is a false economy

Effective emergency response is difficult without a plan. However, Matthews, Smith and Knowles (2009), reporting the results of the 2005 study of 635 libraries, archives and museums in the UK, 'Safeguarding Heritage at Risk', found that a significant proportion of libraries, archives and museums have no written procedure: 28% archives, 26% libraries and 14% museums. The reason for this may be that the institution considers the risk of an incident occurring as low, but most often the reasons cited are a lack of time and a concern over how much planning and preventative measures might cost. One principal aim of this book is to show that the plan process can be fast-tracked and is often much less onerous than initially feared. Budgeting only becomes a major issue for the purchase of emergency stockpile equipment, which will be discussed in Chapter 7, and costs need not be excessive. An effective plan should also prevent damage from escalating, which will save institutions significant sums of money if there is an incident. Failure to plan is a false economy.

Obligation to plan for irreplaceable collections

Should an emergency incident occur, causing devastating damage to a collection, which the staff were ill-equipped to salvage, the phrase 'I didn't have time' would sound very hollow. Time must be freed to ensure plans are composed. Some have argued this is a moral obligation of heads of service for irreplaceable collections. Indeed there is a UNESCO accord, the Radenci Declaration (1998), which states:

> All institutions caring for the cultural heritage . . . should integrate risk preparedness and management within their operations to avoid loss or damage in both normal and exceptional times . . . . The goal is to avoid loss or damage to cultural heritage in the event of emergencies by improving prevention, preparedness, response and recovery measures. It is achieved by developing, implementing and monitoring strategies which assess and reduce risk, improve response capacity and ensure co-operation of all relevant parties in local, national and international emergency management.

The declaration goes on to require that adequate funding is provided, good working relationships with the emergency services are fostered, manuals of emergency procedures are produced, emergency supplies are provided and training is held regularly. Emergency planning is essential and it is incumbent on those with responsibility for cultural heritage to ensure appropriate measures are in place. This process need not, with appropriate support and guidance, become unmanageable and unwieldy, but rather be completed efficiently, quickly and sustainably, in a manner which will maximize the chances of successful implementation in real emergency situations.

Environment of increasing risks and threats

Those working in libraries, archives and museums are well aware of the importance of the collections for which they are responsible and the requirement to protect them from damage. Standards exist, such as BS5454, which provide guidance on how to minimize threats to collections from perils such as water and fire, as well as long-term issues associated with poor environmental conditions. Collection custodians strive to ensure that the building environment poses minimal risks to their assets as far as is practically achievable within building constraints and budgets.

Nevertheless incidents occur and a residual risk will remain. The abovementioned study 'Safeguarding Heritage at Risk' found 30% of respondents in the last five years had suffered an incident they would categorize as a disaster, of which 21% had suffered more than one. Water damage accounted for 68% of incidents, with other perils much less common, notably fire at 11%. Residual risks persist because of external factors that cannot be controlled and the capacity for human error. A large proportion of water-damage recovery projects handled at Harwell Document Restoration Services are attributable to building contractors' human error, where there is no intention of causing collection damage, but their presence certainly heightens the risk of escapes of water through the nature of their activity. An external contractor may not be aware of the nature of the collection, nor consider fully the repercussions and implications of even a small leak. There may also be impacts as a result of bad housekeeping and bad practice in neighbouring institutions.

Figure 1.2 shows damage to an archive store caused by a fire in the neighbouring workshop of a different organization.

There are some, although thankfully few, examples of arson and deliberate damage to organizations in the heritage and information services sector. Two UK libraries have been significantly affected by deliberate damage: a library store was affected during the riots in Salford in 2011 and an arsonist attacked a library in Kent in 2005, both causing damage to thousands of books. National institutions are high profile and potential terrorist targets, and higher education libraries have been targets for civil disobedience such as occupations.

Figure 1.2 *Damage to an archive store caused by a fire in the neighbouring building of a different organization* © *Harwell Document Restoration Services*

In addition to these risks, there is the background of a changing climate and the impact of extreme weather on buildings. The Intergovernmental Panel on Climate Change's 2007 report (Pachauri and Reisinger, 2007) states:

> There is *high agreement* and *much evidence* that with current climate change mitigation policies and related sustainable development practices, global greenhouse gas emissions will continue to grow over the next few decades. Altered frequencies and intensities of extreme weather, together with sea level rise, are expected to have mostly adverse effects on natural and human systems.

Many buildings were not designed or constructed to cope with such extremes, heightening the risk of damage through water ingress, particularly where collections are housed at ground level or below.

Figure 1.3 shows flash flooding as a result of a month's typical rainfall falling in three hours.

Definition and terminology

For these reasons, planning is essential to protect vital, irreplaceable records and cultural heritage. There is a question though as to what kind of plan is required: there are many terms currently used in public and private spheres, which all broadly refer to the procedures an organization will follow if there is an emergency. 'Disaster planning' was historically the term most widely used in the heritage sector in particular, but in recent years 'emergency planning' has superseded this. The content of such documents is broadly the same, but avoidance of the word 'disaster' is seen as more positive and, indeed, disastrous situations can be averted if emergency plans are successfully implemented.

The term 'emergency planning' outside the heritage sector usually refers to the 'blue-light' phase of an incident. Indeed only incidents sufficiently serious to involve the

Figure 1.3 *Flash flooding in the city centre of Londonderry in July as a result of a month's typical rainfall falling in three hours*
© Harwell Document Restoration Services

emergency services would qualify as an emergency in other sectors. It also refers to wider civic response to major incidents such as the aftermath of an earthquake, flood or other natural disaster. 'Crisis planning' is another phrase that is used for response to emergency situations, although it usually typically refers to the communications sphere and public relations issues generated in such circumstances.

'Business continuity planning' is a term used in the commercial field for incidents that cannot be managed through normal working procedures and which pose a serious threat to an organization through injury to staff, damage to buildings, or an interruption to systems and IT. The scope of business continuity planning is discussed more in Chapter 9, where it will be argued that libraries, archives and museums must include business continuity strategies in their planning. Where heritage and information services organizations differ is that small-scale incidents, outside the scope of a business continuity plan, would require a prompt and effective response, and must therefore be captured within the plan. Dealing with damage to a shelf of books or files may not threaten business as usual, but if those are valuable, irreplaceable or contain vital business information, effective response is required.

Definition and scope of plans

All these elements should appear in emergency procedures for libraries, archives and museums. For the purposes of this book, the term 'emergency plan' will be used, which is intended to encompass the procedures to 'any incident which threatens human safety and/or damages or threatens to damage or destroy an institution's buildings, collections, contents, facilities or services' (Matthews and Eden, 1996). This is the definition of 'disaster' that was used in the abovementioned 2005 study 'Safeguarding Heritage at Risk' (Matthews, Smith and Knowles, 2009). This definition works effectively because it is broad, encompassing not just the collection, but also the building, the service provision and most importantly the people.

Practical disaster recovery experience has shown that although many emergency plans work effectively for collections salvage, they are less successful in dealing with the wider implications of the incident, such as damage to the building infrastructure, impact on services and communications. The focus is often narrowly on preservation of collections. The reason for this is that often the impetus for writing plans comes from collections, curatorial or conservation staff whose main concern is for the objects. In major incidents, however, response is much more complex as, while collection salvage is important, many other issues must be concurrently considered and a more holistic approach is required.

Those institutions whose existing document is not known as an 'emergency plan' need not amend the title provided that all aspects of people, collections, services and buildings are considered in the content. Indeed, for those organizations embedded in a larger institution such as a university or local authority it makes sense to adopt the corporate term so that plans are appropriately integrated and fully used in major incidents.

Will your existing plan work in practice?

Where organizations already have emergency plans, theoretically the hard work is done and dealing with emergency situations should be simple. However, many users find that plans do not work as effectively as they had hoped when they are required. Ostensibly the boxes are ticked: priority lists, salvage guidance notes, telephone numbers of key staff and suppliers are provided, but real emergency response is chaotic and the plan's performance a disappointment.

Implementing an emergency plan is not as simple as following a recipe, as common sense and an element of interpretation are required. Because of their scale and related strained resources, salvage will be delayed and damage to collections will worsen unavoidably in some situations. Even with a good and well functioning emergency plan, response and recovery is not easy work: it is potentially physically demanding, unpleasant and upsetting. However, some plans either fail completely or only work in a limited way in a real emergency. Why do some plans work ineffectively in real fire or flood situations?

Plans are not used properly

When an emergency plan is not actually implemented in an emergency it can be extremely frustrating for the plan author. In all likelihood, it contains good quality information but, through a lack of communication about its existence or location, response is made without reference to the plan. Plans are sometimes used initially, but if the content or layout is not user-friendly, users cannot find the information they need quickly and disregard the plan. If the last time someone looked at their plan was over two years ago, its efficacy will be compromised. Training, testing of the quality of the content and maintaining that process would have averted this scenario. This outcome can also be the result of senior staff not being involved properly in the planning process. They have no ownership of or trust in the content of the plan and therefore choose to operate in their own way in an emergency. This underlines the importance of gaining buy-in to the plan, as explained elsewhere in this book.

Plans do not tell users what they can and should do

Some plans amount to little more than lists of information that will be useful in an emergency but give no guidance on how such information should be used. Salvage guidance notes, priority lists and lists of equipment in disaster kits are all important but they provide no structure detailing how to organize the salvage operation, or how roles and responsibilities should be allocated. Successful emergency response relies on a collaborative approach with staff working together in clearly defined roles, with guidance on what they need to organize and what they are authorized to do. Failure to provide firm guidance can cause dithering. The plan must give clear guidance on emergency expenditure – what is permissible and if limits are exceeded who should be approached to release funds? The cost of hiring a dehumidifier for two weeks, for example, is a tiny fraction of the potential cost and operational disruption triggered by a mass mould outbreak because an area has not properly dried out. Roles and responsibilities are discussed in Chapter 3.

Plans are inflexible

Major incident disaster recovery is demanding even for well prepared organizations simply because of the scale of the incident. As is explained in Chapter 6, salvage techniques appropriate for small-scale incidents can be totally counter-productive in the context of a much bigger incident given time constraints. A flexible approach is required so that organizations can manage a range of incidents effectively, which requires training and confidence among the team of staff managing the incident. Plans must consider the spectrum of possible incidents and be scalable and flexible. Similarly they must be resilient for the absence of key individuals. Emergency incidents often happen when it is least convenient and if plans presuppose that certain individuals may be available in person to deal with the situation there is a strong possibility of the plan failing due to the absence of that key person.

Plans are not integrated

Over-reliance on other departments within a parent organization (such as the wider public authority or academic institution – see Chapter 3 for more on this), most particularly facilities, can cause problems too, particularly in the context of a surge event where multiple buildings are affected in your area. The level of support from a parent organization depends on the assessment of managers in that organization of your importance within its wider interests and priorities, and they may not afford you the level of resource you had expected. Managers of organizations have to target limited resources on high priority areas. Those in local authorities prioritize people before they consider heritage or other assets. Pumps and dehumidifiers, which will be in limited supply, are more likely to be targeted at civic infrastructure such as power sub-stations and medical centres than towards public libraries and archives, and justifiably so. Pre-incident negotiation can help ensure awareness is raised about the nature of collections, but inevitably they will not be the top priority in an incident where human safety is threatened. If the primary source cannot help, what is the back-up plan?

A poor relationship with the facilities service is immensely problematic for incident response, as well as overall risk management. Anecdotal evidence in training and real salvage situations indicates that many working in the heritage and information services organizations find the relationship with facilities challenging. Often this relates to a lack of mutual understanding. The library service must understand the number of sites the facilities section is responsible for, as well as budgetary and resource constraints, but the facilities section must understand the special circumstances and speed of response required for an incident involving objects that will deteriorate quickly if there is fire or flood damage. This is discussed in Chapter 10.

It is not uncommon for plans for large organizations to be very thorough for the main repository but to fail to cater for satellite sites, such as off-site stores and branch libraries. An integrated approach is essential at all locations where collections are kept and from which services operate.

Plans lack testing and training

Above all, a lack of testing of the plan content and staff training thwart effective response. Testing a plan and rehearsing its procedures will usually throw up minor niggles, which are much more easily rectified in a dry run. In one training scenario, the location given in the plan for the emergency kit was outdated, and when eventually it was found it could not be moved as it was too heavy. This problem was rectified immediately and shortly afterwards a real flood occurred. Without the training, the response to the flood would have been impaired. Training in the procedures will give greater confidence to individuals in their role. Although this does not make disaster response easy, it is less overwhelming if the issues have been considered in advance, rather than first considered in the midst of a real emergency. Even good quality plans do not work well if individuals cannot navigate them rapidly to find the information they need. Make an effort to provide a user-friendly, intuitive layout; the more familiar the plan is to the user, the more effectively it will be used.

The remainder of this book provides guidance on how to avoid these pitfalls by showing what information should be available in a good emergency plan, how to present it to best effect, how to communicate the content of the plan effectively to potential users and ensure their proficiency in its application, and finally to ensure the plan is properly maintained.

Writing an effective plan – how to use this book

The type of plan required will be one that ensures the following:

- Problems are identified and reported to the appropriate people quickly.
- Staff and user safety is prioritized throughout.
- There is swift control and containment of damage to building and collection.
- Service disruption to users is minimized.
- Affected stock is salvaged, treated for damage and reinstated.
- Building fabric is restored.
- There is a return to business as usual as quickly as possible.

Figure 1.4 on the next page is a possible template for the contents page of a disaster plan.

Using templates

Each of the elements listed in Figure 1.4 is discussed in the book as indicated. Some checklists are also included. These are obviously generic and will require adaptation to specific set-ups, but they broadly outline key issues to be considered and indicate how response can be managed safely and sensibly. Remember that for effective planning, it is not possible merely to fill in the blanks of a template or to ask colleagues in other institutions to see their plan and copy their structure and content with only cursory adaptation. One size does not fit all. Such plans are not tailored and rarely work in practice: your facilities team may have a different remit; you may hold different types of object and more or fewer items in total; you may have entirely different working patterns and staff dynamics. They may have a different strategy, and, while it is useful to compare their approach, plans should be written as bespoke documents.

The guidance in this book must be applied and adapted to the specifics of your own organization: some organizations may find that the emphasis on business continuity is unnecessary for them; others may choose to take emphasis away from salvage onto business continuity because of differing core missions and priorities. Each element should be considered carefully,

Title page (Chapter 9)
1. **Introduction** (Chapter 9)
2. **Emergency Management Team (EMT) contact information** (Chapter 3)
3. **Initial procedures for emergencies – during working hours** (Chapter 4)
 out-of-hours procedures (Chapter 4)
 incident assessment and control instructions (Chapter 4/5)
4. **Salvage and incident management tasks for the Emergency Management Team:**
 Emergency Response Manager (Chapter 3)
 Collections Salvage Manager (Chapter 3)
 Building Recovery Manager (Chapter 3)
 Service Continuity Manager (Chapter 3)
Appendices (all discussed in Chapter 7 except where indicated)
 Personnel contact lists
 Priority lists
 Floor plans
 Emergency equipment
 External suppliers and utility companies
 Salvage and treatment guidance by object (Chapter 6)
 Risk assessment form (Chapter 5)
 Prepared press statement (Chapter 9)
 Damage record form (Chapter 6)
 Incident log form
 Accommodation and sites for salvage
 Instructions for isolating utilities
 Insurance cover details
 Contacts directory
 Business continuity – business impact analysis and targets (Chapter 9)
 Incident report form

Figure 1.4 *Possible template for the contents page of a disaster plan*

however, as the content included is included on the basis of practical experience. Nothing listed above is suggested arbitrarily: somebody has needed this information before in an emergency and benefited from its inclusion or regretted its omission.

It is important not to be put off by how much material is listed above and grow concerned about how much time it will take. The section that requires most work is the selection of priorities for salvage and deciding on how your Emergency Management Team is composed. Everything else can be achieved through the adaptation and fine-tuning of guidance notes in this book (for example identifying suitable contractors from suggested lists here using online directories, filling in telephone numbers and staff, and fine-tuning material such as floor plans probably already in existence).

It is possible to have a plan that has a lot of information in it which is nevertheless clear, succinct and easy to use. Remember that access to office space may not be possible. Sometimes a plan with fewer sections and pages may seem attractive, but critical information may be missing when required, and the layout may be too compacted to be user-friendly. An emergency plan should be a single point of reference, well laid out and thoughtfully presented, prompting individuals about what to do and providing critical information that may not otherwise be accessible. The remainder of this book will demonstrate how this can be done.

Project management

The process of plan composition or redraft can become protracted if a timetable is not established for completion at the outset. Although with appropriate support none of the tasks involved is especially difficult, the process of gathering information can be time-consuming and frustrating. Momentum can easily be lost, draining initial motivation to complete the plan and ensure it is a plan tailored to the individual organization. In these circumstances the plans can linger in incomplete draft for months, sometimes years. Alternatively, through frustration at lack of progress and support, plans can be completed hurriedly with key content lacking and poor layout. Such plans rarely work well in practice.

Getting initial buy-in

In some organizations, the planning process is deferred until complete buy-in to the process has been achieved with all senior management. This is often the case in the corporate sector where the first step in the business continuity 'life-cycle', designed to ensure that the business continuity concept is embedded in business practice, is for the executive of the organization to write a policy document, endorsing the process and requiring staff at all levels to participate in planning.

It is important to gain the buy-in of a group of people to endorse the plan if the plan is to be used in a real emergency. Without this ratification, the plan may not be used in an emergency and prove a paper exercise, which does not translate to any meaningful contribution to disaster recovery. A formal policy may not be necessary for libraries, archives and museums but can be a useful tool if keen, committed individuals find they are simply not being provided with information and input when required and top-down support would be helpful. Even if a policy is not deemed necessary, meeting senior colleagues before the work commencing to garner their support will smooth the information-gathering phase of plan composition. As will be discussed in Chapter 3, senior managers are likely to be allocated an emergency role. At the beginning of the planning process, the Emergency Management Team exercise described on page 46 can quickly convey why their involvement is essential. Inviting speakers from similar institutions that have suffered real incidents also demonstrates how a major emergency could happen and provides some context to the planning process.

Who should write the plan?

The question remains as to who draws the plan together into an initial draft. In some organizations the research and composition are completed by one individual, for sign-off and approval by senior management. In other organizations, the tasks are delegated to a larger group. Each approach has its advantages: one person focusing on the task may result in a faster completion than a larger group with other competing priorities, but a collections manager will not necessarily have the detailed knowledge to write guidance for health and safety, or business continuity procedures which other colleagues would have. A group approach may mean that the persons who would ultimately be responsible for tasks draft the procedures, which may result in less iteration, but often results in a more protracted composition period.

It may be that some individuals cannot contribute time to writing the plan, but they must at the very least review draft content and take ownership of the elements that involve them. Even if one person co-ordinates the information gathering and collation of the plan, this is made much easier if colleagues elsewhere within the service and in other departments such as facilities understand why the information is required. The profile of the plan will be better and the ownership of senior staff in its content will be greater. On balance, it is often best if one person co-ordinates the planning process and composes the document, but interviews and involves all those likely to be involved in an emergency process during this time, and that their sign-off is sought for all sections pertinent to them. The whole process requires the input and stewardship of the senior manager of the organization to ensure the composition process is kept to a reasonable schedule.

Schedule

Having agreed the content and author(s), set deadlines. The priority tasks to begin with are to determine:

- the Emergency Management Team and contact information

- priority lists
- procedures for isolating utilities
- external suppliers (especially salvage suppliers).

During the composition process, risks remain. Consider what information would be most crucial if an incident were to happen tomorrow and prioritize the completion of these sections.

The second advised phase will be to draft instructions on what to do if there are emergencies and to commence discussions with external agencies and departments from whom you'll need support. Development of these relationships may require some time before they come to fruition. At this stage, to establish rapport with local fire services personnel invite them to meet you and tour the building (see Chapter 4, and the Royal Horticultural Society case study) and discuss issues such as insurance, finance arrangements for suppliers, and business continuity objectives. Start the process of procuring emergency kit and recruit additional personnel to assist in emergencies beyond the Emergency Management Team.

The final stage will be to fine-tune the roles and responsibilities for the EMT for salvage and incident management, and adapt material such as salvage instructions, filling in the remainder of the blanks. Many plans copy and paste this information into their plans, but do not remove instruction on object types they do not retain, or add in those object types they do have but were not included on the copied list. Minor niggles like this can become magnified in implementation as they add to the size of the plan and can undermine its quality and credibility.

CHAPTER 2

Case studies

In this chapter a variety of case studies highlight the importance of preparedness and the potential severity of the challenges in emergency response situations, and how particular problems have been overcome in the planning process. They emanate from libraries, archives and museums from around the globe, which have faced incidents including earthquakes, fires and floods. Their experiences and learning points convey the reason why the emergency planning content outlined in this book is essential.

CASE STUDY: Flood recovery at the State Library, Queensland, Australia

Grant Collins, Linda Barron and Rory McLeod, State Library of Queensland, Australia

Context

At 4 pm on Tuesday 11 January 2011, the State Library of Queensland's clients and staff evacuated the building after days of torrential rain had fallen in the regional catchments of South-East Queensland resulting in flood waters rising from the Brisbane River. The State Library of Queensland (SLQ) is located directly adjacent to and overlooks the Brisbane River. The river levels rose to 4.46 metres resulting in the basement level of the State Library being inundated. The Counter Disaster Plan (CDP) was implemented with relocation of collections from the basement to upper building levels before the building evacuation.

Much of the Brisbane Central Business District (CBD) and low-lying river areas were inundated; this included the State Library's loading dock, which was covered by 1.9 metres of river water. The State Library building was closed for a month while the car park was closed for several months. This led to significant disruption while recovery was carried out to power substations,

Figure 2.1 *Clearing out the sediment left after the waters receded in the library's loading bay*   © *State Library of Queensland*

the river pump room, the State Library of Queensland loading dock, lower level staff areas, audio-visual store, cold storage vaults, quarantine facility and the suite of general storerooms all located on the lower level (see Figure 2.1). From 7 February, staff made a graduated return to the building to prepare for a 'soft' opening to the public on 16 February and a full publicized opening for the weekend of 19–20 February.

Once flood waters reduced it was clear that this was a disaster that had affected the building infrastructure and library services to clients became a business continuity challenge. Having a detailed and tested Business Continuity Plan (BCP) was our greatest asset. The BCP is activated once we reach the maximum outage levels of any service or system. We had spent considerable time and energy developing and testing our BCP. The plan included detailed descriptions of evacuation and salvage procedures including individual plans for critical systems. In addition the BCP included the nominated members of the Crisis Management Team (CMT) and their backups.

Before the flood – evacuation

On the day before the river levels inundated the State Library, the CDP was activated. This was triggered by alarms in the river pump room indicating that levels were on the rise. It included the evacuation of large quantities of photographic materials from the cold storage vaults and collections in the quarantine facility located on Level 0. The SLQ Disaster Recovery Coordinator coordinated 40 staff to relocate all collections from the cold stores on the basement level to the upper level cold stores. Overflows of the 64 portable units which housed the predominately photographic negative collection were then located into the conservation facility which has critical climate control. Fifteen trolley loads of incoming collections earmarked for quarantine inspection were wrapped and relocated to the auditorium in The Edge building adjacent to the main building. We needed to insulate each one of the 64 portable photographic storage units with felts in order to negate the risk of condensation occurring on the collections when removing from the cold store without conditioning. We had time-trialled this previously, but we were aware there can be a disparity between planning and what happens in high-pressure situations.

The early projection of flood-level peaks resulted in an action plan where replaceable stock (not accessioned stock) was elevated to higher-level shelving in the basement. The flood levels proved to be much higher than the projected levels and the stock though elevated was damaged. The permeable stock such as packs of archival paper and board which did not come into direct contact with the flood waters was rendered unsuitable for archival purposes due to being subjected to high levels of relative humidity where it had absorbed moisture and become distorted.

Our staff were exceptional during this time and there are many stories about the staff's commitment to the library. One particularly memorable story is a small number of staff moving heavy equipment up flights of stairs at 3 am in the morning by flashlight as the river visibly rose into those spaces just vacated.

Business continuity

A strength was our capacity to quickly get some electronic services up and reassigning the majority of staff to meaningful off-site duties. Another was the setting up of a somewhat curtailed but workable information service in difficult circumstances. The speedy restoration of e-resources, access to print and electronic collections were difficult so staff delivered services by phone, IM (instant messaging) and online. Extended enquiries services were handled initially by staff at home and then limited numbers on-site before public reopening.

Our technology worked in many respects – we could use our internal servers to allow staff to work from home while the building was closed (once limited power had returned). This, however, caused the system to become busy and unresponsive. We have now obtained a comprehensive list of staff personal e-mail addresses so that we can contact them without having to log in to the work system.

Areas for improvement

Greater clarity about essential services was required. Although we are precise regarding our information about the priorities for collections, we have not been so rigorous about precisely detailing essential services. The Library is a reasonably complex place with various business units each having views about what is essential. Future revisions of the BCP will address this.

The maintenance of more detailed inventories in those areas that are least visible (e.g. the basement) is something we have focused on. It is important to know exactly what is present when things go wrong and this was reinforced to us during the floods. Less visible areas in an organization can be less rigorously described than others. A reliable description of what is where in an asset inventory and storage plan is required for collating insurance claims.

Competing priorities

Another learning point for us was in the recovery period. We realized that we are not always priority one and that the other affected institutions – Gallery of Modern Art, Queensland Performing Arts and Queensland Museum in our immediate vicinity – all had major recovery works to be done. Co-ordination of recovery of State Library stock, equipment and furniture was made more challenging by competing arrangements with government partners, as all the while they worked with contractors in getting the massive-scale infrastructure (power, lifts, mechanical services, etc.) back up.

Communication

We were also constrained by processes and procedures activated by the nature of the event including departmental protocols which influence what you can say and when you can say it. Although the communications lines from the CMT to the staff worked fine, there were definite areas for improvement including:

- The staff hotline and web notices were inaccessible due to phone and web services being down.
- The staff hotline was made public which undermined the intention.
- Our phone and internet service provider had a problem with their systems making these services unavailable.

Communications with staff and the public was especially challenging. Organizations like the State Library have a complex set of communications requirements covering hundreds of staff and hundreds of thousands of clients as well as board and government responsibilities. It is a strange situation to be in when the communications systems you rely on every day are no longer available to you. Although our essential network equipment was away from water, the flooding in the basement levels across the city meant that we were without power for a period of time, impacting on our communication systems. This made it impossible to communicate with dispersed staff, many of whom were isolated by flood waters and experiencing similar difficulties.

Social media, in particular Facebook and Twitter, worked well as they were not reliant on our infrastructure. There was a need to ensure timely and accurate messages on Facebook with more information, more frequently, to avoid proliferation of inaccurate comments and conjectures.

Equipment

Even though we had substantial salvage equipment and consumables in the disaster store and kits, the sheer volume of mud and slush that remained in the lower building level from the riverine flooding was overwhelming. There were insufficient squeegees for our teams to create pathways through the very slippery floors to gain access to commence salvage work. Disposable gloves were also used up quickly as the risk of infection from sewerage was high. We also had a limited access to trolleys and torches. All of which has now been addressed in our review.

Welfare

Staff, as stated, were outstanding; however, we have also now added responsibilities to a staff member who will carry out the role of health and well-being coordinator in the case of future disasters. This position is responsible for liaising with the disaster recovery coordinator to ensure that disaster responders remain positive, receive encouragement and ensure that there is appropriate acknowledgement of even the smallest 'wins' during and post recovery. Disaster responders were at times called on to work in unsavoury conditions and for extended periods of time. This work can impact on an individual's health and well-being. It is essential that this aspect of managing people be given a priority in the recovery response process as often the individual is too caught up in the moment to be aware of the toll it may be taking. Responsibilities of this position would also include ensuring workers take necessary breaks away from work stations and ensuring ready availability and access to drinking water and other sustenance away from the work stations.

At times of crisis, while we need to respond practically, we also need to remain level headed and remember the principal purpose of our organization – why we are here. Existing collections' security, monitoring and maintenance are vital, but our role in capturing and remembering the events unfolding comes into play as well. Collecting and retaining Queensland's documentary heritage of this event was not always easy both emotionally and practically.

From 7 February, staff made a graduated return to the building to prepare for a 'soft' opening to the public on 16 February and a full publicized opening for the weekend of 19–20 February. Since the floods we have reviewed our experience, shared our learning and modified plans and procedures. We have now condensed the CDP based on what we now know; it is a shorter and slicker document. We are often asked for copies of our BCP, which we are pleased to share; however, our experience has been that the value of the plan is the journey the organization undertakes in articulating its priorities and the determination by its people to respond to crisis.

Key lessons learnt

These were the key lessons we learned:

- Paper-based material above the flood line can be damaged from increased relative humidity.
- Use social media for communication.
- Look after the welfare of the staff.
- There are competing priorities on central resources in a major city-wide incident.

CASE STUDY: The fire at the Royal Horticultural Society Lindley Library, London
Debbie Lane, Systems and Documentation Manager

At about 12.45 pm, the small 'bleeper' pre-alarm warning device sounded and flashed, and I looked at it. The text on the device, which provides a short warning before the main alarm goes off, read FIRE STACK. I went at speed downstairs. As I went towards the door to the stack room, I told staff and readers that there was a problem and that we should evacuate the Library. The fire alarm started to sound at this moment.

I reached the door to the stack room and entered. Once I was just inside the door I saw (and smelled) swirling black or brown smoke in the air, coming from the rolling stack area. This was a very odd moment when a number of things went through my mind simultaneously. Almost immediately a member of the Building Services staff appeared from around the corner of the rolling stacks, emerging from the smoke. He had read the computer printout initiated by the fire warning system. He said, very tensely, 'There are flames on the ceiling' and rushed passed me.

I said to everyone in the room, 'We must leave the library now.' Library staff immediately defaulted to their well rehearsed roles for checking that secured doors had released and making absolutely sure that public and staff areas were evacuated. My colleague Lucy saw the stack room at this time and recalls, 'I saw a wall of thick smoke coming towards me at speed. I couldn't see flames as the smoke was so thick. The speed was terrifying.'

Once I had checked the various areas of the library, I briefly joined my colleague from the Building Services staff at the main reception desk. He was speaking to the Fire Brigade. Shortly afterwards I left the building and stood on the pavement at the front of the building with other members of the library staff. Everyone in the Library had been safely evacuated and no one was injured. We waited at the front of the building for the Fire Brigade to arrive. I did not have my handbag, which contained my mobile phone, so I borrowed the phone of a colleague and attempted to contact the Head of RHS Libraries. In the event I could not reach her immediately but spoke to my colleagues at our Wisley site and told them what was happening.

The next few minutes were a difficult and anxious time; we knew that the stack room was on fire, but the Fire Brigade had not yet arrived. The possibility that the whole collection might be lost was at once inconceivable and yet alarmingly possible.

The Fire Brigade duly arrived, and though it seemed that they had been a long time coming, in fact they had taken something like 6 minutes. They headed straight in with breathing apparatus and laid hoses. Lucy liaised with them at this point:

> We had met this crew a few weeks before so they knew who I was, the nature of the collection and that they needed to minimise the water used. As the fire was emanating from a light fitting, they were able to use CO_2 extinguishers to control the fire. The extinguishers were pulled from throughout the building using plans in our fire box to locate them quickly. When the mains current was switched off, again using plans, a minimal amount of water was used to put the fire out. Our building services manager has fostered very good relationships with the Fire Brigade and even though he personally was away that day, this

preparatory work made a significant difference. They knew the damage that water would cause and so minimized the use of water as much as they could.

It was at this time that I was told that the Director General would like to have an update on events. I borrowed a phone and rang the Director General, telling her what I knew and again later when I received the news that the Fire Brigade had contained the fire, and had used only a minimal amount of water. Someone from the Press Office asked me for information at this point, and I provided minimum details, uncertain about what should be said.

The firefighters eventually brought some badly burnt and still smouldering material out and placed it on the pavement. During this time I spoke to colleagues who were with a volunteer who had been working in the stack room at the time of the outbreak of the fire. This volunteer was shaken by the experience. My colleagues took her to a café to rest and have some food and coffee.

The stack room was a terrible sight. Apart from pools of illumination provided by portable light units, it was pitch black; soot, a small amount of water and a large amount of unidentifiable debris covered the floor, crunching underfoot as we walked, and the air was acrid and heavy with the smell of burning. Everything was covered with soot and grime.

The main concern of the firemen was reignition. They used heat guns to check the tightly packed boxes on the stack room compactor shelves. Some of the boxes were so hot that smoke was coming from them. These were isolated on the floor to cool. Other hot items were taken outside (Figure 2.2).

At about this time the rest of the staff re-entered the Library. After briefly showing them the damaged areas, we discussed how to proceed with the day, with cups of tea. While I was seated at the issue desk, a man came in wanting to find some information about a watering can he had brought with him. It took quite a while and quite a bit of persuasion to get him to leave! I was still at the issue desk when the Head of Libraries rang. She had been working off-site and had just been informed about the fire. I explained the situation to her and she told me that she would leave for London immediately and would arrive in about an hour.

The members of the Fire Brigade continued to liaise with us about what was going on downstairs. I asked for masks for the staff and they brought several. The Fire Brigade's investigator took statements from all library staff members who were present. The Head of Building Services advised there would be a 24-hour guard in the building that night and over the weekend, and that the basement would be checked every half hour.

The Head of Libraries arrived, and took over management of the situation. Our senior manager arrived during the late afternoon and the Head of Libraries, Lucy and I went with him to see the fire damage and the lights that

Figure 2.2 *Small proportion of heavily damaged stock from the Lindley Library, removed from stacks because of risk of reignition* © *RHS Lindley Library*

appeared to be the cause of the fire. He thanked us for our efforts. He was positive and encouraging and it was good to see him.

All library staff members (apart from the Head of Libraries, Lucy and I) eventually left. Before they left, the Head of Libraries told them how much she appreciated what they had done, and been through, and extended her heartfelt thanks for their calm and professional handling of the incident. They were all very reluctant to depart.

Eventually the initial response firefighting team, members of the Westminster Red Watch A251, was replaced by a second unit. To a man they were friendly, considerate and helpful. At 8 pm the second unit departed, telling us that they would return to check the area of the fire again at 10 pm. The three of us packed up our things, left the Library and went for a meal at a nearby restaurant before returning home. It had been quite a day.

We alerted Harwell on the day of the fire as to what had happened. As soon as we saw the scope of things, it became obvious that we had a major issue on our hands. In the following days and weeks, Harwell removed the books and other material from the stack room for off-site cleaning. The rare book collection was cleaned on-site, as were all other collections housed in the

Library lower ground floor. Water damage to stock was very isolated and limited – most of the books, periodicals and other material were dry but smoke-contaminated.

The Library was closed for just under a year due to cleaning of the building and the collections and to reconstruction and refurbishment work on the stack room area. New storage facilities were established and a new Inergen Fire Suppression system was installed. During the period of closure library services were operated from the RHS Garden Wisley Library, allowing access to stock unaffected by the fire.

The staff of the Lindley Library is a close-knit group. Their calm, efficient and highly effective responses on the day of the fire reflected their familiarity both with the collections and premises and with established emergency procedures. The high level of organization of health and safety services within the Society also played a very positive role: fire drills are frequent and are taken seriously, the fire alarm system is tested regularly, fire marshal training is kept up to date and regular inspections by the Fire Brigade are scheduled. Fire regulations are respected to the letter, a process that includes regular testing of electrical equipment and fittings. On the day, all of this was seen to be well worth the effort.

Key lessons learnt

These were the key lessons we learned:

- Fire drills are essential.
- Pre-incident liaison with the fire service is valuable.
- Floor plans showing location of utilities and fire extinguishers save time.

CASE STUDY: The New Zealand earthquakes
Lynn Campbell, Conservator, New Zealand

At 4.43 am on Saturday 4 September, 2010, the Canterbury district in New Zealand was shaken by a 7.1 magnitude earthquake. The epicentre was located 40 kilometres west of Christchurch and had a focal depth of 10 km causing widespread damage which affected the whole of the South Island with vibrations felt as far away as the North Island. No one died during this earthquake but buildings were badly damaged including many heritage buildings. However, on 22 February 2011, at 12.55 pm there was a 6.3 magnitude aftershock centred in the port of Lyttelton that devastated central Christchurch and killed 188 people, most in the central city district. The severity of this quake was caused by the fact that its focal depth was only 5 km. It was the shallowness of the shake that caused the major wide-scale destruction.

New Zealand is known as 'the shaky isles' because minor tremors are not uncommon; however, Wellington was the city considered to be most at risk, not the Canterbury region. This unknown fault came as a complete surprise to the earthquake experts around the country and overseas. Particularly after the February 2011 aftershock I was asked to help many cultural institutions to salvage their collections.

Issues that were apparent included:

- no disaster preparedness plans
- no use of lifts or stairs
- dust and dirt
- liquefaction
- mould growth from leaking water pipes
- dangerous situations involving toppled shelves
- no prioritizing of the collection ensuring the most important objects are safely removed first
- no location list as to where these were stored
- lack of adequate supplies
- no specific teams were set up to do specific jobs
- no labelling of objects therefore salvage took much longer than the team anticipated
- packing materials being limited delaying the salvage.

Figure 2.3 *Historic building immediately after the earthquake* © *Lynn Campbell*

These are some important points we learned from the Canterbury experience:

- Prepare for significant aftershocks for up to at least two years. One earthquake does not mean the disaster is over. The worst loss of life and damage to buildings was caused by an aftershock six months later.
- If a city-wide disaster occurs the museum or gallery will very likely be on its own with little outside help including staff members who will be more concerned with their family and homes.

- If a state of civil emergency is declared museums and galleries will have no power or access.
- There could be a possible takeover by Civil Defence of cultural buildings such as public libraries and museums, as these buildings tend to be built to a high standard to protect the collection within so will stand up to earthquakes better.
- Communication is essential in the disaster recovery of collections.
- The building must be declared safe by the emergency services.
- It is vital to have up to date contact details for everyone that you need to communicate with such as a disaster telephone tree.
- Efficient preventive procedures can save your collection from major destruction and safeguard staff in the process. It cannot be over-emphasized how important this is.
- Be aware that some staff may be severely traumatized by seeing the collections damaged.
- This earthquake highlighted, for many cultural institutions, the need for improvement in storage and health and safety.
- Do not leave it until a disaster occurs to think about the risks to personnel and collections. Having a disaster recovery plan in place that all staff have access to that has been approved by senior management is vital.

The preparation of a disaster recovery plan is the most effective method for ensuring the safeguarding of collections. Thinking about the issues that are unique to museum or gallery collections is vital. There is no one size fits all, and coming up with a plan that incorporates fresh ways of managing any potential disaster will be of immeasurable assistance should disaster strike. Risk assessment is also a vital part of this process. Another essential tool that can be used is training in disaster preparedness. This can be achieved by participating in hands-on workshops that can be done in conjunction with your local friendly fire-training school.

These are essential requirements for preparing for disaster:

- clear communication
- a disaster plan for all staff
- allocated set roles
- adequate materials in disaster bins.

After all the big aftershocks a state of civil emergency was declared by the New Zealand Government and Civil Defence. This state of emergency gave the local council and Civil Defence special powers. This included the demolition of buildings without the necessity of a building consent. In terms of heritage buildings this has had a catastrophic effect on the historic areas of Christchurch and many heritage listed buildings have been demolished under these new laws in the last couple of months. In some instances museums in the area lost buildings and collections, not to the earthquake, but to the decisions made immediately afterwards by Civil Defence personnel with different priorities.

With hindsight, it is clear that the one issue not considered when disaster plans are written for heritage salvage is the lack of input that museum staff may have in relation to saving their collections in the event of a region-wide catastrophe such as the Canterbury earthquakes. This is something to consider and negotiate for future disaster planning protocols.

Key lessons learnt

These were the key lessons we learned:

- Advocate for heritage buildings with civic authorities to avoid demolition where possible.
- Investment in better quality storage before an incident may reduce damage to collections.
- Museums likely to be on their own need their own resources and to be resilient through planning. Even staff may not be in a position to help if their homes are affected.

CASE STUDY: Wider recovery from a river flood at the University of Sussex, UK

Deborah Shorley, University Librarian at the University of Sussex

I took up my post as University Librarian at the University of Sussex at the beginning of October 2000. Ten days later the River Ouse burst its banks at Lewes and submerged much of the lower part of the town for several days. By the time we realized what was happening Lewes was closed off, so we could do no more than watch helplessly from afar as the flood forced the steel doors of the store open and all our material was submerged in 13 ft of muddy, contaminated water.

Many of us are relatively well informed about the physical problems of book restoration and we know where to go for help. But there is much less information about how to deal with insurance claims of this magnitude or of the importance of public relations when something like this happens, both within the university community and more widely.

At Lewes, in accordance with our well formulated disaster plan, we prioritized a certain amount of material for immediate salvage – and then dithered.

I was no expert, but it seemed to me not worth trying to restore the mass of material which had remained under dirty, contaminated water for several days.

But, given the scale of the damage, this decision could not be made by the Librarian alone. When the loss adjusters appointed by our insurers realized the potential for a large claim, they thought it prudent to have the material boxed up and deep frozen until more informed decisions could be made.

We quickly established a good and close relationship with our insurers. (In my first three months at the University of Sussex I spent more time with loss adjusters than I did with my professional colleagues.) In the event we spent about a year preparing a very detailed insurance claim for everything that had been lost.

I cannot stress too much how time-consuming and difficult this task was. Nobody before had, for example, tried to put a value on BBC World Service monitoring reports, or the papers of the Society for Visiting Scientists. We took advice, used our professional knowledge, and made informed estimates, but we were conscious that there was frequently no single right answer. Fortunately, our insurers took an eminently reasonable approach and trusted our judgement.

Right at the beginning, as all the volumes lay sodden in the store, I had declared, as confidently as I could, that we would seek to 'restore the knowledge base' for the university library, rather than try to replace the material item by item. It has to be said that this suited all parties. We were well insured, and had we sought to have all the material restored, the insurers might have had to pay us upwards of £6.5 million.

By choosing to restore what we had lost in broad terms, but not title by title, we could expect a much smaller settlement, but one which would give us the freedom to develop the library in ways appropriate for the beginning of the 21st century. In the end we received approximately £2.6 million in compensation and used most of the money to help finance a long overdue e-strategy for the library.

I learned a good deal about working with insurers and, above all, about how loss adjusters are the key players in large claims of this sort. I also realized how important it was to record absolutely everything. From the outset we kept a file (e-mail helped a good deal) which became the record of our negotiations from the beginning of October for the 18 months thereafter. The importance of this discipline cannot be over-emphasized.

Meanwhile, as we worked through the long drawn out insurance-claiming process, we had to ensure that the effect on the library and its services was minimized. This flood could not have happened at a worse time. I knew none of my colleagues, and the new term had just begun. We immediately issued news bulletins through all the usual channels including, of course, our library website. And we promised staff and students that we would do all we could to make sure their studies and research were not compromised by what had happened.

In practice, since most of the material held in the store was not frequently used, I don't believe that our students were disadvantaged at all, and we provided every assistance to researchers, by acquiring material for them either on inter-library loan or by replacing it immediately. Demand was in the event minimal.

Had the library flood been an isolated incident we would have had far more publicity. As it was, people all over Lewes had lost their homes and livelihoods, so what had happened in the library store was, in some sense, not newsworthy. The University took the view that there was no need to publicize it loudly and, in any case, we were, above all, anxious to ensure that no potential students were discouraged from coming to Sussex by what had happened. I remain convinced this was the right decision.

So what did we learn? Above all, I am convinced disaster planning is absolutely essential – but not much use when something as bad as this happens. The plans we had would have been invaluable had one section of the library been flooded, but they were of little help when we were dealing with a large store full of contaminated water and 40,000 soggy books and newspapers. In the end, you just cope. You cope by keeping cool, not panicking, and seeking help from colleagues you can trust. You also hope you will never be called upon in the same way again.

Key lessons learnt

These were the key lessons we learned:

- It is essential to understand the role of the loss adjuster and the importance of a good insurance policy.
- There are timescales involved in valuing and replacing damaged stock.
- Incident log and meticulous documentation is essential for insurance claim.
- The incident occurred when the University Librarian was new in post – plans should be resilient for incidents at inopportune times.

Note: this case study was originally published in *Library + Information Update* March 2003 Vol 2 (3) p46–7. It has been considerably amended and updated for this book.

CASE STUDY: Fire and flood recovery at Norfolk County Record Office, UK
Susan Maddock, Principal Archivist of Norfolk County Council

On Monday, 1 August 1994, at 7 am, attendants entered Norwich Central Library to begin opening up the building. The fire alarm sounded around 7.20 am, and one attendant went to investigate. When he opened a door into the main part of the Library, he was thrown back by an 'explosion' of fire.

Subsequent investigation showed that the cause of the fire was dangerous wiring, as an electrician had discovered the previous Thursday, but poor communication prevented his report being acted on promptly. The fire leapt immediately across the ground floor covered courtyard space, which had been baking for many days in exceptionally hot and humid weather.

The fire service was called at 7.30 am, but the fire-fighting operation was delayed for several minutes because a member of staff was believed (wrongly) to be trapped inside the building. This delay gave the fire time to gain a hold. By 8 am, it was at its height: windows were exploding and the site was cordoned off. By 9 am, fire hoses extended one-quarter of a mile from the fire.

By 10 am, the fire was beginning to come under control, and fire-fighters entered the building via a rear door at basement level, using a set of keys held by the county archivist. By 11 am, it was apparent that the basement, which held the Norfolk Record Office strongroom, searchroom and working areas, had kept the fire at bay, but air-heating ducts had allowed scalding, fire-polluted, water to shower the shelves in the strongroom, while the searchroom, offices and conservation workshop had been soaked by fire hoses directed through their windows in order to fight the fire from below.

One member of staff was allowed into the strongroom with a team of fire-fighters; together they spread sheets of polythene over those shelves in areas where water was pouring in. An offer by the fire service to begin evacuating archives was gratefully accepted; staff assisted by taking armfuls of records as they emerged, and a first vanload of records left the site around 11.30 am, while fire-fighting operations were still going on in the Library above.

During the course of the following ten days, all the records in the strongroom were evacuated, as were the catalogues and books in the searchroom, the offices' working files, all the equipment of value, most of the archive shelving and much of the furniture. Everything was affected to some extent, if only by the atmospheric damp, dirt and the smell of the fire, but only around 10% of the archives were damaged, and only an estimated one per cent sustained damage serious enough to affect their usability.

The Record Office's subscription to Harwell proved its value from the start. A first vanload of wet records was sent off on the day of the fire, and during the evacuation period several more vanloads were despatched to Harwell.

This took care in the short term of those documents which were seriously wet, enabling Record Office staff to concentrate first on the evacuation process and then on the identification and controlled drying of those records which had sustained more minor water damage.

Equally vital was the provision of transport and alternative premises, and in these areas unsolicited offers of help from local businesses kicked in almost immediately, even before the County Council's risk section had time fully to mobilize. A local removal firm sent the first removal vans and also provided short-term accommodation for records removed on the first day, while the owner of a large empty wastepaper warehouse rang on the day of the fire to offer his premises as an archive store. This warehouse was to provide a temporary home for most of the archives during the main recovery period (ten months) while interim premises were being identified and adapted for the provision of a full archive service.

Once the County Council's insurers were involved, they engaged a disaster recovery agency. This helped ensure the speedy provision of (for example) sufficient crates, transport and labour for the evacuation, enabling Record Office staff to concentrate on packing, preliminary assessment, unpacking and air-drying of records.

The provision of a public service was never wholly interrupted, even during the fire, as we had a microfilm searchroom in a separate building, which stayed open as usual. Dean and Chapter archives were made a priority as a book to commemorate the 900th anniversary of the cathedral was under way at the time of the fire and access was needed by two or three of the authors who had been commissioned. We also made an effort to deal with (for example) legally vital and personally critical enquiries and to help those with academic and publishing deadlines. People were generally sympathetic and patient. Today, vast numbers of popular documents are accessible on microfilm or fiche in the Norfolk Heritage Centre and also online, so one could help very many people simply by redirecting them to the Library and/or the internet – as we do when we close for stock-taking each year.

We learnt many lessons from this experience. Whatever emergency plan you might have, you may not be in control of the situation. For example, a plan to prioritize the evacuation of pre-selected blocks of archives is irrelevant, if only parts of the building are deemed safe at any one time, and if only a certain number of people can work efficiently in a confined area.

Flexible, resilient, experienced, committed staff are an asset for which there is no substitute. Archives which are well packaged – in particular, which are in boxes – proved to be much better protected from water than we might have expected, and this has been a priority for us ever since. Dealing with the media is one area in which advance planning could be especially valuable.

Key lessons learnt

These were the key lessons we learned:

- It is important to communicate about building problems and prompt remedial action.
- The fire services will be in control, not you, though they will probably try to help limit damage so far as is safe and practical.
- A damage management contractor for major incidents gives valuable support.
- There is a need for access to alternative secure premises for decanting and temporary storage.
- Good quality storage can protect collections.

CASE STUDY: Impact of power loss on an archive service in a UK local authority

A paper conservator

We suffered a major power failure due to mains current entering building's supply – insurers later identified impure materials in mains fuse which melted and ceased to work; it allowed current to flow across it, at mains energy! This triggered a loss of security and fire alarm system because the telephone circuitry was disabled (so although there was a distinct smell of smoke in the building, no alarms rang and there was no call out); we also lost the building management system, lighting and HVAC (heating, ventilation and air-conditioning) to two strongrooms, some electrical equipment e.g. deep freeze, and some computers which were plugged in.

Initially the plan was not invoked other than calling an electrician, but after an hour we could see the enormity of what had happened (it wasn't just a case of changing light bulbs and hot-desking!) and we did go into disaster mode although our plan did not cover power failure. However, we realized we had to shut the archive to the public, cease any other activity, and focus on this problem. The disaster plan helped to structure thinking and provided some useful contact details. Teamwork went really well at the beginning, e.g. with council property services and contractors.

In retrospect somebody should have done more recording of events as they unfolded, as this would have been a help with the loss adjusters – there was so much information to gather at a later date and their questions were extremely detailed, so better records of the first few days would have been a help.

Our plan changed a good deal after the disaster. We hadn't realized our alarm systems were so vulnerable and had a back-up panel installed in a different part of the building, connected to a different power intake. We realized that although our key control was good, only one person knew where the key to manually operate our electronic security gates was. The security gate couldn't be opened manually without it and would have prevented access to the fire hydrants, had they been needed! Also our building contained the servers for the entire organization, not just the Archive. These had to be switched off in a particular sequence, and only one person at the Archive knew that sequence. This made us realize how vulnerable and valuable our servers were and they became the number one items for salvage in our disaster plan. Also forms for recording and reporting on events were included in the disaster plan and in the disaster response kits.

Key lessons learnt

These were the key lessons we learned:

- Loss of power results in loss of security and HVAC – it is not just an IT issue.
- Know where keys are.
- It is helpful to log events for the insurance claim.
- Put details of instructions for dealing with IT infrastructure such as servers in one place.

CASE STUDY: Wider impacts after flooding to a university campus, including the archive
Dr Richard Heseltine, University Librarian at the University of Hull

We had lots of disaster reaction processes in place that worked well, but even so we learned some significant practical lessons. At a trivial level, we have disaster reaction cupboards with equipment, but found that all the wellies were the same size and we didn't have enough flashlights and batteries. We have now re-equipped to an appropriate level.

Generally speaking we were pleased with the reaction and were fortunate in the fact that we had Harwell to deal with all the damaged material. Had we not had that arrangement in place we would have been in serious difficulty given the amount of material affected.

We felt there were lessons to be learned about some of the processes. Among library staff, there were hardly any difficulties in getting staff involved. Staff were willing to help with the salvage efforts and moving stock. The connection with other parts of the University was not as clear as it could have been. What we could ask from other sections, particularly facilities, was not entirely clear. That has since been improved. The University's Disaster

Reaction Plan has been developed to take account of issues of coordination.

The one thing that we were not prepared for was the full impact of a power loss. The electrical sub-station for the main part of the building was housed in the sub-basement which, being flooded floor to ceiling, was out of action for five weeks. This meant there was no lighting and there were no fire alarms in the main tower block, where most of the book stock is kept – the east part of the Library was unaffected by power loss. Although the entire building was closed for a day during the rescue of the material from the basement, the tower block remained closed to the public for the full five weeks at the insistence of the University's health and safety office, primarily because there were no fire alarms. As it was summer the loss of lighting was not a serious problem, although it would have been during the winter.

The service was only shut completely for one day. After that, staff ran a retrievals-only service as a means of providing access to the material in the tower block, and the risk assessment required staff to carry hand-held fire alarms and torches, and always work in pairs. Fortunately this occurred in the summer vacation. It would have been much more difficult had it occurred in term. As we did have power to one area of the building, this could be used as an information point, to issue material and as a public point for access to the catalogue points. Electronic journals were still accessible and our website and servers were unaffected. Study space was lost but this was not a major problem given the time of year.

As a result of that we formalized what was implicit in our minds: the most important thing is to continue to provide access to the book stock. Our procedures are to prioritize this and to shift staff into that front-line role. This principle underpinned our approaches to pandemic planning, too, shifting back-office staff to a front-line role in the event of 50% of staff being absent. All of this has resulted in more thinking on preventative measures. The University has invested across campus in flood prevention measures and taken as much plant as possible out of the basement. There was a lot of learning all through the University particularly in our facilities department, and we have better forms of liaison than were in place previously.

Key lessons learnt

These were the key lessons we learned:

- We need effective communication with our own team and the wider organization.
- Power loss has a large impact on staff's ability to provide a service for undamaged materials.

- It might be necessary to work in a building with no functioning fire alarm system.

CASE STUDY: Strategies for preparedness at the Library of Congress

Dianne Van der Reyden (Director for Preservation) and Diane Vogt-O'Connor (Chief of Conservation) at the Library of Congress, Washington DC

In the Library's continuity of operation planning (COOP), a group of stakeholders determined that sustaining the collections immediately after an event had the second highest impact immediately after that of administrative functions. Therefore, sustaining collections was given second priority of several dozen services provided by the Library. We formed volunteer teams of our expert preservation staff with liaisons from the Library's curatorial divisions to address special collections at risk, as well as teams to address actions for our most treasured collections, those on exhibit, as well as our general collections. Those actions include, but are not limited to:

- 'shelter in place' (or SIP) certain collections (for example to ensure there is plastic sheeting available to temporarily cover collections if necessary, etc.)
- 'relocate in-place plan' (or RIP) to temporarily move certain collections to more 'hardened' centralized and concentrated locations within our buildings
- 'display emergency plan' (or DEP) to address loaned items on exhibit, as well as our own items on display in the Library, etc.

We have practised these plans and have done telephone drills. We've even developed a charter with other federal libraries to provide mutual assistance (with a template online for others to imitate) and we hold annual training sessions for these colleagues as well as basic preservation training for federal libraries.

In preparation for a high-risk (but highly unlikely) event, and to mitigate more ubiquitous minor risks, the Library has developed a special isolation room for recovery of collections at-risk. The collections recovery room is a secure space dedicated to enhancing the Library's capabilities to safeguarding its collections if there are emergencies. Meeting both practical and educational functions, the room's efficient organization provides a model setup for preservation training and drills in collections salvage and recovery work related to the Library's recovery, as well as similar initiatives.

Figure 2.4 *Library of Congress Collections Recovery Room, showing isolation cabinet, furniture and space*   © *Library of Congress*

The collections recovery room also stands ready for actual salvage operations should collections be inadvertently exposed to water, mould, insects or other conditions that may threaten safe accessibility by researchers.

The collections recovery room allows preservation staff to isolate wet or mouldy items, dry items affected by water in a controlled environment, minimizing risks of mould growth and cross-contamination. Staff can also safely examine and inventory contaminated items away from other collections and clean affected items without posing risks to staff.

The space has a number of special features that facilitate emergency response work, including modular furniture (to maximize the drying space and quickly reconfigure the room), two freezers (with a blast freezer available offsite), and a biological safety cabinet for cleaning mould and other fine particles in a high-efficiency ductless cabinet, which prevents biological residue from spreading throughout the space. The ductless system is fitted with alarms that alert users when airflow is low or when filters need to be changed.

The collections recovery room is well organized and always stocked with the supplies and tools needed for recovery work to enable rapid start-up times during incident responses. The supplies are maintained by a careful inventory and replaced when used so that staff members are fully prepared for the next incident.

In addition to the recovery and training procedures performed in the collections recovery room, the Library has developed special emergency notification protocols when incidents involving collections are discovered, as well as a salvage contract in the event of a large-scale incident.

Key lessons learnt

These were the key lessons we learned:

- It is useful to have a facility to deal with mould safely and in-house freezer capability, which can double up as a quarantine area.
- Have a salvage contract and scalable response to major incidents.
- It is useful to have a detailed plan of items that should be moved and those better to protect in situ to avoid wasted time in emergency situations.

CASE STUDY: The Tohoku Earthquake and subsequent tsunami of 11 March 2011 and its impact on library and archive collections

Tokuda Seiko, currently a librarian at the University of Tokyo Library, recounts the experience of the Tohoku Earthquake and subsequent tsunami of 11 March 2011 (see also pages 144–6). This is based on his experience, official reports at the time, and the translated excerpts of two internal documents and other related information released online by the University of Tsukuba Library (www.tulips.tsukuba.ac.jp/shinsai/ fukkyu0516.pdf).

The University of Tsukuba, founded relatively recently in 1973, is one of Japan's leading national research universities. More than 300 km from the epicentre and 60 km north of Tokyo in a non-coastal area, the earthquake recorded there had a greater seismic intensity than elsewhere. The University's library, consisting of the central library and four branch libraries, was one of the campus facilities that suffered severe damage (Figure 2.5).

Upon the earthquake, supply of electric power was terminated until 14 March in many campus areas. The library staff urged all the patrons to stay away from the bookshelves and protect themselves, and when the quake temporarily stopped, the staff asked them to evacuate. There were no casualties inside any of the libraries, but the buildings' interiors and exteriors were heavily damaged. The Art and Physical Education Library was the most severely damaged of the five libraries: part of the walls, windows and ceilings were destroyed, and debris was scattered dangerously on the floors of its four-

Figure 2.5 *Fallen shelving after the earthquake in Tohoku*   *© University of Tsukuba Library*

storey building. At the same time, the bookshelves on the first floor fell down one after another. It was nearly one year later before the thorough and quake-proof reconstruction of this library began.

Even after the electricity supply resumed, there was a possibility of the planned rolling blackout scheme in Central Japan to avoid a national power shortage due to suspension of many power plant operations. Since it was hard to keep the on-site servers running, the library staff started tweeting via its official account (@tsukubauniv_lib) on Monday 14 March to explain the situation and provide information. With intermittent downtime, the library's temporary website opened on Wednesday 16 March, returning to the normal one on 29 March, and the off-campus proxy access to the subscribing electronic collections was restarted on 17 March. These services online had to be resumed step by step in accordance with the recovery process in the buildings.

As for the damage to the collections, there was minor water leakage from the ceiling that affected a small part of the holdings in the Medical Library. In addition, in most of the libraries, huge volumes of books were de-shelved by the quake, and the ones physically damaged were later repaired in-house, or by external bookbinderies when the nation's supplementary budgets were allocated.

It was estimated that approximately 60% of all its collections (1.5 million shelved items) fell from the shelves. Soon after the library uploaded the photographs of the situation via the web and Twitter, a group of student volunteers was organized with faculty and staff members of the university acting as advisers, and they helped to reshelve the books. The library started to open limited areas to the public on 29 March, but thanks to the contribution of these volunteers, almost all the floors of the central and other branch libraries, except of the Art and Physical Education Library that had suffered more structural damage, were completely reopened on 16 May.

Key lessons learnt

These were the key lessons we learned:

- Use social media to communicate with staff and users.
- Appreciate the timescales involved in reshelving fallen stock.
- Consider using student volunteers to help with some aspects of recovery.

CHAPTER 3

Roles and responsibilities

Introduction

This chapter is designed to help readers work out how best to organize their team to manage the various activities that need to be completed if a plan is activated. If there is a major emergency, the tasks required for completion will broadly be the same regardless of the type of the institution: restoring the building and its contents, resuming services, and taking care of staff. Although the tasks are the same, one size does not fit all. Differences will emerge related to the varying sizes of institution and their staff, and differences in emphasis given to salvage of collections and business continuity. Some organizations have certain activities, particularly facilities and press functions, completed by colleagues in other departments. Each institution must work out how best to divide the tasks that are required for completion.

The roles and responsibilities outlined here must be adapted when formulating or reviewing your emergency plan: the dissemination of the responsibilities will vary. The detail of how to approach this is discussed throughout this book. Practical experience indicates that giving individuals a clear notion of their role and what they are required, able and authorized to do makes response much quicker and clearer. Referring back to the template guidance referred to in Figure 1.4 (page 12), this chapter provides information on how to formulate your own Emergency Management Team and generic advice on what their roles should entail.

Emergency response activities

Consider an emergency such as a burst pipe, causing damage in a public area of a library across two floors. What will need to be organized in order to respond effectively to this incident? Someone will need to deal with the source of the water itself and try to isolate it. Services may be interrupted as people cannot use the affected area, rendering some parts of the collection inaccessible and limiting workspace. Items within your collection are becoming damaged and need to be protected.

What about a power cut? What demands would that place on an archive? IT would be down. How long can services run on emergency lighting? Can a retrieval service operate? Is there any impact on the collections as a result of the sudden cessation of the environmental control system? Would telephone systems be functional? What about security? Is it safe to open or is it best to close for the day? Who could make that decision?

Arantza Barrutia-Wood, Collections Project Co-ordinator at Museums Sheffield, comments on her experience after a major flood at a museum store:

> We realized that each department needed to know very clearly what their responsibilities were as well as what their role would be in a disaster. They also needed to know what they are authorized to do. So for instance the front of house team knowing whether they should release staff to support the response team, whether they should make the decision to close sites to the public and where to find the information they need, so what the hierarchy of responsibility is. This applies to every department. Who can release funds, who can release staff, who keeps the press/public informed, who keep staff informed, etc.

Often, the catalyst for emergency planning in libraries, archives and museums is a concern for a collection which is financially valuable, unique, irreplaceable or of historical significance, or contains vital information. Therefore the process of emergency plan composition is driven by collection managers whose primary concern is the preservation of that collection. Many of the plans are therefore very strong in the content that directly relates to dealing with damaged objects: priority lists are completed, salvage guidance provided and equipment sourced to provide first aid to objects.

However, if you consider the realities of an emergency situation, the impact will be felt not just by the collection that is under threat. There will be service disruption, potentially including IT failure. Someone will have to deal with the buildings and facilities issues that are triggered. Security concerns, public relations issues, and financial and administrative tasks may be generated.

It is vital that a cross-section of staff is involved in the planning stage, as they could be affected by an incident and involved in the recovery process. If a plan is written without their involvement, even if they have received some training after it is completed, their ownership and stakeholding in the plan will be minimal. A plan imposed on them without their input, even if they were not particularly keen to provide input, may not work effectively in a real incident, with response proving disorganized and disjointed as there will be a lack of familiarity in and trust in the plan. Some members of staff will follow the plan, others may not. Individuals may be unsure of their role, question the rationale behind the prioritization and waste time in the recovery process.

Whose input will be needed to manage a real incident successfully? Often the existing management structure will give some direction as it indicates broadly the general areas of responsibility in an organization. This reflects what key business or service areas are important to the organization and may require attention in an emergency situation. Many institutions will have roles such as 'collections manager', 'user services manager', in addition to other roles and an overall manager, giving a clear delineation between the stock and the service. It can be difficult to deviate very far from existing management structures as subverting existing hierarchies in real emergencies may not be practical, although this can be resolved to some extent through training and giving robust support to individuals selected for roles through their obvious capability, resourcefulness and technical suitability for a role.

An exercise that can be useful is to write down all the activities that you can think would be required in managing a major incident, as shown in Figure 3.1 (overleaf).

Against each of the activities listed in Figure 3.1, write the name of the most obvious person within your existing staff to conduct this role. Clearly the collections manager will need to manage the salvage operation so that person cannot simultaneously be doing everything else. Similarly the user services manager can be sorting out communication with customers, but cannot be simultaneously filling crates with wet books. Some functions may be carried out by another department in your organization such as facilities or IT.

When this exercise is carried out certain names usually occur frequently. This will help you to identify what your staff structure for emergencies should look like. In small-scale incidents, as is discussed in the next chapter, possibly only one or two people will be involved, but as the scale of an incident grows more people are required as the complexities and service impacts escalate. A team of people is required to help minimize the impact of the incident on all aspects of the organization. This could be referred to as an Emergency Management Team. Ideally, the people identified must participate in the process of composing your initial plan or scrutinizing an existing document before a rewrite. Inevitably they will be involved in a real incident, so their ownership in the process is vital. Even if one person collates information and drafts the plan, the people you identify must review it and agree with the document if it is to work effectively in practice.

Every institution is slightly different, and these variables are discussed below, and the division of roles as set out below is a suggestion, not a blueprint. Large organizations require a bigger team, with additional roles;

Activity	Primary person	Secondary person
Deciding to close the building and service		
Risk assessment for safety of salvage staff		
Contacting other institutions in the area for support and assistance		
Dealing with concerned owners and depositors		
Updating website and e-mail circular to users and staff		
Isolating the electricity to the areas affected		
Liaising with stakeholders and trustees		
Organizing salvage of stock		
Sourcing and installing dehumidifiers		
Securing the building and the temporary salvage areas		
Determining salvage strategy (air-dry or freeze)		
Liaising with insurers		
Organizing emergency budgets or cash flow		
Deciding text for press release		
Clearing up standing water and arranging pumps		
Prioritization of items for recovery		
Working out a documentation process for tracking damaged items		
Staff log and site control		
Rebooting systems and IT recovery		
Organizing catering and rest breaks for salvage helpers		

Figure 3.1 *Emergency team identification exercise*

small institutions may need to streamline these activities into one or two roles. The Building Recovery Manager role, as set out below, would overwhelm an individual working in a national museum, given the scale of the operation. However, for the majority of institutions it would reflect the multifunctional role of a facilities manager, incorporating elements of building, health and safety and welfare.

Emergency Management Team roles
Emergency Response Manager

The role of Emergency Response Manager usually suits the person who in normal circumstances is in overall charge of the service: the director, head of library services, archives manager, medical records manager and so on. This person decides the overall recovery strategy, the implementation of which is carried out by those in the other roles described below. This role is the liaison point between the service and the wider organization (for example the local authority, the board, the trustees, the vice chancellor's office) and the insurers. Given their budgetary control they are able to make authoritative decisions about spending money, including authorizing overtime, which colleagues may not be in a position to do. Speaking to the media may be a role for this person, as well as authorizing press releases (although in a larger organization communications and press may be a standalone role).

It is a pivotal role, and ideally the person who naturally fills it will be a calm, rational, authoritative individual who can lead in these situations. If this is not the case, then reassignment of certain tasks may be necessary, although given the importance of liaison between this person and senior managers in the wider organization or trustees, the senior member of staff must be incorporated into the Emergency Management Team somehow.

This person also has an oversight over the services as a whole and can decide how resources should be managed appropriately based on the specifics of the incident. This may mean that in a higher education library, they decide to allocate most staff to helping users with enquiries because of the service disruption, reducing the in-house human resource for salvage and necessitating external support. In an archive service, the reverse may happen, where the building is closed to the public so more staff can concentrate on salvage.

As will be discussed in subsequent chapters, this role may not be involved in small to medium-scale incidents which can be managed locally by others in the Emergency Management Team. Certainly a director of a national museum would not ordinarily expect to be called in on a weekend to deal with a minor leak affecting a handful of objects but would certainly be required for a large-scale incident. However, in most institutions, there would be an expectation that an Emergency Response Manager would attend and assist in most emergency incidents.

To some extent the actions in this role are determined by the specific circumstances of the incident but the responsibilities can be set in advance. A suggested checklist for Emergency Response Managers is set out below. The specific activities can be amended as required. All checklists for the Emergency Management Team are set up to indicate:

- responsibilities of the role
- immediate actions to be completed (where appropriate)
- tasks as the salvage operation progresses
- tasks after the salvage operation is completed.

The bullet points are supported by appendices in the remainder of the document. The points below and on all the responsibility checklists detailed in this chapter should fit on one side of A4, making it user-friendly. The checklists rely on common sense. In some situations, certain activities will not be necessary. For a medium sized flood in a basement, non-public area with no immediate impact on service provision, a press release would be unnecessary. The Emergency Management Team must be prompted on the key tasks but decide in the specific circumstances which activities are actually necessary.

Where the checklists presented below allocate a responsibility to one role, it can be transferred to another role if it is more appropriate to your organization. Transfer, rather than deletion, is crucial though: it does not really matter which role takes responsibility, for example, for arranging catering for salvage workers, but it is crucial that somebody does.

Figure 3.2 shows a checklist for the Emergency Response Manager.

Checklist for the Emergency Response Manager	
Responsibilities:	
Liaise with the emergency services.	
Liaise with governing body (e.g. trustees, council, university executive).	
Liaise with insurers.	
Liaise with depositors and stakeholders.	
Take overall responsibility for health and safety.	
Communicate with members of Emergency Management Team; organize meetings.	
Liaise with other institutions for assistance (space, people, equipment, expertise).	
Have financial control for the salvage and recovery operation.	
Contact and muster staff for the emergency operation.	
Immediate actions to be completed (where appropriate):	
Notify all relevant personnel who will be required for the recovery effort.	

Figure 3.2 *Checklist for the Emergency Response Manager*

Checklist for the Emergency Response Manager	
Ensure funds are available to procure equipment and secure suppliers to make the building accessible and facilitate the recovery of collections.	
Set up a financial system and code for expenditure associated with the recovery operation.	
Increase balance on organizational credit cards.	
Notify the insurers.	
Notify governing body and other key personnel (insert cross reference to page).	
Notify sensitive depositors.	
Ensure that a risk assessment has been carried out before the salvage operation commences.	
Maintain an incident log (see form on page 175) and arrange for the salvage operation to be photographed.	
As the salvage operation progresses:	
Support the Emergency Management Team in arranging resources identified as required for the recovery effort.	
Arrange for regular meetings of the Emergency Management Team.	
Closely monitor the timescales for recovery and identify solutions to speed the salvage process up where necessary.	
After the salvage operation is completed:	
Declare the emergency phase over.	
Appoint someone to liaise with the insurance company over the insurance claim.	
Ensure that appropriate remedial work is undertaken to avoid repetition of the incident source.	
Conduct a review of the performance of the plan.	
Thank those members of staff who were involved in the recovery operation. Consider whether any form of additional support such as counselling may be necessary.	

Figure 3.2 *continued*

Building Recovery Manager

The Building Recovery Manager deals with the impact of the incident on the building and its facilities: pumping out water, temporary power and emergency lighting, health and safety, accommodation and sourcing extra space, parking, security, long-term drying out of the building and so on. This role is very heavily front-loaded in that other vital activities, such as commencing the salvage operation, are contingent on the completion of tasks such as pumping out water, turning off stop-cocks, conducting risk assessments and so on. In very large organizations it may be necessary to split the role up further into sub-roles of 'security manager' and 'welfare and safety manager'.

In some organizations many of the functions of the person carrying out this role would most naturally be conducted by a facilities department or subcontractor which is not exclusively tied to the library or archive but serves your entire institution, potentially responsible for dozens or even hundreds of buildings. Some of the challenges caused by this are discussed below in Chapter 10, but even where this function exists it is often helpful to have someone from your own team liaising with the facilities department. Some issues may still fall under this person's direct responsibility (accommodation for the salvage operation, salvage risk assessment and so on) and if liaison is necessary with several different departments within the wider organization, facilities, health and safety, fire officer and so on, this often becomes a complex and time-consuming job in itself. The implications of floods in libraries, archives and museums are unusual when compared with the approach in a general office, for example, where much of the contents will be discarded and replaced, rather than restored, and an advocate strongly conveying these points may minimize miscommunication with facilities and ensure response is appropriately scaled. It is recommended that one person focuses on these issues wherever possible.

When drafting incident control procedures, particularly for flooding (Chapter 4), often this individual would be the most suitable person to call to attend first, assess the nature of the problem, then call on other members of the Emergency Management Team as appropriate depending on the situation, before going on to control the source of the leak. Other members of the Emergency Management Team and the Deputy Building Recovery Manager must also be able to control an incident quickly; provide training as this individual cannot be guaranteed to be available at all times.

Figure 3.3 shows a checklist for the Building Recovery Manager.

Checklist for the Building Recovery Manager	
Responsibilities:	
Render the building accessible and safe to salvage and work in.	
Containment of the building after the incident (sourcing contractors).	
Control the environment of the affected area after the fire or flood to reduce humidity.	
Secure and control the site.	

Figure 3.3 *Checklist for Building Recovery Manager*

Distribute personal protective equipment, conduct risk assessments and monitor staff welfare.	
Source space suitable for the recovery effort and logistical support.	
Immediate actions to be completed (where appropriate):	
Create cordon if necessary to limit access.	
Determine any structural risk to the building with the appropriate professionals (insert cross reference to suppliers' page).	
Conduct a building check to ensure that all areas of damage are identified and reported.	
Arrange for standing water to be removed from building (insert cross reference to suppliers list). Use pumps and wet vacs. If utilities are turned off, you may need to hire a generator.	
Isolate utilities if necessary.	
Risk assess salvage operation and render building safe and accessible for salvage (insert cross reference to risk assessment form). Source and distribute personal protective equipment. This may include a fire risk assessment if alarms are off and temporary fire alarm signal measures are implemented.	
As soon as the building is risk assessed and entry is possible, ensure that any undamaged collections are protected from further damage (e.g. seepage of water). Actions may include covering shelving in polythene sheeting or moving items (in consultation with the Collections Salvage Manager).	
Implement a site register system or badges for contractors and staff.	
Make arrangements for the security of the building and any decant areas.	
Make arrangements for any breaches to the building to be covered over and temporarily contained (e.g. covering gaps in roof, boarding windows).	
Source space for materials removed from the affected area; clear a route to this area.	
Establish a rest and first aid area if usual rest areas are inaccessible.	
Remove electrical equipment from the affected area for testing, repair or replacement.	
As the salvage operation progresses:	
Remove wet non-accessioned material (wet carpets, furniture, etc.) from area.	

Figure 3.3 *continued*   *(continued on next page)*

Install dehumidifiers and air movers in the affected area to ensure environmental conditions are stabilized and returned to pre-incident levels.	
Reassess risk assessment periodically and monitor the usage of personal protective equipment by staff working in the salvage area and take action if necessary. Be aware of the risks of mould growth developing.	
Contact contractors to repair building functions such as environmental control, lifts, racking.	
Ensure catering is provided for the staff rest area.	
Provide logistical support to the salvage operation, including giving assistance with moving items from the salvage site to the assessment area.	
Manage parking and access to site for contractors.	
After the salvage operation is completed:	
Arrange for the sanitization of the affected area if necessary.	
Continue to monitor levels of humidity and temperature in the affected area. If environmental conditions fail to return to normal, appoint a specialist contractor.	
Make arrangements for the replacement and redecoration of the fixtures and fittings of the affected area.	
Make assessments of any further repair work that is necessary to the ingress point to prevent a recurrence of the problem.	
Re-evaluate the risk assessment of the building to establish risks of occurrence of this problem in other areas.	
Liaise with utility companies on the restoration of services.	

Figure 3.3   *continued*

Collections Salvage Manager

This role usually sits best with someone in a collections management or collections care senior position. The task is to organize the recovery of damaged stock but this is potentially complex in a major incident given the short time you have to work with and the evolving situation. It may involve leading a large group of people so some consideration will need to be given to the interpersonal, leadership and management skills of potential candidates. Another key attribute is to be able to work quickly and pragmatically, adapting usual best practice for handling objects in the constrained circumstances of a recovery operation. These issues will be discussed more in Chapter 6.

In some emergencies there is a potential conflict between people with curatorial responsibility for the collection and those who are responsible for its preservation or conservation. These issues are discussed in Chapter 7 in the section on priority lists. In a real emergency, there needs to be a balance between the collections that are a priority because of their value, and those that might deteriorate most quickly and need fast intervention. This is made yet more complex in a museum setting where there may be several different curatorial departments all concurrently trying to arrange a salvage operation, each of whom regards their own collection as the most important and deserving immediate attention, against a backdrop of a finite conservation capacity.

The person selected for this role must be able to bridge these issues and robustly manage the salvage process. The role will be made much easier in an emergency if there are predetermined salvage priority lists, whose drafting all parties have been consulted on and agreed to.

Figure 3.4 shows a checklist for the Collections Salvage Manager.

Checklist for the Collections Salvage Manager	
Responsibilities:	
Protect and avoid damage to unaffected at-risk collections.	
Minimize further deterioration and secondary damage to the damaged material after the point of discovery through prompt action.	
Manage the salvage, removal and appropriate treatment for the damaged material.	
Prioritize the damaged items for recovery.	
Communicate handling techniques to staff.	
Immediate actions to be completed (where appropriate):	
Establish a policy on the materials to be salvaged, including identifying priorities and a salvage schedule. Consult priority lists (insert cross reference) and consider high-demand stock (e.g. short-loan) and swiftly deteriorating formats (e.g. coated paper, parchment, leather, photo-graphic material). Discuss with curators, archivists and subject librarians.	
From initial projections of the damage count, decide on whether specialist contractors or external assistance (e.g. local emergency support networks, your emergency salvage contractor, conservators) will be required to assist; contact them as appropriate. Cherry-pick items to be treated in-house and items to be sent away for freezing.	
Source labour for moving material and, In conjunction with the Building Recovery Manager, make sure there is sufficient space.	
Source all materials required for the salvage operation. This may include crates, trestle tables, blotter, tags and polythene bags.	

Figure 3.4 *Checklist for the Collections Salvage Manager*   *(continued on next page)*

If appropriate, establish a system for weeding either at the point of salvage or at the treatment area in discussion with curators, archivists and subject librarians. Pack separately materials not to be salvaged, and discuss with insurers how these items are to be listed for the purposes of claiming.	
Establish a documentation system for tracking items (insert cross reference to documentation page).	
Create teams of up to four people for the salvage operation and ensure that conservation and collections handling skills are mixed. Ensure that staff are briefed on health and safety matters, personal protective equipment, documentation and handling techniques before salvage begins.	
Photograph scene before any items are moved and try to take photographs throughout.	
As the salvage operation progresses:	
Monitor timescales and work rate very carefully – if the timescale for removal of all materials is likely to exceed two to three days, look for ways in which they can be improved and be prepared to change tactic (e.g. reduce material to be air-dried because of space or time constraints).	
Think ahead about the requirements for equipment such as crates and ensure they are delivered to schedule.	
Work with the Building Recovery Manager to monitor the environmental in situ conditions in the store affected with a view to the protection of unaffected material.	
Remove the polythene sheeting from shelving when the immediate threat of damage is over or replace with fire-retardant polythene.	
Keep staff motivated throughout the salvage process.	
After the salvage operation is completed:	
Obtain quotations from restoration companies and conservators for any drying or cleaning work that can be outsourced and discuss with insurers.	
Replace all used equipment from the disaster kit.	
Ensure that appropriate remedial work is undertaken to avoid repetition of the incident.	
Do not reshelve anything that was water damaged into the store until you are satisfied that it is thoroughly dry. It may be advisable to quarantine for six weeks and monitor for signs of mould growth.	
Conduct a review of the performance of the plan.	
Thank members of staff who were involved in the recovery operation.	

Figure 3.4 *continued*

Service Continuity Manager

The Service Continuity Manager ensures that, despite the incident that has occurred, business carries on as usual, as far as is practicable, and the interruption to customers and users is minimized. The content of business continuity is discussed in more detail in Chapter 9. The priorities of the person in this role in particular are very site-specific rendering it difficult to provide general guidance on them. In this book the general function of media relations and communication has been allocated to the person in this role although it may belong to someone in a separate role in larger organizations. The Emergency Response Manager should sign off any statements.

Figure 3.5 shows a checklist for the Service Continuity Manager.

Checklist for the Service Continuity Manager	
Responsibilities:	
Manage business continuity and resumption of service.	
Restore administration systems (phones, post, etc.).	
Restore internet connectivity and access to servers and web-platforms.	
Communicate with users and stakeholders about the incident.	
Communicate with staff.	
Deal with the media.	
Immediate actions to be completed (where appropriate):	
With the Emergency Response Manager, make an initial assessment of whether any service can be operated in the next 24 hours based on whether any part of the institution is unaffected and has power, any collections are unaffected and any online materials can be accessed. If the decision to close is preferred, seek approval from or advise the necessary line managers.	
Ensure that telephone lines are diverted either to a mobile telephone number or a switchboard and that those receiving these calls are aware of the current status of whether the service is open or closed.	
Update the institution's website on the current status of opening and send a circular note to all registered users via e-mail. Social media accounts (such as Facebook or Twitter) may also be used, especially if servers are down.	
Issue a statement to the press either directly or via your marketing or public relations office. Ensure that the press-release wording is approved by the Emergency Management Team before issuing it.	

Figure 3.5 *Checklist for the Service Continuity Manager*

(continued on next page)

In conjunction with the Emergency Response Manager, notify all depositors and stakeholders about the status of the institution.	
Where possible assess whether IT infrastructure, including internet access, is operational.	
Notify any institutions with which you have reciprocal arrangements of your situation and that you may need to activate these arrangements for a period of time. Find out how many extra students each partner institution can accept.	
As the salvage operation progresses:	
Keep the press updated on progress and remember to include updates by e-mail, social media and via the internet to users.	
Ensure that any staff not involved in the recovery effort are advised at home of any alternative locations to report to when they are next due at work.	
Arrange for directing and transporting users to temporary sites.	
Ensure that servers and off-site copies of essential documents are unaffected.	
Contact a data recovery company if electronic records or infrastructure require recovery (insert cross reference to suppliers list).	
After the salvage operation is completed:	
Make the necessary arrangements to minimize disruption to users, based on the anticipated timescales for complete recovery.	
Participate in the debriefing and revise contingency arrangements.	

Figure 3.5 *continued*

Emergency Management Team additional roles

The four roles described above would broadly fit the majority of organizations in the information services and heritage sectors, balancing concerns about people, collections, buildings and business, but there are exceptions. Some organizations are too big to fit this model precisely and require additional roles and perhaps a command structure in the vein of the gold, silver and bronze model structure operated by the emergency services.

In very large organizations, small incidents are managed by an operational response team, often known as an Emergency Response Team, comprising perhaps the Building Recovery Manager and, if collections are involved, the

Collections Salvage Manager. This corresponds to the bronze level in the emergency services – the team first on scene. Those in this team manage the incident but have the capability to escalate large or complex incidents and make senior colleagues, the silver command or Emergency Management Team, aware. This may be appropriate where tactical decisions are required as the implications are not isolated, thus necessitating a co-ordinated response. There may be wider consequences from the incident and management input is needed.

The silver command can escalate to gold command any incidents that threaten the wider parent organization, or where the situation is especially complex and stretches the silver command and a strategic approach is needed. The gold command can then provide top-down support for incident management and strategy, supporting the silver command. The gold command could also be called on if there was more than one damage site and deployment of resources was an issue. This would be the major incident or crisis team for the organization.

This model works in very large services that are part of large parent organizations, for example a university library with the senior managers responding only to major incidents, with small-scale incidents managed locally by library staff. The senior managers, the Emergency Management Team, can escalate the incident to the wider university incident management team where necessary, or come under their command if multiple university sites are affected.

In situations such as public records management, museums, archives and libraries, there is more of a blur between the silver and bronze level as the organizations are smaller and there is no separate Emergency Response Team and Emergency Management Team. Nevertheless, the capability to escalate to the highest (gold) level (for example the emergency or contingency planning officer for the local authority) exists. These matters are expanded in Chapter 4 when discussing categorized response.

Often in larger organizations security, IT, administration, finance and human resources become roles in themselves and cannot be managed adequately by one person in any of the main four roles identified above because of the scale of the task. In such situations, be aware of potential problems in effective communication: a very flat management structure can make it difficult for the Emergency Response Manager to manage information effectively and support more than five or six people given the demands of a disaster recovery situation.

Typically, in the fire service, command and control is managed hierarchically. An overall incident commander is appointed, who then appoints sector commanders either to lead the fire-fighting in a particular area or to manage a particular task. Given this structure, the flow of information is managed very effectively and the incident commander is not overwhelmed.

Consider in a large organization whether tasks can be grouped. Under the role of Building Recovery Manager, the tasks of welfare for staff, health and safety and security fit thematically. Under the Service Continuity Manager, the roles of dealing with the press and IT can also be grouped. The Emergency Response Manager can be supported by someone leading administration, human resources and financial issues. Some organizations also identify the role of quartermaster, a title borrowed from the military, whose responsibility is to co-ordinate supplies and provisions. Operationally, in the salvage operation it may also be helpful to have identified salvage team leaders, who are not part of the Emergency Management Team but are identified in advance as people who will supervise the air-drying and object assessment process.

Ensuring your Emergency Management Team works effectively
Smaller organizations or units

In a small organization with only a handful of staff and a large collection it is not viable to have more roles on the Emergency Management Team than members of staff. In some cases, a small staff is not a problem for the recovery operation to be effective, particularly in the case of a records management service embedded within a company, local authority or hospital setting where substantial internal support is available via IT, facilities, the press and marketing office, and so on. This enables staff to focus on the salvage operation itself and the overall co-ordination of all the various parties, with the result probably that two roles will suffice, and tasks that are not managed externally can be split evenly between the roles. In these scenarios, given the limited numbers of people and the volume of collections potentially to be salvaged, for anything other than a very small-scale incident it is most sensible to assume that external support will be required for salvage, such as a restoration company or a local group of salvage volunteers where those exist.

Some small museums have only a very small number of professional staff, if any at all, and they do not have the luxury of the resources of a parent organization such as a local authority to provide reinforcement. In volunteer-run institutions there may not even be certainty about who will be available on the day to lead the salvage operation and the museum cannot compel individuals to be involved. The role of Emergency Response Manager should still exist, and a list of responsibilities drafted, but it must be expected that a number of people could carry out this role. Seek external support to deal with the building and collections via a comprehensive insurance policy if possible. Failing this, establish reciprocal links with other institutions in the local area.

However small the organization, it is always worth separating the role of Emergency Response Manager and Collections Salvage Manager. In a very small-scale incident, one person may easily be able to manage salvage and incident control, but as the scale of an incident develops, it becomes increasingly challenging for one individual to be simultaneously filling crates, documenting, prioritizing collections for salvage while also liaising with facilities, insurance and other agencies by telephone.

Multiple sites

There are also situations where a service operates across multiple separate sites. Often in these circumstances there is one main site or central office with the majority of collection holdings (e.g. a university library) and smaller satellite sites with fewer staff and collections located elsewhere. It is sensible to provide a scalable emergency plan for each location, with managers in each site capable of responding quickly to small to medium-scale incidents locally and independently, with emergency action checklists detailed and equipment provided, but with the flexibility to request support from the central site should the incident prove too large or complex for them to manage alone. Here there may be multiple local Emergency Response Teams for the individual sites, but a central Emergency Management Team for major incidents such as fluvial floods and fires, with additional equipment and expertise to provide where necessary.

Caveats

In real emergencies, a solid management structure where people know what they are doing makes a significant difference to the efficiency of the recovery operation, which in turn minimizes the disruption to the service and damage to the collections. Avoid duplicating tasks and omitting key activities, for example, two individuals each assuming the other had contacted their insurers, whereas in fact nobody had.

Nevertheless, some flexibility is required. A deputy is required for each role. Perhaps if the Emergency Response Manager is unavailable, the Collections Salvage Manager can step up to this role, and someone else steps into that role. Having a 'roving deputy' may help in a situation with a small staff, so rather than having four roles and four deputies, there are four roles and one deputy. Restrictions need to be placed on when key personnel take leave. Imagine a scenario where the Emergency Response Manager and the Collections Salvage Manager were simultaneously on leave when there was a major emergency. In some large institutions, it may be necessary to state a line of succession for the person in charge, the Emergency Response Manager, if the pre-allocated person is unable to fulfil this role. Certainly in the immediate phase of incident response and control of a major incident, senior staff may not be on-site initially and so incident control should be something that a wide group of staff are trained in so the Emergency Management Team can assemble and then take over.

Practical workings of the team

The team may tick boxes on paper but does it work in practice? Experience shows that this may require some rehearsal and refinement. It can be a challenge to involve senior staff who are not involved in the Emergency Management Team (particularly in very large organizations) who are present on the day of an incident and wish to manage the recovery process for their collection in their own way, without any reference to the plan, or awareness of the wider implications of their actions or the overall scale of the incident. Some individuals may feel that their collections have not been allocated sufficient resource because other priorities have been selected by the Emergency Management Team.

Such situations require firm personnel management by the Emergency Response Manager. Similarly consider the implications of two colleagues who do not get on well having to work together at a time of great stress. Can that be managed? If you have the luxury of enough people wanting to participate then managing personalities may also be important. Does it work to have junior staff given a senior role, particularly that of leading salvage operations, and be required to ask senior colleagues to perform menial tasks, or make compromised collections salvage decisions, which the senior colleague may not agree, without background training and context? Often the sources of such friction can be anticipated and the techniques for managing them rehearsed. Involving all staff in training in the rationale behind the emergency plan should minimize such scenarios as discussed in Chapter 10.

The semantics of job titles are not of great importance. Some organizations call managers leaders, others call them officers. There is no need to change these if you have an established plan. The vital issue is to ensure your emergency plan covers all areas – buildings, services, people and collections – and that there is buy-in from the staff who will fulfil these roles.

CHAPTER 4

Incident control

Introduction

The procedures an organization uses to report and respond to an incident – so that it is controlled and contained as quickly as possible – are discussed in this chapter. It examines how to organize a response to an emergency safely and sensibly in order to limit damage and subsequent impacts, and considers which incidents might constitute an 'emergency' and therefore fall within the scope of the plan.

The impact of successful incident control

If the first phase of incident response is managed successfully, its discovery, reporting and immediate control, the potential for reduction in damage and subsequent service disruption is significant. If 100 litres of water discharge from a burst pipe each minute, obviously swift control of the leak, containment of the seeping water, and protection of collections will all serve to minimize the impact of this emergency, potentially averting substantial damage to the collections and building.

Unfortunately, this emergency phase can prove very challenging and very overwhelming. Some individuals can panic and start taking immediate action without any recourse to procedures, or even consideration of their own safety or that of others. Sometimes the shock of the situation can make individuals freeze, making action very difficult as the individual cannot think clearly or act decisively, as demonstrated in this account by Carrie Taylor of the Wordsworth Trust:

> No coherent thoughts raced through my head, only to contact the curator even though it was a Saturday. Within a minute other members of the security and estates team were assembled. Stop-cocks needed to be located and at first no-one could remember where they were, only the horror of uncertainty. We thought

the main one was located in the road way under the snow and ice and it took
some considerable time and effort to locate the grid.

It can be very difficult to predict how individuals will react in these suddenly
pressurized situations. Some individuals can remain composed and think
about safety sensibly and take appropriate actions to contain the incident as
quickly as possible with or without a plan. This is where a plan should fit in:
it can corral a diverse group of people into responding to an emergency
situation in the most appropriate way, which will ensure damage is
minimized and safety risks are assessed and reduced.

All organizations should already have instructions for evacuating if there
is a fire, which will be practised and marshalled properly in order to comply
with local fire safety legislation. Ideally the emergency plan will draft equally
efficient and safety-conscious instructions to guide response to other
emergencies. Institutions should consider carefully which types of incidents
to include in their emergency plans, factoring in issues such as whether the
building opens to the public (not in the case of a closed archive or records
management service). Not all procedures listed will necessarily be required
for every library, archive or museum, but – as will be argued later – threats
other than just fire and water damage should probably be considered in an
emergency plan.

Categorized response?

In drafting emergency control procedures, organizations need to make sure
it is clear when it is appropriate to notify the Emergency Management Team.
Generally there are two approaches that organizations adopt: categorized
response, or a uniform procedure for all incidents. In the first, an incident is
categorized by staff on the ground who notify a predetermined set of people
according to the incident category, with specific procedures followed
depending on the level of incident. This system is often adopted in larger
organizations. The presumption is that small to medium-sized incidents are
handled locally, using emergency plans but without necessarily the invocation
of the entire Emergency Management Team. This system can be cumbersome
for institutions with a smaller team, however, and a more common-sense
approach is required, as was outlined in Chapter 3.

In the categorized approach, the members of staff who respond to
emergency incidents make an assessment at the scene, or in some cases
remotely, about what level of response is required, as illustrated in Table 4.1.
This decision can be made on several criteria:

- the nature of incident (isolated leak, fire, water-main burst, gas leak, utility failure)
- human safety
- the quantity of material reportedly affected
- the value of material affected (strongrooms, galleries).

Depending on the type of incident, a predetermined level of response can be provided.

Table 4.1 *Sample incident categorization table*

	Type of incident	Approximate quantity of material	Who to contact
Level 1	Minor incident, unlikely to result in personal injury or major damage to collections	< 10 items unless high priority area such as strongroom or server room, which automatically elevates to Level 3	BRM*; CSM** (if needed)
Level 2	An emergency that may result in personal injury or damage to collections but can be managed internally, e.g. localized leak	> 10 < 500 unless high priority area such as strongroom or server room, which automatically elevates to Level 3	BRM; CSM (if needed); inform EMT***
Level 3	An emergency that cannot be managed internally or might generate harm to the collection, buildings, staff or users, or any incident however small that affects high priority items, e.g. a fire, substantial flood, utility failure	>500 < 10,000	EMT convenes; inform Major Incident Team
Level 4	An emergency that cannot be managed internally and threatens all aspects of the institution; co-ordination with wider emergency response plans necessary, e.g. terrorist incident, major natural disaster, explosion	10,000+	EMT convenes; Major Incident Team convenes
* BRM Building Recovery Manager ** CSM Collections Salvage Manager *** EMT Emergency Management Team			

The response can then be tailored to the specific nature of the incident. If a leaking air-conditioning unit has caused an isolated leak in a public area, affecting relatively low-value stock, a response by the entire Emergency Management Team could be deemed excessive. If such incidents are rare, then the opportunity to practise emergency response may be enthusiastically received, but if, as for some organizations, leaks are a common occurrence, notification of all senior management every time may lead to a 'cry-wolf' effect of complacency, where perhaps serious emergencies are not responded to with sufficient urgency. The alternative solution might be for the first responder to elect to notify the Building Recovery Manager who would then manage the small-scale salvage operation and notify the Collections Salvage Manager if objects are affected.

If however the leaking air-conditioning unit was located in a strongroom and high-value material was affected, the Emergency Response Manager should probably be made aware. The categorization should make this clear – any flood, however small, affecting a high-priority area, means the Emergency Management Team should all be made aware. Decisions may be made to involve a higher number of salvage volunteers to ensure salvage is completed not just within 72 hours, but as quickly as possible. Similarly, if the collections affected were short-loan stock, there could be an impact on service and perhaps both the Service Continuity Manager and Collections Salvage Manager should be notified.

Training is critical to ensure that those dealing with the emergency can identify the level of the incident accurately. It is not appropriate to say an incident involving 100 items is minor and there is no need to call out staff over the weekend. It will depend entirely on the circumstances and the areas and assets affected.

Further criteria to consider are whether the building should be closed and who can make the decision to close it. Utility failure may result in IT systems crashing, lighting failure and non-functioning alarm systems, posing safety and security issues. The decision to close in those circumstances will need to be made by a senior manager and the business continuity issues must be managed. There are potential impacts on all aspects of the building, including the collections, in such circumstances so all members of the Emergency Management Team would need to be called.

There is also the potential for a very serious incident to occur, which will not only make it necessary to notify the Emergency Management Team, but also lead to wider plans for the parent organization to be invoked, and the response will need to be integrated and cohesive. Such major incidents include mass flooding across a wide site, an explosion and terrorist incident. In such circumstances, a local emergency plan cannot operate in isolation but must be supported by the parent organization, whose staff will control access to the site, safety issues and so on. To some extent the emergency response will be taken out of the hands of library staff for a period of time at the beginning of the emergency. A categorized response can accommodate these constraints.

An advantage of this kind of categorized system is that busy people are not involved in dealing with minor incidents unnecessarily, which can diminish patience for emergency planning in general. The response is proportionate but channels exist to call on additional resources where appropriate. Disadvantages include the fact that plan maintenance is more complex when there are several paths of response to maintain and the senior staff who would inevitably be involved in dealing with major incidents sometimes do not appreciate the logistical constraints of salvaging water-damaged materials as they have few activation experiences and opportunities to practise. This can be remedied through training and constant supervision.

Uniform approach

The alternative method is to have a uniform approach to emergency response. Here, the first responder attends and assesses who is required to assist in the recovery process and notifies colleagues on the Emergency Management Team. As the response is one-dimensional rather than graduated, individuals need to determine what action is required. So in attending an incident such as a leaking pipe in a stack area, the first responder (usually most appropriately the Building Recovery Manager, as discussed in Chapter 3) would decide whether or not to notify or request the assistance of the rest of the Emergency Management Team.

As with a categorized response, training and rehearsal is critical to ensure that all members of staff in the institution can recognize an incipient emergency, and that those responding from the Emergency Management Team can determine which colleagues to involve and what actions should be taken. The response is still categorized, but in an informal way. The advantages of this system are that it promotes a good team ethic in the Emergency Management Team and there are usually more practical opportunities to test the dynamics of the emergency plan. The problem is that it is open to interpretation and common sense can sometimes be a relative term.

The categorized response often works very well in very large organizations but can prove more difficult for smaller and medium-sized organizations, where a uniform approach and common sense usually works better. The guidance for incident control detailed below in this chapter is written for a uniform response but can be adapted for a categorized response. The underpinning principles of the phased approaches to incidents involving water damage in the next section should also be integral to any procedures for a categorized response. The checklists for the Emergency Management Team detailed in Chapter 3 also adopt this uniform approach: not every activity will be required in every emergency and it will be up to the individuals concerned to assess whether some actions are necessary. A Building Recovery Manager will not always need to organize a rest area for staff; a Service Continuity Manager will not always need to update the institution's website if the incident was not obvious and has had no impact on services; a Collections Salvage Manager may not need to organize freezer facilities for damaged stock if the incident is small in scale; and the Emergency Response Manager will not necessarily need to involve insurers if the incident is small. Crucially, the plan provides a prompt, and the individuals can use their common sense to decide what actions are necessary.

Immediate responses to water damage

Response to water damage could involve dealing with river or ground water flooding, drains backing up, leaks, escapes of water, water ingress through the building fabric such as the roof, or ingress due to water main bursts. These incidents are the most common cause for plan invocation and so the process for incident control will be discussed in some detail.

When responding to an incident such as an internal burst pipe, it may seem counter-intuitive to some to suggest that one of the last actions to consider in the immediate response phase is to move damaged items out of the path of the cascade of water. However, in a situation where an individual discovers a leak, sees boxes getting wet and then spends ten minutes moving those wet boxes out of the water, then that response has been well intentioned but poorly planned. The instinctive reaction has been to protect the collection but this person's action has not only worsened the damage to the collection in all likelihood but also put the individual at substantial personal risk.

In that ten-minute period other activities should have taken precedence. At this stage, nobody else knows there is a problem. How much more quickly could those boxes be moved with an extra three pairs of hands? It is not yet obvious where the water is coming from. Simultaneous damage could be occurring somewhere else as a result of the same problem, perhaps where more important collections are housed. Nobody currently has turned off the stop-cock to cease the flow of water and in those ten minutes perhaps an extra 1000 litres of water have discharged unnecessarily. This will result in more objects getting wet (perhaps because of build-up of water on the floor) and a greater impact on the environment (relative humidity), which might put the rest of the collection at risk of mould growth. If the stop-cock can only be turned off by a member of staff in the facilities section, those staff need to be notified and travel to site, which will take time. Consider the impact of a delay in notifying facilities or your drain clearance contractor if there is flooding after a heavy rainstorm – in all likelihood yours will not be the only building affected and there is a chance that facilities staff may operate a first-call, first-serve response to callouts. In order to gain support at the earliest possible juncture, it is critical to be among the first wave of people to call for help when facilities and suppliers operate with a limited resource.

An additional problem is that while you are moving the wet boxes the flow of water may move or increase, or the build-up of water on the floor might rise to such a level that initially unaffected material starts to get wet. Your first priority from a collections perspective is to ring-fence the damaged material at the outset, so that nothing that is currently dry gets wet, and nothing which is only damp at the point of discovery sits under water for a prolonged period and eventually gets saturated. Therefore the cascade of water should be diverted away from the collections if possible, or if this is not possible, collections should be covered with polythene sheeting to shield them from the water. If there is a risk of water building up on the floor and tipping over the level of the bottom shelf, soakage cushions, wet vacuums or puddle pumps should be used to prevent it happening. If these resources are not available, the bottom row items at risk could be moved to prevent damage that would increase the scale significantly from the initial quantity of damaged boxes.

The greatest concern of a rushed response is the failure to consider issues of health and safety. No form of risk assessment, even mental, in this scenario has been conducted, which is putting the individual taking action at very high risk. Water is falling over live electrical points, which have not been isolated. Short circuits could be triggered, which present a fire risk. No one necessarily knows that this salvage operation is going on as the work is being conducted alone without raising the alarm. There is water all over the floor, causing slip hazards. The water could be coming from a foul pipe, which has not been investigated. No personal protective equipment is being worn. Health and safety in salvage situations is discussed more fully in the next chapter but it is critical that before salvage begins and work in the area affected is authorized that area has been made acceptably safe and that those engaged in salvage are fully aware of the hazards and the precautions needed to make the area safe to work in.

There is no universal way of responding to such an incident in any institution. As ever, there will be specific circumstances to be considered, such as whether facilities staff must be called to turn off stop cocks or whether this is something that can be done by trained staff who possess the plan and know what the correct procedures are. However, there are some basic principles, which should render the alarm raising process as efficient and safe as possible.

Phase 1 People, reporting, organizing

These are the immediate activities to undertake if there is water damage:

- Refer to emergency plan once report is received of water damage taking place.
- Notify Emergency Management Team (usually the Building Recovery Manager, who will notify others as appropriate).
- The Building Recovery Manager takes charge of the situation and investigates the situation in the affected area.
- Consider people's safety – evacuate area and restrict access if necessary.
- Notify other members of Emergency Management Team as necessary (so Collections Salvage Manager if there is collections damage, Service Continuity Manager if IT equipment for example).
- Establish a control point.
- Ask extra staff to report to the control point to help.

Whoever discovers the incident may need to clear the affected area of users, if in a public space, before the arrival of the Building Recovery Manager, for safety and security reasons. The procedures listed assume that other action should await the Building Recovery Manager, but if possible empower *all* staff to take the actions listed under phases 1 to 3, as it will limit the amount of damage significantly by cutting out the potential for delay. As staff may try to take action anyway in good faith, it makes more sense to train them in safe and appropriate action – basic dos and don'ts at the very least. A balance must be struck between being over-precious about objects and protecting them. It is absurd to have competent people available to take action to contain an incident but unaware of the correct procedures or locations of equipment and therefore unable to take action.

The Building Recovery Manager should visit the scene to verify the situation and assess if further members of the Emergency Management Team should be notified. All members of the Emergency Management Team could be called automatically by the person discovering the incident, without the verification step, but this may lead to a number of false alarms and frustration with the plan. It should be clear in the procedures who to contact if the Building Recovery Manager cannot be reached.

It is worth visiting the affected area to identify the source of the water by looking at its colour and speed. The decision whether or not to clear the area must be made on the grounds of safety and security. Many people's safety must be taken into account, not just that of members of the public in the area. It is important that staff are prevented from going into the area where there has been water damage, and any contractors not connected with emergency response should be kept out to prevent accidents from occurring. In a very serious situation the entire building may need to be evacuated but the Emergency Management Team should make this decision, as it may prove excessive and unnecessarily disruptive to public services.

The logic of establishing a control point is to maintain contact with key personnel should the problem subsequently escalate due to further leaks, and the water seeping through the building. Communication by mobile phone may be possible, but reception can be intermittent and individuals may have forgotten their handsets initially, so it may be helpful to have a control point, to which information is fed and individuals report for action, and then return when they have completed an assigned task. Additional staff who may be required to assist with salvage can report to someone at this point in order to be allocated a role. If people attempt to salvage items on their own it can lead to chaos and safety risks, as the well meaning action is not necessarily directed to the most pressing or important task.

Phase 2 Incident containment

The next phases are incident containment and damage limitation to the building and collection. At this stage, the Building Recovery Manager usually remains in overall control (unless they consider the incident sufficiently serious to warrant notifying the Emergency Response Manager) and this person will supervise the operation to control the source of the problem. If damage to collections is also occurring, then the Collections Salvage Manager will have been contacted in Phase 1 and will lead the operation to limit the damage to objects. These phases can happen in tandem as soon as the electricity to the affected areas has been isolated.

Actions may include:

- isolating electricity to affected areas of the building if water is coming into contact with electrical circuits, appliances and installations, including lighting and hidden wiring
- identifying the cause of the leak
- isolating the source of the leak if possible (turning off stop-cocks, closing windows and so on)

- redirecting the flow of water and stopping further entry (diverting the leak, using absorbent cushions)
- checking all areas within the building for signs of further leakage.

The source of the water will need to be investigated and the source traced. The water could be coming from clean or foul water pipes within the building, an external source from the roof, a blocked gutter or an open window, for example, a horizontal source such as a burst water main or power washing of paths, or from drains, sewers or fluvial floods. It may not be initially obvious as water can move vertically and horizontally through a building, taking the path of least resistance.

In many organizations only facilities staff are allowed to complete the tasks necessary to control an incident, even if it involves relatively simple tasks such as turning off stop-valves and isolating electricity. In some organizations this does not cause problems, but in many others it causes extreme delays to salvage starting as it is not safe to enter an area affected by water if the electricity is still falling over live electrical points. Given the potential impact of delays to the start of salvage, it is worthwhile negotiating to see if some staff (including all members of the Emergency Management Team) can be trained in the locations of distribution boards and stop-valves. Turning supply off should be straightforward when clear instructions are provided, but restarting supply requires input from an appropriately qualified technician.

If facilities staff are not content with this suggestion then it reinforces the need for there to be a clear understanding for the need for a prompt response to an emergency involving your building and it is crucial to foster a positive relationship before there is an emergency. If turning off power may lead to knock-on impacts (such as trapping people in the lift, taking out your alarm systems), it is helpful to have a checklist on the relevant appendix and to have a laminated version of it by the distribution board.

Remember in the case of a vertical flood from a higher floor, water may also have come into contact with hidden electrical cabling, which also poses a safety risk as there might be an electric shock and short circuits triggering fires. For floods coming from the side or underneath (e.g. storm or river flooding), electrical risks may be less of an issue if only the ground floor is affected and the height of the water is well below socket level, although if water has gone from ground level to a basement area, then there is both vertical and horizontal flooding, and precautions will be necessary.

If the water is from the mains water system or from a sprinkler system turn off local stop-valves and pumps to prevent further discharge. If the problem is due to a roof leak then diversion of that water will be necessary initially after which attempts can be made to repair the fault or remove the blockage.

This will necessitate facilities staff doing the work or an emergency contractor being found.

Problems associated with drains and water coming in from the sides are more difficult to stop independently, although water entry can be limited using soakage pads that act as sandbags, and trying to pump out as much water as possible. If external support is required beyond facilities staff (for example it is necessary to contact a utility or drain clearance company), ring quickly to avoid delays occurring because of other people in the same situation as you calling them more quickly. Michael Hodgson, Conservation Officer from Glamorgan Archives, had this experience during a heavy rain event affecting many buildings locally: 'In a situation like widespread flooding there is of course going to be competing demand for certain services so the quicker you can respond the more likely you are to secure what you need. We were able to secure the hire of a pump but it was the last one they had in stock.'

It is not appropriate to enter an area that has leaking water until the electricity has been isolated for safety reasons and risk of electrocution. Arguably if the electricity can be isolated in a few seconds this should be done even before the source of the water is identified as at least then salvage and incident containment work can begin, thus minimizing the damage. If it takes ten minutes to trace the water back to the source and the electricity is only isolated then, there are ten lost minutes where the salvage team could have been preventing damage. It is important to retain some power if possible as extension cables may be needed to run emergency lighting in the area that has been flooded, and where the power is now off.

Think through definitions of what a 'flood' and a 'leak' are for reporting purposes. One curator has commented in a recent training event that when she reported a leaking pipe to facilities staff, eventually someone attended with a mop and bucket. The leak she reported was substantial and required wet vacuums and a much quicker response. The staff in this library have since agreed that anything where water is discharging at speed will now be referred to as a flood. When reporting incidents to facilities staff, ensure that everyone is using the same terminology to avoid lost time. The nickname by which you know a particular gallery or store may mean nothing to a facilities person who knows it just as a room number. Clarity over vocabulary and terminology is important to avoid delays.

Another key activity at this stage is to conduct a thorough building check. Damage has been discovered in one area but it is not known if this is the only area of damage or one of multiple sites. It may be that an area that houses more vital material is simultaneously affected. A thorough building check is therefore essential in order to ensure that salvage activities are targeted appropriately. Water can move laterally as well as vertically through a building so check all areas on the same level and beneath the known source of the damage. Those conducting the checks should take torches with them to check rooms without natural light rather than turn the light on on entry.

Phase 3 Damage limitation

This phase can take place at the same time as Phase 2 if facilities and collections teams can work successfully in parallel. Actions may include:

- risk assessing the salvage operation (once electricity is isolated)
- assembling the disaster kit for containment
- pumping away standing water (if applicable – this task may also require the Building Recovery Manager)
- protecting unaffected at-risk collections
- covering wet materials if water is continuing to seep
- clearing surface water (using mops or wet vacs)
- photographing the scene (before this stage if possible but at least before anything is moved).

Before staff are permitted to enter the affected area, electricity needs to be made safe, or indeed an assessment made as to whether this is a safety issue at all. With this issue neutralized, then the next phase is to undertake a more general risk assessment. There is often a temptation to attempt to salvage materials as soon as possible but a risk assessment must be conducted first to ensure that the salvage operation can occur with risk of injury minimized. The process for this is discussed in the next chapter. In order for salvage to progress safely and sensibly, remove standing water. Although salvage can begin with personnel wearing wellington boots, this is hazardous as it might put the salvaged collections at greater risk through being splashed and/or dropped. Surface water should also be vacuumed or mopped up. Further seeping water should also be cleared continually.

   With the risk assessment undertaken, safe systems of work identified and all salvage participants appropriately briefed and attired in personal protective equipment, damage limitation can begin. Where possible, divert the water away from the collections but this often proves challenging in buildings where records and collections are typically stored. Leak diverters or tarpaulins can be used but they require exposed pipes from which to hang the inverted umbrella. Polythene sheeting can also be used and rigged with twine.

Sheeting

If this proves too difficult, the shelving itself can be covered with polythene sheeting to go up, over the top and down the other side, with the bottom of the sheeting tucked under and taped as much as possible to the bottom of the shelf. For shelving against the wall, if possible tuck the sheeting down the back of the shelving, or the polythene can be taped to the wall or top shelf itself. This can prove difficult when surfaces are wet, even with gaffer tape, and staple guns may be better or weighting the polythene with battens or another weight (although with all these products, care must be taken with historic interiors and signage should be arranged if weights are above head height).

This task is ergonomically awkward so rehearse it as part of the training procedure, and provide a laminated sheet of instructions in disaster kits, with photographs. It is sensible to buy pre-folded polythene (4 metre widths folded to 1 metre, or 2 metres folded to 1 metre). Measure the length of polythene required with string before to avoid wastage. Cut the length required and then roll it towards the middle from each end. Make sure that any protruding bits of metal that might tear the sheeting are covered (foam insulation for water pipes is useful for this, cut into lengths). Using ladders, place the middle of the rolled polythene on the top of the shelf in the middle of the area to be covered, then roll down each side. Unravel the width and cover the shelving. Finally, tighten the polythene and tape either to the ground, or to the bottom shelf, ensuring approximately 40 cm overlap to any subsequent sections and that these are fully taped. Simple things such as tape guns with gaffer tape preloaded make this process much easier.

It is worth covering shelving with sheeting also where collections have obviously already got wet to limit further water penetration if water is continuing to seep through. If water is rising, you may wish to consider installing pumps (puddle pumps usually have a low inlet and may be more suitable in this situation than submersible pumps) and wet vacuums to try to control the rate at which the water rises, or alternatively also consider moving collections, although this is more labour intensive.

All these activities are labour intensive so recruit as many people as possible to assist. Make sure they are working in groups. For cutting and rigging polythene at least three per group works best as the sheets of polythene can be unwieldy with fewer people, and you have a third person to cut tape. Simple considerations also such as making sure taller people are split between teams will help, as they are able to reach further. If there is a large amount of standing water, it must be removed first before any substantial salvage work begins as it can be impractical to work while it is present, and it may exacerbate the damage to have ten people wading around, splashing water everywhere.

With this task completed, the damage has been ring-fenced. There will be wet material to deal with but crucially the overall quantity of damage should not rise further and the extent of damage and saturation should not increase either. Although it may seem that a lot of activities are required before damaged items are dealt with, the principle of controlling the situation and preventing additional damage is critical. Additional quantities of damage will put further pressure on the salvage operation and should be avoided.

Consider how you can factor high-priority, high-profile objects into these principles, especially in gallery spaces. Although the principle of ring-fencing damage before commencing the removal and salvage operation is usually the most appropriate course of action, salvage staff may feel it appropriate to make safe and remove from risk high-priority valuable items within their collection, even if they are not affected. This issue must be decided for each item individually and in the knowledge that 30 minutes spent protecting or moving priority items may mean that the damage increases more generally within the collection. Usually high-priority items are encapsulated or housed to a high standard and may be fairly resilient left in situ. It may be considered more appropriate to protect museum objects that are breakable or subject to handling damage in situ, even if they are high priority, rather than to move them. The main exception to this is unglazed watercolour paintings, which degrade immediately if exposed to leaking: remove them as a matter of priority. Salvage operations consist of decisions designed to emerge with the least worst outcome or, put more positively, the best outcome in the circumstances, and those responsible for the collection must decide how best to allocate resources. These issues are expanded in Chapter 6.

Out-of-hours response

For water-damage emergency situations that are discovered outside normal working hours, the same activities will be required, but there may be a longer lead time as the resources and people needed must travel to attend the scene. Procedures need to be written for those likely to discover an incident at these times in order to rouse the Emergency Management Team appropriately. These people may include security guards, contract cleaners, key-holders and weekend staff. For an institution open from 9 am to 5.30 pm Monday–Friday, out-of-hours constitutes 75% of the week, and it is vital that out-of-hours staff are fully aware how to report even the slightest concern they may have with a drip of water. A drip of water that is dismissed as minor and not worth reporting by a contract cleaner on a Friday evening at 5.45 pm could be a substantial flood by Monday morning. Communication and training is critical. Those discovering incidents out of hours are likely to be alone or working with a small number of colleagues in the building. Their safety should obviously be of paramount importance when drafting procedures. Make clear that no one should take action on their own or without appropriate risk assessment. If training and a list of key dos and don'ts can be provided on how to stop leaks and contain incidents potential damage may be reduced. Facilities personnel need to be available on a 24/7 callout system if possible.

Generally, the best protocol for someone discovering an emergency out of hours is to raise the alarm with a member of the Emergency Management Team. Members of the Emergency Management Team may benefit from having a series of questions to hand at home or in their purse or wallet as an aide-memoire to help to gauge the severity of the problem and determine the best course of action and whether they should visit the site or whether the problem can be left. Questions to answer include:

- What has happened?
- Where is the damage (with a prompt for areas to check)?
- Who is on-site?
- Who has been contacted?
- Is the normal meeting point okay?

Once the Emergency Management Team member has got the necessary information she or he should tell the caller what to do until they arrive (for example, tell them where to find the disaster plan, to liaise with emergency services until your arrival, not to enter any affected areas alone).

The Emergency Management Team will need to decide from this initial information what the best course of action is. Should the entire Emergency Management Team be asked to visit the site immediately, perhaps in the middle of the night? It may be better to ask people to attend site first thing in the morning having had a proper night's sleep, as their work rate and overall capability may be better. This decision will rest on common sense given the particular circumstances on the day and the individual circumstances of the institution. If facilities staff cannot attend until morning to isolate electricity and stop the leak, what can be achieved in the middle of the night by the Emergency Management Team?

In order to make the decision-making process as clear as possible, it may be helpful to give details of the circumstances in which it is necessary for an Emergency Management Team representative to visit the site. Any fire requires the presence of at least one member of the Emergency Management Team, as does a situation which cannot be brought under control (by stopping the leak or protecting collections from further damage) by those who found it, especially if important collections are affected and the Emergency Management Team can isolate the utilities without having to refer to facilities staff. If the leak has stopped and no further damage will occur, attendance by someone from the Emergency Management Team could arguably wait until morning.

Personal safety issues should also be considered and it may be more appropriate for people to meet at a hotel and travel together to the site than arrive on their own in the middle of the night. If the fire service are in attendance someone from the Emergency Management Team should go to the site to liaise and provide information for the incident commander, but in most circumstances the remainder of the Emergency Management Team may be more effective by attending first thing in the morning, as it is not likely that they will be able to do anything of practical benefit while the fire services are in attendance. Make sure that any reference material the fire services need is in the plan.

Procedures need to be clear for key-holders for alarmed buildings without a physical presence overnight, particularly if they are not members of the Emergency Management Team. If alarms go off in the middle of the night due to what is ostensibly an electrical fault, the ultimate cause of this fault could be a leak that has caused a short circuit, so a thorough investigation is required. Any unusual activity in environmental conditions could also be the sign of a leak, and security staff and weekend teams should know when to investigate these situations, perhaps checking building management system data. Out-of-hours staff, security staff and key-holders should also know where to find building plans, stop-valve instructions and any other vital information to provide to the fire service if there is a major incident.

It should also be made very clear to out-of-hours staff that it is acceptable to make contact with the Emergency Management Team, whatever the hour, whatever the time of year, if damage is occurring. It may be that the person they reach decides it is not necessary for them to attend the building immediately, but at least the problem has been reported. In a recent survey conducted on emergency response, several responders mentioned that security staff had been unwilling to call on senior staff at the weekend as they had not wanted to disturb them unnecessarily. In one case this was over the Christmas period and this well intentioned action resulted in substantially worse damage occurring through the failure to follow the plan and key activities not being completed. Rehearse the callout procedures regularly and give instruction on what to do if the first attempts to contact the Emergency Management Team are not successful. The message must be to keep trying those on the contacts list rather than just give up.

Maintaining awareness of procedures can be challenging in environments where security teams are sub-contracted or where there is a high turnover of staff, but efforts invested in these areas pay dividends if there is an emergency. Make sure that time is provided for meaningful emergency-procedures training in the contracts for security contractors and it is included in induction training for new staff.

Immediate responses to fire
Phase 1 Discovery, reporting, evacuating, roll calling

It is highly probable that organizations will already have documented and well rehearsed procedures in place to respond to the outbreak of fire in order to comply with legislative requirements. Fire marshals will have guidance already which will be designed to maximize human safety and prevent the spread of the fire. In addition to contacting the fire service (including a confirmation call if the fire is verified), instructions may include sweeping areas such as toilets and rest areas, disconnecting electrical equipment and closing all windows and doors (not locking) on evacuation, which may limit fire spread. There may be instructions not to open hot doors and to feel doors near the top with the back of the hand before opening them – if the top of a door is hot or smoke visible, it should remain closed as fire may be behind it. In addition lifts should not be used. Having evacuated all people from the building, the fire marshal will be responsible for conducting a roll call, including staff and signed-in visitors and contractors. The Emergency Management Team should defer to the fire marshals during this phase, taking over from them, if they are on-site, once the roll call has been completed and results reported to the Fire Brigade.

In some cases, there may be an opportunity to evacuate collections from the path of the fire while the fire is still burning. It is not recommended that this is attempted without the express authority of the Fire Brigade and their endorsement and support on the day. These issues are discussed below under Phase 3. Similarly it might be possible to use fire extinguishers to control the fire. This would be subject to internal risk assessments about the use of fire extinguishers and pre-incident training on using them safely. Advice varies from region to region but in interviews several fire service professionals have expressed a preference for civilians to evacuate the building if there is a fire rather than to try to fight the fire themselves.

Phase 2 Liaising with fire services

When fire services arrive, fire marshals should confirm whether anyone is unaccounted for. Thereafter Emergency Management Team staff should take over liaison if they are available, but the fire marshal should continue to liaise with the fire services pending the arrival of the Emergency Management Team. These individuals should be able to direct the fire services to:

- stop-valves and main switches for all services to the building
- the location of any chemical cupboards and contents (particularly conservation studios)
- the location of fire extinguishers within the building
- information about any fire suppression systems, particularly gaseous suppression systems
- the location of the nearest fire hydrants and other water sources
- the nature of the collection within the building, particularly any areas with special or irreplaceable collections
- locations of priority collections (snatch lists) and disaster kits (for polythene).

The example of the Royal Horticultural Society fire response in Chapter 2 shows how critical these procedures are for life safety and the avoidance of substantial damage. They will depend on the fire service's familiarity with the building, liaison on the day between the staff and crew (Figure 4.1), and their awareness of the nature of the collection.

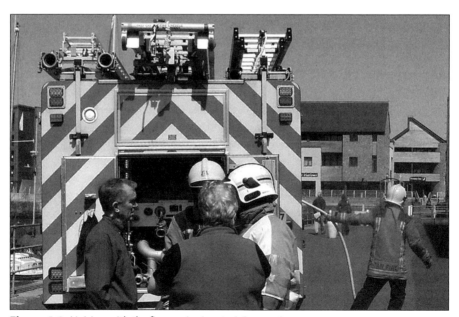

Figure 4.1 *Liaising with the fire service in a training session*
© *Harwell Document Restoration Services*

The work of the fire service will be aided by having a person with knowledge and responsibility for the building at all times. Emergency Management Team members should be able to provide access to the fire panel showing the fire zones of the building and the information described above. In some areas specialist secure containers called Gerda boxes can be used, containing information such as snatch sheets and floor plans (Figure 4.2).

Phase 3 The Fire Brigade in control
Possibility of salvage of objects during fire-fighting

When the Fire Brigade arrive, they will be in control of the building, and human safety is their top priority, followed by fire-fighting, environmental impacts and salvage. Priority or snatch lists are prepared by some institutions, particularly historic buildings and museums, with the intention that the fire service will permit

Figure 4.2 *Secure Gerda box containing information useful to the Fire Brigade, accessible outside the building but in a secure location*
© Harwell Document Restoration Services

some form of evacuation of objects away from the predicted path of the fire if there is a major incident, with fire service staff moving items or allowing members of staff inside to move them. Institutions must be realistic: the priority of the fire service must be to extinguish the fire, as this is the most effective means of protecting objects. Wet objects are much more easily restored than charred ones. The fire service will not and should not risk the safety of their own personnel or staff members from the library, archive or museum for the sake of salvaging objects, however much some people may want to commence salvage.

However, salvage work is part of the fire service remit in most countries. For example, section 7.1(e) of the Fire Services Act 2004 for the UK requires fire authorities to 'make arrangements for ensuring that reasonable steps are taken to prevent or limit damage to property resulting from action taken for the purpose mentioned in subsection (1)'. So as far as is reasonably practicable the impact on contents and buildings of water used to extinguish the fire should be limited.

Nicole Targett of the Royal Berkshire Fire and Rescue Service described the importance of salvage to a fire-fighter's job:

Salvage is actually a key part of a fire-fighter's job at an incident, whenever it is feasible to do so, and teams can be allocated specifically for this task. However, removal of items is only permitted when the risk to life and limb, for example danger from fire, smoke or heat, building structure collapse, explosion, gaseous release or other 'hazards', is deemed to be acceptable and relevant.

Where the level of risk has been deemed acceptable, then salvage would be undertaken. Who does this will again depend on circumstances, for example it may be safe for trained firefighters wearing protective clothing and breathing apparatus to go into a smoke-filled area to rescue paintings, artefacts, etc. but it would not be safe for civilian personnel, hence the use of on-site personnel with the knowledge to direct fire crews to relevant areas. This is normally detailed within the site-specific tactical plan. For example, Windsor Castle has salvage crews, trained to wear breathing apparatus, who can work alongside our teams to save the historic items.

Dynamic evacuation of objects is more likely in large historic properties such as Windsor Castle than in most typical libraries, archives and museums. Where organizations train alongside the fire services and are known to them through pre-incident drills, and have appropriate personal protective equipment, they may be allowed to work inside the affected building during the fire. It would be highly unlikely for the fire service to allow civilians into the building to evacuate objects themselves otherwise, without fore-knowledge of their training and protective equipment, but if the fire-fighting is adequately resourced, fire-fighters may offer to evacuate objects for the institution themselves.

Snatch lists

Staff in museums and historic buildings should consider drawing up 'snatch lists' giving an order of priority for items they would want removed in an emergency. These form part of standard priority lists (as explained in Chapter 7) and describe the priority of objects in room groups or individually so that items can be found in the shortest time possible, potentially in a smoke-filled room, if the fire service can permit access for salvage. They may also be referred to for situations where flooding is imminent and a limited time is available to move items above the predicted flood line. Fire service staff usually conduct this work, because of the risks to the organization's staff if they were to do it. Snatch lists also serve the salvage operation when the fire service has handed control of the building back to the organization's staff.

In drawing up snatch lists, staff should consider including not only the value of items but also their portability and fragility. It may not be possible to remove an item which is very heavy, such as a piece of sculpture or a bronze statue, even if it is valuable. Such items can be protected in situ with fire blankets or fire-retardant polythene sheeting, but moving the item would not be possible under a time constraint, even if it is a very valuable item. The possibility of dropping a fragile item must also be considered, and it may be better either to leave a large ceramic item in situ or position it under a table or something that will protect it from falling debris rather than attempt to move it from the room. The case study below details how one museum developed its own snatch lists.

CASE STUDY: Writing emergency snatch lists with fire service input
Kathryn Riddington, Grosvenor Museum, Chester

The Museum keepers initially decided what was on the priority list: very high, high, and medium, everything else is considered low priority. Initially we were just looking for objects to protect them from fire, but later this was expanded to include other eventualities. We went through a lengthy process in consultation with the Fire Brigade (Figure 4.3), most particularly Matt Lewis, White Watch, Chester Fire Station, to decide how best to mark objects, especially those on display where we were concerned about security issues:

- Display – using cards with pictures of the object on the front and maps on the back
  - Coloured border, dependent on priority level (red [very high], orange [high], green [medium], blue [loans])
  - Matt laminated: so that torches do not reflect off the surface and obscure info and to protect from handling or weathering, etc.
  - Picture on front
    — Object image 'cut-out' so that its outline is distinguishable if the object is covered in smoke
  - Locality information on back
    — Instructions to the gallery at the top on the back
    — Map of the gallery on back, showing the location of the object marked with a yellow box
    — Instructions about the location within the gallery beneath the map
    — Approx. dimensions
    — Any other relevant info, e.g. two-person handling shown by stickmen
- In store – using fluorescent numbers for top priorities
  - we have cards showing the layout of the store with the position of objects marked on them

Figure 4.3 *Fire Brigade practising the removal of a sample painting from a gallery*
© *Grosvenor Museum*

- Shelf markers are used for entire shelves. Tabs are used to mark the exterior of cupboards, and then individual objects marked inside. Boxes are marked with cut-out numbers.

We went through a lengthy process to sort out the cards for objects on display. The maps were especially difficult as the building is complex; you need to check out the Fire Brigade's 'way of thinking', e.g. keep left. We decided that as well as the copy of the cards on-site, we needed one set off-site and that they needed to be easily distinguishable in case anyone 'helpfully' fetched the second set and sent firefighters in for objects already salvaged. Different coloured paper was decided as easiest, in terms of production and recognition.

The building was split into zones. Maps were drawn of these zones with the priority objects (very high, high, and medium) marked on. The folder was then split into these zones, which in turn are split into individual galleries or stores. We ensure all curatorial staff are aware that they need to tell us when a priority object is moved so that we can update the sheet. We tape a temporary map to the back if it is returning to the original position and we do new sheets for important loan objects that need to be salvaged.

We provide training so that callout staff are familiar with the system and know what would be expected from them.

- Make sure your callout staff are familiar with the system, and what would be expected from them if there was an emergency (expect lots of questions).
- Have a section at the front of the folder that includes useful things like images of the marking system, so that you can show these to firefighters who may be unfamiliar with the system: assume that all will be.
- We have established that firefighters would only remove objects before museum staff arrived if they would otherwise be destroyed. They would try to move them to a safe area within the building if at all possible.

Immediate responses to flood or storm warning

Where buildings are located in a flood or hurricane prone area, there may be an automated notification system, which advises when there is a risk of an extreme weather event, providing people with an opportunity to minimize damage to their collections, such as Floodline in the UK. Details of the action to take when such warnings are received should form part of an emergency plan.

Even if you consider yourself not to be in a flood risk area, it may be that you are at risk of secondary flooding if drains are overwhelmed by a volume of water; consider including procedures in your emergency procedures document even if you assume the risk is small. If warnings are provided about likely flood times and river peaks, there may be a window of opportunity to protect the building (by limiting the entry of water) and evacuate objects. The ability of salvage volunteers to get home safely before the flood peak must be given paramount importance.

These are some key steps that can be taken to minimize the damage in advance of flooding:

- Turn off gas, electricity, and water supplies at mains (these should not be reconnected after flooding until checked by an accredited person).
- Unplug all electrical items and move to higher area.
- Move priorities off-site or higher.
- Empty cases if possible and move drawers.
- Raise large items on bricks or blocks.
- Leave internal doors open.
- Weigh down or tie together items that cannot be moved.
- Move items away from windows.
- Move kit, emergency plan or catalogues off-site.
- Arrange for night-watchman for security.
- Limit entry of water with sandbags or plywood or metal sheeting on outside doors, window frames and airbricks until waters recede. Use silicone sealant to increase resistance.
- Put plugs in sinks and lids down on toilets, then weigh them down with a heavy object.
- Weigh down manhole covers.
- Move any dangerous chemicals or objects that may contaminate flood waters further.
- Move away from site to safe area and do not re-enter until directed by someone in the Emergency Management Team.

When waters recede and access is possible, you would revert to the procedures for re-entering a building, which emphasize safety and getting most of the water out. These issues are discussed in Chapter 5.

Immediate responses to other types of incident

There can be a tendency for emergency plans for organizations in the heritage and information services sectors to focus on physical threats to their collections exclusively and to provide guidance on response and recovery only to incidents such as fires and floods. However, the definition of an emergency (see Chapter 1) encompasses not just collections but also services, people and buildings. Should threats other than fire and flood response be included in emergency procedures too?

Consider the likelihood and implications of discovering:

- a utility failure
- a suspect package
- a bomb threat
- a systems failure
- vandalism or break-in
- bad weather
- civic disturbance or a nuisance visitor
- there is a pandemic illness.

Kristie Short-Traxler, Preventive Conservation, Bodleian Libraries at Oxford University, points out that it might be necessary to deal with incidents that are not typical emergencies:

> When someone mentions emergencies for library and archive collections you immediately think; fire, flood, particulates, vandalism, etc. It is important to include response mechanisms for those incidents which may fall outside the typical emergency situation that threaten collections.
>
> As a high profile, higher education university, there is a necessity for the Bodleian Libraries to plan for incidents where the health and safety of employees and clients or the reputation of the institution are at risk. These include occupations, civil unrest and accidents. We have included guidance and advice on occupations in our plans and are working to implement table-top training scenarios.

If any of these other threats could cause a negative impact to any aspect of your organization's building, collections or service, pose a safety issue, or potentially lead to reputational damage if managed poorly, give guidance on how to raise the alarm and control such incidents. The individual member of staff who discovers the incident should have guidance on:

- appropriate action required to contain the problem
- who to contact for support
- who to notify for public relations reasons
- when and how to escalate action
- when to shut or suspend the service.

Should a situation such as a sit-in occur in a public library, promptly calling the appropriate people should ensure that the incident is dealt with as quickly as possible, minimizing disruption to customers and denying access to more protestors. These incidents seldom result in any damage to collections but the emergency phase needs to be managed effectively so that the control of the incident is decisive and resulting disruption minimized.

If the emergency response plan is to be the touchstone document for staff to respond to in emergency situations, it makes sense if all emergency information sits in the same place, rather than there being separate processes for different emergencies in different documents. All members of staff need access to it, so that the appropriate action is taken and the best people are contacted as swiftly as possible to resolve the issue.

Obviously the potential for some threats will be less likely if the institution is not open to the public and so procedures for dealing with a nuisance visitor may not be necessary. Plan authors should risk-assess what incidents are possible. Whereas previously those managing heritage collections may have felt somewhat immune from this type of threat, incidents such as the occupation of the area outside St Paul's Cathedral in late 2011 and early 2012 underline that such threats are not entirely impossible as libraries, archives and museums often have a high profile in the eyes of the public and media.

In responding to these incidents, it is crucial that staff know who to notify within the service and when to call either security staff or the police directly. Staff in independent institutions would normally escalate the incident by contacting the police, if it cannot be safely resolved or there is a breach of the peace. The procedures outlined below presuppose that the security or facilities staff of organizations such as local authorities, universities and so on will have considered the issues provoked by these types of incidents.

Utility failure

Utility failure could involve the failure of gas supply or boilers (loss of heating), loss of power (loss of IT, lighting, telephones, possible loss of fire and security alarms) or failure of water supply (loss of toilet facilities). The key question will be to determine the likely duration of disruption and whether it is safe and appropriate to continue to work in the area so that user services can be maintained. One of the case studies in Chapter 2 demonstrates how although a utility failure may not initially appear to be an emergency, it can rapidly limit the service that can be provided and threaten collections and security.

These are some of the actions that might be necessary if there is a utility failure:

- Alert the Building Recovery Manager and Emergency Response Manager on the Emergency Management Team.
- Decide whether or not to evacuate or close in light of the failure in discussion with the appropriate institutional authorities. This decision is usually made by the Emergency Response Manager.
- Although emergency lighting should activate, open all blinds or curtains to receive more outside light.
- Provide assistance to people in your area.
- Find out if there is anyone in the lift.
- Call the relevant utility company (*insert cross-reference to the relevant section of your plan*) on its emergency number and seek further advice.
- Tell users what has happened and update the website if possible.
- Divert telephone lines.

Facilities staff may need to make contact with the utilities provider on your behalf, or the contact may need to be made directly by independent institutions. These contact details should be in your appendices. Emergency arrangements will also need to be made to ensure that IT services are maintained if there is a back-up battery supply on your servers. Telephone lines will need to be diverted if they rely on a mains supply. Make detailed instructions site specific, and consult IT departments when procedures are drafted.

There may be an impact on collections following utility failure even if there is no visible threat. If a store is environmentally controlled and there is going to be a power failure for a long time, notify the Collections Salvage Manager to decide whether temporary environmental control systems (e.g. dehumidifiers) should be used. Air-conditioning units may fail and leak, so conduct thorough checks. In many modern libraries, systems of swipe cards are used to maintain security and access control, and these may fail if there is loss of power. This may necessitate improved physical security to areas affected.

Nuisance visitors

Examples of anti-social behaviour include violence, threats, derogatory remarks, excessive foul language, drunkenness and theft, any of which could involve a concern for safety given the unpredictable situation. Staff should have guidance on how to handle such situations appropriately.

These are some of the actions that might be appropriate if staff have to deal with nuisance visitors:

- Remain calm and contact a member of the Emergency Management Team or security staff.

- Restrict access to the affected area.
- Give the visitor a verbal warning that their behaviour is unacceptable and does not meet the expected standards of behaviour.
- If the visitor does not change their behaviour call security staff, who should ask him or her to leave. If the nuisance visitor is a library member ask for their library card.
- Await the arrival of security staff for the physical removal of the person. Do not engage in physical contact.
- Secure any CCTV which may be useful.

Occupations

There is the possibility that some high-profile institutions will be occupied by groups of individuals who wish to disrupt the institution's operations and attract publicity as a result. Any organizations deciding how best to respond to such potential threats, should consult institutional authorities and the police. Try to limit the disruption to the building, though this may prove difficult for health and safety and legal reasons. Appropriate action could include alerting security staff or the police, telling them:

- when the occupation started
- the number of people involved
- of any damage, violence or unruly behaviour that has occurred.

Security staff at this stage may elect to contact other officials within the institution such as the press office, legal section or executive office for support and to advise them of the situation.

If there is an occupation:

- Evacuate the building of staff and users. Encourage users to take essential personal belongings and work.
- Consider evacuation of high-priority items. Decide whether to evacuate objects in consultation with someone senior in the Emergency Management Team. If they are removed take them to a safe and secure location.
- Do not use physical force to resist entry. Secure the premises by placing a security staff member on points of entry but do not lock doors as this would prevent protestors from leaving.

Usually the process of liaising with protestors will be left to security staff or the police as will the tactics for the recovery of the building. The health and safety needs of all parties, including the protestors, must be met. In addition to the security impact of an occupation, business continuity concerns will emerge and departmental staff should attend to them. Potential impacts on the collection should also be considered and brought to the attention of the security officers or police, particularly if sprinklers are fitted where the occupation is ongoing and protestors may be smoking.

Mike Heaney, Executive Secretary Bodleian Libraries, Oxford University, commented:

> In situations like these, the premises are often at physical risk (real or threatened) and the circumstances put the same kinds of demands on staff, which include:
> * the need to operate from partial or temporary premises
> * the need to liaise effectively with security staff and/or emergency services
> * the need to communicate effectively with staff and third parties, often with disrupted communications
> * the need to make rapid decisions based on imperfect information.

Telephone bomb warnings

Incidents such as telephone bomb warnings and suspect packages that may be incendiary devices are rare but not impossible. The Emergency Management Team should assess whether these instructions should be included in the incident control documentation:

* Listen carefully to the information given and be polite – the longer the caller is talking, the more information can be gleaned.
* Attempt to get as much information as possible about the device, while if possible gaining the attention of a colleague and writing a note to ask them to contact the police or security staff. A tactic could include pretending the line is bad. Try to find out:
  — the exact location of the device
  — key timings
  — the appearance and size of the device
  — why this is being done
  — the name of the caller.

It may be of use to recall:

* information about the voice – male or female, nervous or calm, accent or well spoken, age
* reading from a text and talking freely

- any unusual phrasing
- background noises.

Suspect packages

Any member of staff could be alerted to a suspect package, so give the following sample guidance to all staff:

- Report the discovery immediately to security staff and/or the Emergency Management Team but not via a mobile phone as it may trigger a device.
- Do not touch the package. Be prepared to describe it to security staff by telephone. The following information may be required:
  — Is there a return address? If so does it match the postmark?
  — Is the handwriting unusual?
  — Are there any signs of grease staining or powder marks?
  — Is there an almond or marzipan smell?
  — Does it say 'private' or 'personal'?
  — Is the weight distribution even or does the package feel heavy for its size?
  — Was it delivered by hand?
  — Is wiring or foil visible?
- Security staff or police will inspect the suspicious item and advise on whether to evacuate the building.
- If evacuation is recommended, sound the fire alarm or use the public address system (if available).
- Members of staff and the public should leave the building in accordance with evacuation procedures.
- Await the arrival and instructions of the emergency services.

You may wish to include guidance on how to deal with a medical incident, such as a member of the public fainting or suffering a suspected heart-attack, or – in some areas of the world – earthquakes and hurricanes. Your plan should give specific guidance for staff so they can respond appropriately to the emergency phase of such incidents. Once the incident has been reported and brought under control, the salvage and recovery process can begin, as will be examined in the following chapters.

CHAPTER 5

Planning the recovery operation

If the procedures for responding to emergencies that were given in Chapter 4 are followed, the emergency will be either under control or being controlled. Now the mitigation of the damage to collections, buildings and services begins. Some assessment of the scale and potential impact of the incident is required to formulate a strategy to minimize further damage. This phase can be simple for small-scale incidents but the response and recovery operation of major incidents must be project managed. In disaster recovery situations, time is limited before additional damage might occur and pragmatic decisions may be required.

Emergency Management Team meeting

Members of the emergency team should meet and decide their approach for managing the incident. If access to the building is possible ask some or all of the team to conduct a site tour, so they can observe the scale of the incident; this knowledge will be important in planning the recovery operation.

If the area is not accessible, set up a control point (pre-identify potential locations in the plan), which is private and where the response can be planned. It may be necessary to set up a separate area for communications, including dealing with the press. Liaison will be required with the emergency service personnel if they continue to control the site, but organization of disaster recovery should start using whatever information can be gleaned, including locations and levels of damage, the status of utilities, when access will be permitted and any anticipated structural damage. The fire service's commander will be positioned outside the building and one person from the Emergency Management Team should liaise with that person. If the damage is severe, it is crucial to ensure that the required resources are in position at full strength as soon as entry is permitted.

If the overall volume of damage, range of objects affected and extent of water penetration inside the boxes are estimated it will help quantify the response required. Include a 'ready-reckoner' in the plan, so that should there be water damage to the whole bottom row of a store, the Emergency Management Team can calculate the approximate number of crates that will be required. This information is very helpful when planning a salvage operation and ensuring adequate resources are obtained. A ready-reckoner can also help to monitor the rate of salvage when work starts, and establish the likely timeframe for the completion of salvage, helping the Emergency Management Team to decide whether efficiencies and/or improved resourcing are required as early as possible on the first day of the salvage operation to minimize the danger of mould developing.

It can be helpful to provide an agenda for the Emergency Response Manager for this Emergency Management Team meeting as a prompt to ensure that all potential issues are discussed, including:

- whether to shut or suspend service (if relevant)
- how to reconfirm roles and responsibilities based on those present
- a communications strategy for staff, users, stakeholders, press
- whether to contact insurers
- what resources are required (redeploying staff to assist with security, salvage and enquiries, equipment and professional contractors)
- finance
- security
- welfare for staff
- risk assessment for those entering the building
- a salvage strategy (discussed in Chapters 5 and 6)
- a business continuity strategy (discussed in Chapter 9).

The fire service may be in control of the site, in which case fire service personnel will determine whether to close or suspend service. However, flooding incidents will not necessarily involve the emergency services and so the decisions will need to be taken by staff. Welfare arrangements may be required for staff, particularly if they have been evacuated from the building and are upset. There may also be situations where people are unaccounted for, in which case next of kin need to be informed. This will probably be handled by an organization's HR department, although, for independent institutions, access to this information may need to be made available to the Emergency Management Team.

It may be best to send all but Emergency Management Team staff home unless salvage is likely to start in the next few hours, in which case provide staff with somewhere warm to rest and wait. It is sensible to notify key contractors and personnel whose services are likely to be required to make it more likely that they provide adequate full-strength resources when required.

The Emergency Response Manager will be responsible for taking a wide-angle perspective on the emergency response and ensuring that resources are being appropriately allocated and delivered, monitoring levels of morale, anticipating problems and identifying emerging new challenges. Regular communication throughout the management process is essential. Mobile telephones are the most prevalent tool, although they may not work universally in the building. Radios and walkie-talkies can also be used but require pre-incident training if the Emergency Management Team are not familiar with them. At least hold regular meetings to monitor progress. These meetings can be brief and direct so as not to delay salvage operations, but ensure that all Emergency Management Team personnel have a chance to step back and reflect on the big picture. Hold a kick-off meeting and a debriefing at the end of the day, but it may be useful to meet in the middle of the day. If an external contractor is required to speed up the rate of salvage, a call at 1pm is more likely to result in a next-day response than if the request is made at 6 pm.

Tactics – in-house or outsource?

At this stage, it is crucial that the Emergency Management Team considers the tactics it will deploy in managing the recovery. As will be discussed in Chapter 6, time is limited in disaster recovery if secondary damage is to be avoided, and a substantial volume of material may need to be treated. In a major incident, a compounding factor may be that human resources available for salvage are stretched if temporary services are being provided temporarily at other sites, or library systems are down, so staff must rely on manual processes, which take longer.

For a commercial or residential insurance claim, if a problem arises, the usual procedure is to hire an experienced, competent contractor to resolve it. This is likely to be cheaper, quicker and more appropriate than using professional staff in a capacity that does not make the best use of their knowledge and skills, or have homeowners dealing with contaminated water. In the heritage sector, the mind-set is often different. The collections in archives, museums and historic houses are not replaceable, so conventional insurance procedures do not apply. However, this does not mean that staff should deal independently with all the salvage tasks without support. With appropriate supervision and their methods tailored to the specific circumstances of these environments, professional contractors can assist and may have considerable experience in the safety issues of disaster recovery. Specialist moving contractors can be used to complete the packing and moving work, freeing up institutional staff to supervise, document and focus as much resource as possible on business continuity and other tasks that cannot easily be outsourced. It is rarely the most efficient strategy to use an institution's own staff for their brawn rather than their professional skills.

In a major incident, it is far better to involve professional contractors from an early stage to assist rather than to strive to manage without support for four days, realize that the salvage operation is only partially complete, and then seek external support. By that stage the objects will have suffered four days of avoidable further deterioration. This is particularly true with library and archival collections that use up a large amount of space for salvage but can easily be frozen and stabilized, and even treated by disaster recovery firms.

Triage assessment

Although priority lists for salvage should have been identified as part of the planning process (see Chapter 7), the prioritization strategy will require revision once the specific sites of damage are known and if the quantity of damage is significant (salvage will take longer than one day). In these circumstances, while the value of top-tier objects remains a major consideration, tough decisions may need to be made in order to make the best use of limited resources.

Triage assessment is widely used in damage management. It is the process whereby items are categorized where:

- rapid deterioration is likely and early intervention is necessary
- items are beyond likely economic restoration
- items require restoration but will not deteriorate rapidly.

Unfortunately the vast majority of items in library, archive and museum collections are all vulnerable to rapid deterioration through mould growth, which makes the triage process somewhat redundant. Additionally the term 'economic restoration' is not always useful where collections are unique and replacement is not an option. In public libraries some items can be immediately dismissed as beyond economic restoration, but again this category is small – usually standard public lending library fiction stock would be cheaper to replace than to restore after a serious flood, but specialist academic material and even reference materials in public libraries justify restoration, given their high replacement costs. Additionally, the prioritization must be seen through the eyes of users, particularly in academic libraries. Is a collection a high priority if local libraries stock similar material and business continuity can be maintained, even if it is costly to replace? Should the focus in these situations not be directed at subject collections where access to similar material would be more logistically challenging? Where theoretically stock can all be replaced, or is digitized or duplicated, consider the most vulnerable formats – which will be beyond restoration if prompt action is not taken – first. Thereafter prioritize on the basis of value. Reference and non-fiction stock is usually more costly to replace; adult and children's fiction relatively inexpensive to replace.

Where collections are all irreplaceable and all important, as in archives, it is difficult to triage on the basis of the collection itself, so it is perhaps better to work out where the time of salvage staff will have the most impact. In these situations, the time is allocated using a triage assessment. Here it makes most sense to:

- Crate and set to one side all material that has fallen from shelves and is on the floor.
- Prioritize reboxing lightly damaged items first. Dry items in wet boxes will ultimately absorb moisture and require stabilization or treatment, but early intervention can prevent this.
- Introduce ventilation or dehumidification to prevent mould growth above the flood level and moisture spread to adjacent areas.
- Pack and remove for salvage all damaged items that can be stabilized that remain on shelves and can be quickly crated.
- Cherry-pick important items that could be stabilized for supervised immediate air-drying on site either because they are of high value, which you would rather not leave the site or freeze, or because they are heavily used objects and if they can be air-dried, service disruption would be minimized.
- Recover and air-dry damp items that cannot be stabilized (e.g. glass plate negatives, cased photographs) that were not previously cherry-picked.
- Recover saturated, heavily damaged items that may have been dislodged and fallen to the floor.
- Recover damaged duplicate material.

Figure 5.1 (overleaf) shows three rows of water-damaged boxes, the bottom two saturated, the third row from bottom saturated on the bottoms only. The prompt removal of contents will avoid water penetration.

It may seem tempting to salvage and recover the heavily damaged, saturated items first. However, these will occupy the available drying space for a significant period owing to their heavier saturation. In 72 hours, perhaps 600 damp books could be dried out, whereas only 100 heavily saturated books

Figure 5.1   *Three rows of water-damaged boxes, the bottom two saturated, the third row from bottom saturated on bottoms only*

© Waterford County Council

could, and leaving 600 damp books untreated for 72 hours could result in 600 books becoming affected by mould. An activity as seemingly straightforward as ordering dehumidifiers for the salvage operation and to avert mould growth on dry materials may only take ten minutes, but early introduction is critical to avert potentially costly and complex long-term problems with the internal building environment, which could spread to affect dry, initially unaffected materials.

Rather than completely ignoring the most heavily damaged material initially, it may be possible to allocate resources in a proportionate way. So, if 20 people are available to assist with salvage, two people could start on the saturated heavily damaged material with the other 18 people treating the damp material, then, upon completion of that task, bolstering those who have made a head-start on the heavily damaged items. Front-loading the salvage operation with attention to the most badly affected material, which is the most time-consuming task, may be tempting, but is usually not a very sensible strategy.

In museums the triage process is more complex than in libraries and archives as most items are irreplaceable, but many object types (e.g. ceramics, wood, metal) cannot be stabilized through freezing (see Chapter 6). It is better to defer treatment wherever possible through freezing, to maximize time and resource on those items which must be treated immediately. This could include freezing books, documents, leather, most photographic material and textiles, leaving space to air-dry paintings, metals, ceramics, natural history, wood and so on.

Involving insurers

In situations where the recovery process involves external equipment, professional contractors and building repair, an insurance claim may ultimately cover the costs. It is worth investigating insurance cover in detail with your insurance officer or broker to make sure that all parties are clear about what types of incident insurance provision are in place, and detailing this succinctly in an appendix to the emergency plan so that the relevant information is readily available should the Emergency Management Team not have access to their offices and shared network drives.

Whether or not you can claim for an incident depends on the excess or deductible an institution has in position as part of its insurance policy. An excess or deductible is the sum of money the institution would have to pay on a claim before an insurer would need to pay out. For some organizations this sum is set as low as £1000. In others, most notably large local authorities who seek to reduce the cost of premiums, excess levels can be set very high, in the hundreds of thousands. In these cases claiming is highly unlikely but it is still worth making contact with your insurance officer for clarification in an emergency. Many organizations have separate policies in place for buildings and contents, and others have specific policies in place for individual items or collections of particular value. Some policies have exclusions in place for particular perils, which you should note in your plan. The insurance process is likely to involve the appointment of a loss adjuster by the insurer.

Malcolm Hyde, Executive Director of the Chartered Institute of Loss Adjusters, explained what loss adjusters do in the following way:

> Loss Adjusters are experts in the handling of losses. Most Loss Adjusters are engaged by Insurers and act fairly and justly to ensure that claims are settled in accordance with the policy cover. However, many Loss Adjusters are engaged by policyholders to present claims on their behalf and of course Loss Adjusters may also act in circumstances where there is no Insurance cover in place. The Chartered Institute of Loss Adjusters is recognised worldwide and this is evidenced by the involvement of its members in major world events such as the earthquakes in Japan, New Zealand and Chile as well as the major floods in Australia and the summer 2011 riots losses in England.

If there is a major emergency you should notify your insurers as early as possible. Loss adjusters have access to a national network of specialist disaster recovery contractors who may be able to provide support and additional resource. They are keenly aware of the need to avert secondary damage and are usually easily persuaded of the benefits of the costs of arranging commercial freezer storage for damaged objects if it avoids mould growth, which would be very costly to remove and repair.

It is important that salvage action should take place while waiting for the loss adjuster to arrive so long as it is safe to enter the affected area. Indeed most insurance policies expect that reasonable steps would be taken to minimize further damage. The overall insurance settlement may take months, sometimes years, to emerge and be finalized, and negotiation may be necessary for replacement of short-loan stock, for example, to maintain service and avoid 'business interruption'. Sometimes insurers will request that salvage equipment is hired, rather than purchased, even if outright purchase would be cheaper overall, as organizations are not permitted to benefit materially from an insurance claim.

It is also worth remembering that even if your collections are not insured or you have a very high excess, if the culpable party for your incident was a neighbouring institution or a contractor, ultimately their insurance may cover the costs of your disaster recovery operation. In such situations sometimes a loss adjuster or loss assessor can be appointed who will negotiate with the other party's insurers on your behalf. Insurers require that records and receipts are kept of all expenditure and that logs are kept of staff time that is spent on the incident. A photographic record of the salvage process can add weight to the claim. After the initial flurry of activity in the wake of an incident, it is most effective to appoint one senior person to administer the insurance claim to ensure continuity of information.

Where heritage and information services are part of a wider organization and its general insurance policy, it is worth investigating the detail of cover and how it extends to your collection. Some collections may be replaceable, in which case insurers will make decisions on whether to salvage or replace based on the economics of restoration. In fires, for example, nearly all smoke-damaged library stock can be cleaned cost-effectively, but where collections are not replaceable, insurance can become difficult. What is the value of an archival collection when it cannot be replaced? Increasingly archives are arranging insurance for a minimum conservation and restoration cost based on a worst-case scenario costing. This at least provides some basis for an insurance sum and a professional disaster company can usually provide this very quickly if they have a volumetric figure for the size of your collection.

It is sometimes worth considering procuring separate cover for collections if you are not satisfied with the catch-all policy of the parent organization. Insurers may even be prepared to reduce premiums if better preventative measures such as sprinklers or gaseous suppression systems, which reduce the risk, are introduced. Arantza Barrutia-Wood Collections Project Co-ordinator at Museums Sheffield found this to be beneficial after a major flood in a museum store: 'Having a specialist insurance for the collections was absolutely essential to our recovery and the minimal loss of collection objects.'

Health and safety

People's safety must be at the heart of emergency planning and response. Many emergency plans state this principle but include little formal guidance within the plan on how salvage can be managed safely. In a real emergency situation, the concern to get valuable collections to safety is overriding for some individuals, and a lack of rigour in health and safety procedures may result in high-risk activities being undertaken. This scenario must be avoided by an organization, given its corporate responsibility for the safety of all people within its buildings. Failure to facilitate safe salvage could result in sanctions being taken against those at the highest level if an accident were to take place. Geoff Davidson, Health and Safety Manager, National Museums Northern Ireland, advised:

> Safety shouldn't be seen as a dampener on collections recovery. Looking after collections-focused enthusiastic staff itching to get to their collections is difficult but is necessary. The emergency services will guide you on when and where you can enter any building. Immediately post incident you will be provided with general information relating to the building from the emergency services. General information needs to be built into the risk assessment for the operation. An overall assessment can be built from a series of individual assessments coming together to create a system for working in the environment. Where damage has occurred it may be necessary to get advice from a structural engineer to establish how and where work can commence.
>
> If we view risk assessment as an evil forced on us by far distant people with no understanding of our needs we totally miss the point. If we can view risk assessments as a logical and formal way of thinking about any activity that could harm people so minimizing the potential for injury and damage to collections then we are using the risk assessment tool effectively. Risk assessment offers the opportunity to consider what we need to do taking into account the hazards to people and collections, who and what can be injured or damaged, what controls or help we have available and consequently have we the ability to deliver what we actually need to do or should we do some more

planning allowing us to work around the issues or hazards most likely to injure and damage. We can use assessment as a means to decide what we have the resources to do and what we can't do and where we need to look for assistance.

Certainly personal protective equipment, including hard hats, overalls, hi-visibility vests, gloves, safety spectacles and safety boots, would be appropriate for staff in disaster response mode and particular types and additions will be dictated by the safety requirements of the incident. Remember that this equipment and the ability to undertake risk assessment as circumstances change must be available from the start of the emergency response. Trying to get equipment in the early hours of the morning will not work and you leave staff in a position where they should not be reacting to the situation. Even better is to do the risk assessments in advance and establish how we will deal with emergencies and have people, equipment, materials and appropriate environments available when they are needed.

It may also be worthwhile discussing emergency response with insurers, particularly with regard to any mutual aid agreements so that they are satisfied that the assessments are in place demonstrating that you thought out how to ensure that staff were protected when helping out on someone else's disaster recovery.

The key step is to ensure that there is a risk assessment of the salvage operation. This process will identify the hazards present and the risk of harm and injury that they present, and prompt the assessor(s) to find measures that will reduce the likelihood of any harm emanating from the hazards and resulting risks if existing measures are not sufficient. The process of salvage provides a change from the normal working environment and so necessitates an evaluation of how it may be approached safely. This applies regardless of how small the incident may initially seem.

Risk assessments can be conducted dynamically but it is crucial that the conclusions are documented immediately. It also helps if the emergency plan contains forms that expedite the risk assessment process and provide personnel with a format to follow as it makes the process quicker. For example, it should be possible to predetermine expected minimum levels of personal protective equipment and to specify safe systems of work for predictable situations such as a leak, flood or a fire recovery, and this saves time in a real emergency.

Identifying hazards

A major difficulty with fire and flood recovery is that it may not always be immediately obvious for individuals encountering this type of situation for the first time to identify hazards. If the hazards cannot be identified, then risks will not be assessed and safety measures will not be implemented. An emergency plan must help to prompt salvage personnel about potential hazards in a user-friendly way, and provide guidance about how potential risks can be mitigated.

Hazards may be split into the obvious, time-delayed or hidden hazards, and the unknown. Obvious hazards include:

- slippery surfaces caused by debris or surface water
- obstacles on surfaces making tripping more likely
- twisted or jutting metal
- lack of lighting
- working at height (to recover items from higher shelves)
- broken glass.

These hazards are either visible or familiar to those working in this sector. However, some hazards may not be visible or immediately apparent but exposure to these issues over a prolonged period without mitigating measures will result in a high risk of injury or medical implications. Such hazards include:

- contaminated water
- manual handling
- mould
- stress
- electrical hazards (discussed in Chapter 4, in the Phase 2 response to the immediate reaction to water damage)
- working within a building with no functioning alarm systems (discussed below in the section 'Working safely' on page 107).

Contaminated water

Sometimes it is obvious that water comes from a potentially contaminated source. These are the standard classifications for water:

- Clean water has come directly from plumbing.
- Grey water has low levels of contamination (from the outlet of a washing machine, for example).
- Black water may be contaminated with unknown agents, such as sewage, storm water and even sprinkler waters, which can cause serious harm to health.

Fluvial flooding and storm, or flash flooding, where drains have been overwhelmed, can carry contamination such as raw sewage, rodent-borne disease such as leptospirosis and Weil's disease, petrochemicals and perhaps even other types of contamination from local industrial premises.

As black water contamination poses the risk of infection, take extreme caution when working in environments where there is black water and handling items damaged by black water. However, contamination is not always obvious and so precautions should always be taken unless the discharging source is immediately over the collection and is confirmed to be mains water pipe. Trace the source of the water and investigate the water's journey from source to the damaged material. Even clean water can become contaminated as it travels through a building or down a street. If a clean or grey water flood is left unattended for a prolonged period, it may become black water if microbes grow in it. Furthermore, water used to extinguish a fire may not be clean, as fire services may pump from lakes or rivers to gain the water they need, and the water in wet pipe sprinkler systems may have been standing in those pipes for several months.

Manual handling

Manual handling is a hazard that is managed daily in all heritage and information services collections, but in fire and flood recovery situations the load changes, as does the working environment. A box of documents weighing 12 kg, could weigh 24 kg when saturated. Items may need to be moved from the floor, so involving bending and not working at trunk level where handling is easiest. Furthermore, items may be wet and dirty, causing individuals to carry them at arm's length, which further reduces the load that can be borne safely. Salvage work may involve transporting material significant distances within a building which may not have functioning lifts, which may result in use of stairs. The prolonged and repetitive nature of salvage manual handling can also prove problematic, even if all the loads being transported are within safe limits. Most manual handling guidance such as that illustrated in Figure 5.2 is based on a number of lifts per hour (for example 30), which in disaster recovery operations may quickly be exceeded. Conduct risk assessments where the manual handling risks are reduced as far as possible. Those who have back problems should not participate in any activities that involve excessive bending (filling and emptying crates) or carrying loads long distances.

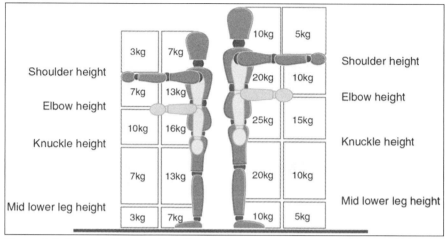

Figure 5.2 *Current HSE manual handling guidance* © *Crown*

Mould

Mould is a microscopic fungus that grows in the form of filaments called hyphae. They grow superficially on substrates, secreting enzymes in order to degrade the cellulose (in the case of paper) so that it can be absorbed as a nutrient source. This activity can cause irreversible staining. Moulds can grow even on inorganic materials such as glass and plastic, usually existing on organic materials deposited on the surface, such as dust. When a mass of hyphae is present, the fungal colony is known as a mycelium. See Figure 5.3.

Figure 5.3 *Mould growth on a piece of wooden furniture after flooding*
© *Harwell Document Restoration Services*

Mould typically, although not exclusively, grows in dark environments where there is low air movement. Varying types of mould require differing degrees of moisture in order to grow. The moulds usually seen growing in library, archive and museum stores in normal conditions are xerophilic moulds, which can grow in conditions under 80% relative humidity, rH (the amount of moisture in a given volume of air, at a given temperature, which is expressed as a percentage of the amount that air could hold at saturation). Other forms of mould are associated with higher relative humidity, such as the stachybotrys species, which is considered to be most harmful. Moulds can grow actively between temperatures of 5°C and 40°C, although the rate of growth is decreased at lower temperatures. Freezing does not kill mould but renders it inactive. The rate at which mould growth develops in the aftermath of a flood varies depending on many factors, including the ventilation in the affected area and the temperature. Mould grows faster if the environmental conditions are warm, humid and still. Certain substrates are more susceptible to rapid mould growth, including glues and leather.

It is important to remember that not all moulds are harmful. There are spores in the air in normal conditions but in the aftermath of floods, wet materials and the raised relative humidity provide an environment for active mould growth. This is problematic as some species can produce mycotoxins, which are hazardous to human health, particularly among some vulnerable groups of people. Inhalation of spores can cause reactions among the elderly, the young, pregnant women and those who have respiratory conditions (e.g. asthma). It is impossible to tell by visual examination alone what species of mould is occurring and so precautions must always be taken, including protection of the skin and eyes, prevention of inhalation by face mask and exclusion of vulnerable groups from any aspects of disaster recovery where they may come in contact with mould colonies. Aside from the toxicological risk, mould spores are frequently allergenic, triggering symptoms such as running noses and eyes and itchy eyes. Personal protective equipment and appropriate controls to the building are required.

Stress

The stress of salvage becomes a hazard in itself. Some salvage personnel may feel very upset by the damage to the collection and their workplace, and are overwhelmed by the enormity of the necessary recovery operation. This may lead to some people feeling compelled to stay and help with the salvage operation and work very long shifts in order to complete the salvage process, taking only minimal respite. Such situations may give rise to greater accidents as individuals become exhausted.

Unknown hazards

Finally there are categories of hazard which would be unknown to the individuals concerned, particularly after a major incident. For example, when PVC cabling is involved in a fire, a film of acidic residue can form as the chemical components react with the humidity and the fire residues. Touching such cables without proper protective equipment can lead to chemical burns. Determining issues of structural safety and asbestos disturbance requires professional advice.

Figure 5.4 shows hazardous melted cabling after a fire.

Figure 5.4 *Hazardous melted cabling after a fire*

© Harwell Document Restoration Services

Risk assessment

There are many hazards and ensuing risks to consider for those wishing to start salvage work. Undertake a risk assessment before any work commences in the affected area. Furthermore, that risk assessment must be frequently reassessed as the situation changes: mould growth may not immediately be a problem but become one in subsequent days. The risk assessment will determine a safe system of work, with a recommendation of the personal protective equipment individuals involved in the recovery operation should wear.

An emergency plan must support individuals in an emergency by prompting them to look for the hazards that are not obvious or immediately apparent, and by pointing them to a predetermined level of personal protective equipment and working practice. It should also provide people with advice on where to go for professional input if necessary. Managers in large institutions and those that form part of a bigger organization (such as a local authority or a university) have health and safety staff to refer to, but managers of independent and smaller organizations might need to ask a consultant for advice.

Conduct a risk assessment in all incidents of physical damage to collections, however small, as there may still be a hazard present as a result of contaminated water, for example. Figure 5.5 shows a sample format for a risk assessment form.

Details of the anticipated hazards and mitigating tactics can be given in advance and then reviewed on the day, when the range of hazards that can be expected is updated, and any hidden or unknown hazards are added to the list.

What are the hazards?	Who might be harmed and how?	What are you already doing?	Do you need to do anything else to manage this risk?
Electrical hazards due to escaping water	Salvage staff, public, other members of staff, contractors	Staff instructed to stay out and electrical contractor in suppliers' list on page x	Isolate electricity before salvage starts; signage
Slip hazards	Salvage staff	Safety wellingtons in disaster kit and wet vacuum available	Clear aisles and pathways before work; clear standing water and puddles

Figure 5.5 *Sample risk assessment form*

Advanced risk assessment

This process is more complicated. It calculates the risk on the basis of hazard severity and likelihood of occurrence. Hazard severity can be classified as 1–5 (or nil to very high), and likelihood of occurrence as 1–5 (or unlikely to very likely). Risk can then be assessed on the basis of the product of the hazard × likelihood of the hazard, e.g. 16–25 = high risk, 9–15 = medium risk, 1–8 = low risk. So something that is assessed as being a moderate hazard severity (3), which could be defined as being quite possible (3) to occur, falls within the medium risk bracket (hazard severity 3 × likelihood 3 = medium risk of 9), suggesting that further mitigating action to reduce the risk is necessary. This is a technical and advanced way of assessing risk, but it can be difficult to use in practice.

Working safely

The building needs to be accessible and safe to work in. The key steps are:

- to confirm that the building is structurally safe
- to remove standing water before salvage
- to isolate electricity (if water has fallen through light fittings or circuits or if it has risen to sockets level)
- to determine and communicate emergency evacuation procedures to salvage staff if alarms are down
- to provide adequate lighting to all areas of the salvage operation
- to use generators or trailing extension cables to provide power safely
- to mark clearly any areas that are out of bounds or unsafe to enter.

Confirming that a building is structurally safe would usually only be required in the aftermath of a major fire, a flood higher than 1 metre, or an earthquake or hurricane. A professional opinion must be sought for this either via your facilities or buildings section, a specialist contractor such as a surveyor, or your building's insurers. Some building types present particular challenges, particularly large warehouse spaces and buildings of cast-iron construction, because of the impact of the heat of a fire and then the rapid cooling of the building structure with the use of water to extinguish it. If possible list the contact details of building specialists, ideally with prior knowledge of your building, in plan appendices.

It is in the interests of people and collections to remove standing water before salvage begins. Although individuals can theoretically wade into a building waist- or knee-deep in standing water to extract valuable items, they may not be able to see what they are wading through, which is hazardous, and there is a heightened risk of items being splashed or even dropped into the water. Damage may be exacerbated if a salvage operation starts while there is lots of water being splashed around as personnel wade around the room. Source pumping equipment to extract the standing water, and when most of the water has been removed, use puddle pumps, wet vacuums and mops to reduce possible slip hazards. In the case of a major flood, pumping is futile until external floodwaters have receded, and take care to pump the water to an appropriate drain. It is likely that institutions will need access to hired pumps or professional contractors rather than fire services, as discussed by Nicole Targett of Royal Berkshire Fire and Rescue Service:

> We attend only incidents where there is a risk to life or limb – usually this is where water ingress is affecting or potentially affecting the electricity supply. This is normally for domestic properties only as commercial premises are usually required to make appropriate provision as part of their insurance assessment. Where flash flooding occurs as a result of exceptional weather conditions, the Fire and Rescue Services may attend a heritage site but only if there was no conflict with providing a response to risk-critical incidents elsewhere. We would expect the premises to have their own plans which would cover areas such as salvage in the event of floods.

Electricity must be isolated if it has come into contact with water, but sufficient light needs to be provided to the salvage operation. This may involve generators or extension cables, which have their own hazards. Extension cables should not be overloaded and the cables must be fitted with circuit breakers. They should also not cause trip hazards. Generators must be properly used, earthed and fumes ventilated.

If the power in the building is off the fire alarms may have been deactivated. Therefore consideration must be given to how staff would evacuate, particularly if re-ignition were to occur. In such circumstances consult the organization's fire officer and conduct a separate risk assessment. Identify an evacuation signal and tell staff what it is before entry, and verify that it would be sufficiently audible in all areas of the building. Sign emergency exits and make them accessible as a matter of urgency.

Other useful tactics can include:

- logging staff in the building and the time they started working
- briefing staff before an evacuation begins, telling them which areas they are to work in, which areas they must not enter and what personal protective equipment they must wear and why
- ensuring routes for moving damaged items are established and cleared, which will minimize manual handling risks
- establishing a shift system, maximum time on-site and break times (at least 30 minutes every 3 hours), to a maximum of 8 hours per day
- planning welfare for staff, including providing hot drinks and snacks, and a warm area to rest and sit down
- determining procedures for working at height
- identifying first-aiders and providing first aid kits.

Individuals must take breaks regularly to take refreshment and have a rest from the salvage process. The organization should provide these facilities. There can be some reluctance among committed salvage volunteers to take any respite in a real situation, but overall people maintain a higher work rate and levels of morale if they take regular breaks.

After a major flood at a museum store, Arantza Barrutia-Wood, Collections Project Co-ordinator at Museums Sheffield, commented:

> The internal communication could have been better and staff could have been supported better. We realised we needed to improve the management of the human aspect of the disaster by providing more support if required and better facilities, food, drink, communications, etc. Health and safety advice should have come from personnel or director level rather than staff on the ground and possibly a check to keep an eye on the effect of the disaster on staff would have been good.

Assess the personal protective equipment individuals should wear in the various stages of the salvage operation. Many organizations will have some stocks of items like masks and gloves in their disaster kits (see the list in Chapter 7). These are lists of the equipment that would be necessary in the aftermath of a very serious incident. Many items listed would not be needed to deal with less serious incidents, such as a clean water burst pipe that was detected immediately, but even in those situations it would be necessary to have gloves and an apron as a bare minimum. Complications such as poor lighting may also alter the risk assessment. This level of equipment may be excessive for the area where damaged collections are decanted for treatment, and nitrile or surgical gloves combined with a protective plastic catering apron might well suffice, along with a face mask if required.

Ending the emergency phase

The subsequent chapters will explain techniques that can be adopted to deal with damage to collections and buildings while minimizing disruption to service. Once all objects have been initially dried or removed to freezer storage, processes are ongoing to restore the building, and temporary measures are in place for service provision, the emergency planning phase is over. However, lessons need to be learned, repairs to the building made, and the possibility of repeat occurrences avoided. Gillian Boal recalls that after dealing with a minor emergency while working at the University of California, Berkeley, 'within a week of this minor incident, the campus initiated the process of changing the wet pipe sprinklers to a dry pipe system, which we had been asking them to do for years'. Write a formal report on the plan's performance so that any crucial lessons are learned. It is courteous to thank those who helped, and replenish equipment stocks in case they are needed again.

CHAPTER 6

Collections salvage

Planning salvage

With the situation now under control and the quantity of damage known, and safety assessed and managed, the salvage operation can begin to recover the affected items and attempt to repair the damage they have sustained.

Averting secondary damage

The objective of the salvage operation is to rectify the initial damage but also to avert secondary damage to affected materials. Secondary damage results from the primary damage (the water, fire or smoke) and gets worse over time. Early intervention can prevent it from occurring. After domestic fires, one of the first actions insurers require is the cleaning of laminated work surfaces and uPVC windows. If they are left with smoke covering them for a protracted period, discolouration occurs, and they need to be replaced, which is an avoidable extra cost. Simple cleaning with a detergent will avoid this costly secondary damage.

In the context of heritage and information services collections, secondary damage is more likely to take the form of mould growth, corrosion, warping and distortion, and an overall weakening of the strength of an item such as a bound volume (e.g. as glues become loose in the presence of water). After the primary damage, secondary damage usually starts to escalate rapidly from 48–72 hours after the damage initially occurred and the waters receded. Secondary damage, which is avoidable if salvage begins early enough, adds extensively to the timescale and complexity of restoration as additional processes need to be applied. It is usually reversible, but at an additional cost. In the case of mould growth, the cost and rate of the recovery process are increased, as additional safety equipment should be worn by salvage volunteers, and mouldy items need to be isolated in polythene bags, which involves additional processes and adds to the timescale. Avoidable staining will also occur, which is costly to rectify, and the damaged items will also need to be sanitized to eradicate any residual growth after drying. These additional processes can be avoided completely if the items are salvaged before mould growth commences.

Secondary damage is much less of an issue in fire damage, with the exception of the reaction of metals and plastics, where corrosion and discolouration may occur. Delaying the salvage and treatment of typical library, archive and museum holdings will not result in escalating damage, although you should attempt to control the temperature and humidity. Any items that have been damaged by extinguishant water, however slightly, will be at risk of secondary damage as described above if they remain in a wet state.

In order to avert secondary damage, the items need to be dried or stabilized within 48–72 hours. There may be circumstances when this is not achievable and mould growth is inevitable, for example if there is a period where access is denied to the building on safety grounds. However, proper planning and resourcing of the process will minimize the risks of secondary damage and maximize the efficiency and rate of treatment.

All items typically stored by a library, archive or museum collection can be successfully restored through air-drying, and if this process occurs within 72 hours, the requirements for additional further conservation should be minimized. There are practical limitations as to how much can be processed in that timeframe, however, given constraints such as staff availability and the space required for air-drying. The timescale for the onset of secondary damage is fixed, but there could be any number of damaged items. The best method for an incident involving around 500 items, ensuring their salvage within 72 hours, may be to deal with the damaged collection solely with internal resources. However, this is not likely to be the case for an incident involving 5000 or 50,000 items, for which a different strategy would be required in order to ensure the collections were salvaged with the minimal amount of secondary damage. A combination of some air-drying and some stabilization of items may be required in mid-major incidents.

Stabilization and salvage strategy

When immediate air-drying of all affected items is not possible or practical because of the scale of damage, there is an alternative option of stabilization for some (but not all) objects. This will not address the damage, but it will defer the urgent need for treatment as it will arrest any further deterioration and secondary damage. For the vast majority of library and archival holdings, this will involve freezing to −18°C. The freezing process does not dry the items, but it prevents mould growth, further adhesions, further dye migration or feathering of inks, swelling or distortion.

Freezing is not suitable for microfilm or audio or video tape. If these items are saturated, stabilize them by submerging them into cold clean water to prevent the contaminants drying onto the tape. Don't keep them wet for longer than a week, but this does buy some time in the salvage process. Items can either be professionally rewashed and reprocessed, or vacuum dried. The only typical library and archive formats where stabilization is not thought possible is the glass plate negative and cased photograph, although conservation research projects are currently ongoing to investigate whether freezing may be acceptable in large-scale flooding incidents as a last resort. These must be air-dried on-site and transportation minimized because of the risks of breakage.

The freezing process is possible for some objects typically found in museum collections (textiles, taxidermy and leather items), but not for others (glass, ceramics, wooden objects, paintings, sculpture, metals and so on). This renders mass flooding in museums much more challenging as so many items must be dealt with immediately through air-drying, which requires a large amount of space and human resource.

Although to some extent it is impossible to know how quickly items will dry and to determine the rate at which they can be treated until the process starts, those responsible for managing the salvage operation must make decisions early on as to the best strategy in the circumstances for dealing with the specific volume of material that they have to process, having seen the work rate that is achieved in the first few hours. It is vital to avoid the sort of situation where an attempt is made to deal with damage with in-house labour and resources for three or four days, only then to discover that perhaps 80% of the damaged material still remains unsorted and untreated, and only at that stage realize that external support is required. Although the affected items will still be recoverable, they will have suffered avoidable deterioration, which will increase the costs and timescales of salvage.

Successful managers of salvage operations make this call much earlier on and are well aware in advance of any incident of tipping points where in-house resources alone cannot handle the scale or nature of the incident. They are then able to assess a salvage operation before damaged items are moved and determine how best to proceed, well aware that salvaged items awaiting space for treatment will continue to deteriorate. These tipping points where external support should be called in are different for each organization: what one library can comfortably cope with, another may struggle with because it lacks staff or space, or for some other factor.

Drying capacity

At the point of planning the salvage operation, the key questions that need to be asked are about:

- the volume of damaged material
- the extent of water penetration
- the formats affected
- the available capacity for air-drying
- the available personnel for air-drying.

The simplest of these is volume and throughput. If 300 items can be air-dried per day and there is a flood affecting 3000 items, it will take 10 days to process all of them. If the number of items that can be air-dried per day cannot be increased, a large proportion of the 3000 items will suffer avoidable deterioration and it would be prudent to freeze some of them to stabilize them and prevent this additional damage. Items can then be professionally treated or batch thawed and air-dried.

The extent of water penetration is the second consideration. Obviously, slightly damp or superficially wet items (e.g. books that are only wet on the outside or cover, but have minimal water penetration inside the text-block), or 2D items such as documents, photographs, microfiche and parchment, will dry much more quickly than fully saturated dense or bound items. Therefore whereas an organization may be able to process 900 superficially wet items in 72 hours, they may only be able to dry one batch of 150 heavily wetted books in that timeframe. In some cases of heavily saturated material, the rate of drying can be so slow that mould growth outbreak occurs before the item has dried. Again, in such circumstances, although you may have capacity to dry a given quantity in 72 hours, heavily wetted material may occupy the available drying space for several days.

The next consideration is the format type and how much space that occupies. Certain formats take up a very large area to dry. Table 6.1 shows how much space the salvaged contents of one packing crate might take to dry depending on the contents.

Although individual documents and photographs dry relatively quickly, the space they occupy for drying is much larger than that needed by bound material. Therefore although an institution may have space for drying 900 books in 72 hours, it might only have space for drying the contents of five boxes of documents or one box of photographs before it is necessary to stabilize the items to avoid deterioration.

Figure 6.1 shows documents placed between blotters. This maximizes the use of space, but is not possible for photographic material.

Table 6.1 *Format type vs drying space*

Contents of one crate	Amount that can be fitted on a 1.5 m trestle table	Number of trestle tables required
Bound volumes – 40	20	2
Individual documents – approx. 5000 sheets	15 sheets laid singly; interleaved between blotting paper, stacked 10 layers high, 150 sheets in total on one table	33
Individual photographs – approx. 5000	15 laid singly as cannot be interleaved as blotting paper may stick	330

Figure 6.1 *Documents placed between blotters*

© Harwell Document Restoration Services

The final two points relate to available personnel and space. List possible locations for decanting damaged items in your plan appendices. It is important to be realistic about what spaces will be made available in an emergency. In an exercise held recently at a national museum, collections and curatorial staff had made contingency plans to commandeer the space of the restaurant for air-drying and treating damaged collections. Although this option was very attractive because it provided floor space, available tables and a ground floor secure location, it was not approved by the managers, one of whom said: 'We have a contract with a catering company who run the restaurant. Therefore in this scenario, we could not and would not close the restaurant. Another salvage location would need to be found.'

Those planning salvage need to be flexible in their approach. The main objective of disaster recovery is to make the best out of a bad situation and avoid as much additional damage as possible. Stabilization is very useful as it enables you to manage the pace and rate of drying without the constant fear of collections becoming mouldy.

Salvage constraints

Further flexibility is required when determining the techniques with which damaged items should be handled and treated. Fastidiously sticking to one methodology, which in isolation would be ideal, can prove counter-productive when dealing with damage caused after a major incident, where potentially thousands of items need to be dealt with concurrently, if it reduces the rate of salvage substantially.

Gillian Boal commented on her experience as a conservator at the Bancroft Library at the University of California, Berkeley, after a sprinkler system broke down:

> We had approximately 200–300 books damaged when an old wet-pipe sprinkler system malfunctioned, which was manageable for us to deal with in conservation. Some of them were clay coated. Our planned approach was to interleave all clay coated materials with release paper, but we realised this wouldn't work due to the time it would take and some items would have stuck together before we got to them. So we decided that we'd try setting them to dry in front of the fans. The fast circulation of air wicks away the moisture and keeps the paper separate. Had there been more we could have frozen them, but given the quantity, air-drying was appropriate. The coated books dried without sticking but we monitored them carefully.

Consider a shelf of 20 leather bound books that are saturated and need to be frozen: there are various levels to which those books can be packed for freezing. The premier method is to bandage them to prevent swelling and preserve the shape and curvature of the binding on the fore edge and spine, or to mummify the entire volume. Then the items can be placed in a polythene bag for freezing and finally crated. Although the bandaging is helpful, it is a slow step. Bagging the items is only really essential if there is a risk of the items adhering in the freezer; it is a further rate-reducing step. Straightforward crating of the volumes without bandaging or bagging (provided there is no migrating ink or loose glue, which may cause sticking) provides lateral pressure to the volumes, which will help preserve their shape in a very similar way.

Table 6.2 shows the impact of different methods of dealing with 20 damaged books before packing them into a crate: placing an item in a bag takes 15 seconds, and bandaging takes 1 minute. There is a nine-fold increase between the straightforward crating and the most involved process. Table 6.3 shows the amount of time it would take to deal with items if there was a major incident involving 30,000 items (approximately 1500 crates), 10 salvage personnel, and an assumed time of 7.5 active working hours on-site for each member of the team.

Table 6.2 *Impact of different methods on timings for packing one crate*

Method	Unit timing	Crating timing for 20 books
Crating	9 seconds	3 minutes
Bagging, then crating	9 seconds (crating) 15 seconds (bagging)	8 minutes
Bandaging, bagging, then crating	9 seconds (crating) 15 seconds (bagging) 60 seconds (bandaging)	28 minutes

Table 6.3 *Impacts of different methods on packing timings, major incident*

Method	Crating timing for 20 books	Hours for salvage (30,000 items or 1500 crates)	Equivalent days (10 salvage personnel, 7.5 hours on-site)
Crating	3 minutes	75	1
Bagging, then crating	8 minutes	200	2.6
Bandaging, bagging, then crating	28 minutes	700	9.3

The problem with the escalation in time is that the application of the bandaging technique is designed to reduce the swelling in the volume, but that that will have occurred anyway because salvage has taken so long, in addition to other secondary damage such as mould growth. The technique is not always inappropriate but it can be rendered inappropriate by the scale of major incidents. In these situations, it may still be possible to cherry-pick the most valuable items for the premier packing process, but this is not possible for all items.

The essential thing is to ensure that when salvage begins, work rates are monitored closely. If the initial procedures seem likely to tip the salvage over four days efficiencies will need to be made. Doubling the number of people helping with salvage will double the work rate, although they will need to be briefed, equipped and trained if they are not expert. If this is not possible compromises may have to be made when packing material, as the best way of treating an item in isolation may not be the most appropriate technique in a disaster recovery context.

Moving damaged items
Setting up the treatment area

Assuming that some air-drying is possible, the affected items need to be moved to a separate area for further assessment and drying out, preferably in crates. It will usually not be possible to dry the material effectively in the affected area. Find decant area(s) as close as possible to the damage site, preferably on the same level or accessible via lifts and trolleys, to reduce the manual handling load of the salvage process. Work out a route before moving damaged items. This is especially important in museums or historic houses where very large items may have to be moved, in order to minimize the risk of physical damage occurring during the moving process, to ensure health and safety, and for security reasons.

Ideally temperature and humidity should be controllable in the treatment room, or a cool room should be selected for the purpose. Consider whether it is possible to secure the room as potentially valuable or sensitive items may have been relocated. Provide as many tables as possible in the room to maximize the drying space available as the space above and below the table can be used. Protect carpeted or wooden floors with medium density polythene (taped down to avoid a trip hazard). Fans and dehumidifiers should also be sourced as these will help to speed up the drying rate.

You may also need:

- archival blotting paper (as a base for drying)
- unprinted newsprint or paper towels (for interleaving endpapers)
- Melinex (or acetates if you do not have Melinex) to support single leaf items
- coated paper (for interleaving clay-coated paper)
- string or tape (for creating washing lines)
- brass or plastic clips (for hanging)

- assorted sizes of polythene bags (for isolating items)
- scissors (for cutting paper to size)
- a clipboard, camera and documentation materials.

Documentation

Before moving any items, establish a documentation procedure. Where materials may have become separated from their original boxes, it is important to record where the items were found so they are traceable. Where possible take photographs of the scene before items are moved. Ideally photograph items individually if they are damaged in galleries but this may not be possible for items in high-density stores because of time constraints. Load items into crates, then number and label them individually, uniquely and sequentially, giving the cross-reference of the location as well. One person should control the crate numbering system to avoid duplication, and should have a master list of all crate numbers, which will help them to trace where the contents of each crate were moved to. It may be helpful to have some pre-printed labels in your disaster kit so that this process can be started very quickly. Ultimately if the contents are then separated at a later stage, this can be recorded too. This crate number can then be used to list the location where material was found, and to list the items within that crate. Count the number of items into the crate. This process also works very effectively for removing items which are still on the shelves, as the crate number can then be cross-referenced with the shelf number that items originally came from. Existing shelf lists can be used, to verify the contents of the crate, rather than having to write down each item.

If time permits, lists can be written at the point of removal of each item that is placed in each crate. It is important not to make the documentation process too time-consuming or onerous, given the time constraints of salvage. In the event of a major incident, detailed item lists can be compiled at a later stage. With the original crate number as a reference point, if items are sent off to be frozen, or treated by an external conservator or contractor, this crate number can be a reference point, even if the contents of crate number 1 are split up.

Figure 6.2 (overleaf) shows how this might work.

Give large items that do not fit in crates or similar containers individual item numbers, attach them with string or Tyvek tags, and photograph them; then they can still be part of the same overall scheme.

However an institution decides to document the salvage process, this process must be agreed before salvage begins and all salvage personnel must work to the same system. Failure to do this may result in a very confused situation and a jigsaw of collections left to match together at the end of the air-drying process.

Crate number	Salvage location	Contents	Location sent to	Contents split? If so details	Condition notes (complete if time permits)
1	Shelf A54 (L-M)	15 bound volumes;damp	Air-drying area	No; dried and sent to quarantine area	
2	Shelf A54 (M-R)	14 bound volumes, damp	Air-drying area	No; dried and sent to quarantine area	Minor cockling observed
3	Shelf A56	20 saturated records (Barker – Bramble)	Freezing	Kept together for freezing	
4	Loose on floor next to shelf B56	10 saturated records	Freezing	No, kept together for freezing	
	Loose on floor next to shelf B56	8 saturated records and 4 damp volumes	Air-drying area	Yes. 4 volumes air-dried and quarantined – crate 4a 8 records – frozen, split to crate 4b	

Figure 6.2 *Sample documentation sheet*

Packing damaged items

With the air-drying decant area set up and the documentation process established, the damaged items must be moved. In a major incident in a library or archive, it will probably be clear from the salvage planning process that a significant proportion of the collection should be frozen to stabilize it, as the volume of material affected cannot reasonably be treated in-house in the time available. In these circumstances, it makes little sense to take all damaged material to a decant assessment or air-drying area, only to be moved again to a van or lorry to transport it to a freezer facility. If this is the case, extract damaged items that require internal treatment because they cannot be stabilized, such as glass plate negatives, when the items are crated at the disaster scene. Similarly set aside items of value or significance which you do not wish to leave site for security reasons, or which you can 'cherry-pick' for in-house treatment. After small to medium-sized incidents it will not add significantly to the timescale of the restoration process if they are transported first to the decant assessment or air-drying area and then ultimately transferred to freezers.

In nearly all cases the damaged items will need to be moved. Bear in mind that they will be fragile and susceptible to additional damage through handling. As a result of the water damage they will be heavy and weakened, and glues may be loose, in addition to all of the other usual caveats when handling heritage and information services collections. There is a need to handle items carefully but quickly; be aware that because of the limited time-frame and risk of mould growth, a pragmatic approach may be needed. Remember the example given in Table 6.3 above, that demonstrates how even a slight additional technique in the salvage and first-aid process can add days to the time-frame for salvage.

Generally speaking, crate items to move them. Human chains are useful as they are quick, but they involve multiple pairs of hands on each item, which may cause additional physical damage. Crating items is generally preferable if the damage has already occurred, but if there is an effort to evacuate material from a building during a fire, human chains may be more appropriate. In such situations, book chutes are recommended by some heritage organizations but they are not appropriate for wet or damaged items.

Starting the salvage packing process

Move any items that have fallen onto the floor (where they may become indistinguishable from wet ceiling tiles and wet cardboard) first to avoid them being trodden on or being a trip hazard. In addition, in racked areas it may not be possible to operate the rolling mechanism if the aisles are not clear. These items are likely to be badly damaged, suffering from heavy saturation and the impact of falling to the ground. Individual wet documents are at risk of being torn if removed from the floor by hand, so where possible press a sheet of Melinex to the item so that the document can be lifted with no direct contact and then transferred to a crate. Given the points raised above about saturated material taking longer to dry than damp material, it may be that these items are not actually treated immediately but other, less wet items are dried first.

Collect and document all fragments of items that may have broken or disintegrated at this stage, while it is comparatively easy to determine where they have come from. Flaked paint can be collected and ultimately reattached to a canvas, for example, and it may be possible to repair broken pieces of ceramic objects at a later stage. These should also be meticulously labelled. Broken glass and ceramics can either be placed into crates on their own, or placed in jiffy-style envelopes and placed with the items they are thought to emanate from.

Having cleared the floor, the shelves and cases may now be cleared. Decide on the order in which to recover items and take them to the treatment area, referring to the priority lists in the emergency plan. If any priority items are affected extract them urgently. It will also be worth considering whether any rapidly deteriorating items – such as books with clay-coated papers – that are not on your priority lists should be extracted urgently, as failure to remove them quickly may result in irreversible adhesion.

Thereafter, after the top-tier priorities have been removed, if damage is universal it is usually best to proceed in a logical and logistically straightforward way, clearing shelves sequentially. This methodology is usually quicker. There may be limitations as to how many people can work in the area at a time, particularly if racking is in operation and only one aisle can be open, or if lighting is limited. Simple strategies may also make the crating process easier. Stacking two empty crates on top of one another to form a makeshift table will allow the working crate to be filled at waist height for top shelves and middle, which is ergonomically easier.

When items become wet on shelves, the absorption of water may cause them to swell on the shelf, with the result that contents become wedged and physically very difficult to remove. In order to remove bound items, if at all possible remove the volumes by placing a hand over the top edge of the books and pushing one book, two or three books from behind, rather than pulling from the front. Support boxed items underneath as they are removed from the shelf, to avoid the contents falling through the bottom of the box base onto the floor. Boxes should then be transferred directly into a crate for transfer rather than the weakened box carried to the treatment area, at risk of collapse all the way.

Clear all shelves that require removal from the bottom up provided that the shelving is fixed in place (e.g. screwed to the wall, rolling racking). The reason for this is that puddles and pockets of water will be displaced as contents of shelves are removed, onto the shelves beneath. If the shelves are cleared from the bottom up, the excess water will fall onto empty shelves, rather than further wetting full shelves underneath. Check all areas thoroughly as water may have seeped around the backs of shelves, which may not be obvious unless the volumes are removed from the shelf to allow for a visual inspection. It is worthwhile repeating this process once the salvage operation is complete to make sure that no isolated areas of damage have been missed.

Moving items

Ideally transfer all items to plastic crates for transfer, so those that are damaged are directly handled as minimally as possible. List crate suppliers in your suppliers' appendix in your plan; they can usually be hired fairly cheaply. If crates cannot be sourced other containers can be used, such as empty boxes, but these are likely to become damp and weakened quickly. Keep wet boxed items in their original boxes for transfer, but place the boxes into crates if they are wet. Bound volumes can be packed flat into crates generally, alternating the position of the binding row by row. If there are concerns about the weight of the text block, the bindings swelling, or if the pages are coated, bound volumes can be packed spine down in the crates with a layer of bubble wrap (bubbles facing away from the spines) or foam at the bottom of the crate as a buffer. Before crating, drain any water as it will only slow down the drying process in the treatment area. Keep boxed items flat and make a small hole in the bottom of the box if necessary to let water out.

Large horizontal drawers of maps, prints, drawings, plans or microfiche may be easier to move by removing the entire drawer from the cabinet and moving it as this involves less handling. Surface-dry the exterior before opening the drawers. Sometimes even filing cabinets may be more easily removed in this method, if a trolley can be found to transport them. It is far less risky to remove 2D large format items in their drawers than to attempt to handle them singly when they are wet.

At this stage, there is no need to place any items into a polythene bag unless dye-leaching is observed and you wish to prevent cross-contamination, or if the surface of the binding appears slimy or tacky and you are concerned that it may adhere to adjacent items. Items that are falling apart (for example, spines or boards may be detaching) can be placed in bags quickly to keep everything together, or alternatively items can be placed into crates on their own. Large format items can be placed on support boards or trolleys to move them, or if this is not possible, carried between two trolleys. Wrapping in bubble wrap (bubbles out) may be an option to reduce the direct handling.

When crating material, packers should remain aware of the ultimate weight of a full crate. Standard-sized packing crates may need to be substantially underfilled if they are to be reasonably portable when it comes to move them. Under UK health and safety guidance, the recommended limit of what an individual can move at waist height, close to the trunk, is 25 kg for a man, 16 kg for a woman. When that load is carried between two, the UK Manual

Handling Operations Regulations of 1992 state: 'As an approximate guide, the capability of a two-person team is two-thirds the sum of their individual capabilities and for a three-person team the capability is half the sum of their individual capabilities.' However, team lifts also bring different hazards if handholds are not good and people cannot fully see where they are going. A full packing crate of saturated documents can weigh as much as 50 kilos. Furthermore, if the crates are over-packed they may take up a larger floor area while awaiting treatment as they cannot be stacked. This will further limit the space available for actually treating the items.

Trolleys, dollies, sack-barrows and other aids can be used to make transporting the crates easier. Wherever possible avoid moving items up and down stairs given safety issues and increased handling risks. Dollies, trolleys and slings can be used for moving large and heavy items such as paintings, and it will be useful to involve in your salvage team staff who are experienced at moving such items. These large items should rest on foam blocks while awaiting treatment if possible.

Dealing with large or heavy items

Although it is advisable for most items to be removed from the damage scene for treatment, it may be less risky to attempt to dry some very large or heavy items (sculpture, bronzes, large paintings) or fragile items such as ceramic vases in situ than to take the risk of moving them within a building. Industrial dehumidifiers (with controls) and fans can be used. The drying process for objects may need to be slow to prevent cracking and overdrying, and this may inevitably conflict with the preferred tactics for drying out building fabric. As a result, avoidable damage to the building fabric may occur through mould growth, but this must be weighed against the needs of the objects and the risks of moving them when they are wet, heavy and fragile.

Assessing damaged items

In the assessment area, salvage staff will need to decide whether the crated items should be air-dried or stabilized. The assessment can be made at a sort of checkpoint by the Collections Salvage Manager or a nominated deputy at the entrance to the treatment room. Establish separate teams for dealing with saturated materials, damp materials, and/or different groups of formats – an audiovisual team or a books team for example. Clearly this depends on the people and the space available. An alternative method is to have each crate assessed and treated by one team and when their space is exhausted by material that is in the process of drying but not yet dry, they can move to assess crated material for which there is no space at present. The logistics of this process need to be thought through for each site and rehearsed to avoid backlogs and work out how the volunteers can be most effectively deployed.

An assistant archivist from a higher education institution in London described her experience of attempting to rescue soaking wet boxes:

> The trolleys were being filled too quickly for me to empty meaning soaking wet boxes were sitting on trolleys getting wetter. I think I could have done with another person unpacking them.
>
> I also think we could have done with two people assigned to running the trolleys up and down to the disaster area. This was hard work as we had to run them along the corridor on level 3 due to the lifts being out, and so the job should probably have been rotated between members of the team. Given that our recovery area is always likely to be far away from the disaster area it might be an idea to rotate this task between team members as a matter of course, even if just one person is assigned to it at a time.
>
> It didn't really feel like anyone took the overall role of managing the team, perhaps this should be looked at. The process of getting damaged items out of the room can be done very quickly but the follow-up assessment and re-boxing takes longer and therefore needs more people doing it.

All staff participating in the salvage process need to be briefed on dos and don'ts of salvage and the techniques to be applied, the documentation system being followed, who to ask if they have questions, and safety issues to be aware of, such as required personal protective equipment to be worn, evacuation signals and when breaks are to be taken. The Collections Salvage Manager needs to oversee this entire process, and if numbers suffice, nominate other people to supervise the less experienced members of the team and answer questions as they emerge. Salvage can work equally effectively with 12 people working simultaneously but on their own and concentrating on their own batch of material, with supervisors available if questions emerge, or pairs, or teams of three or four working on a larger amount of material simultaneously. The best process will depend on the dynamics and experience of the staff.

Salvage work can become monotonous so an advantage of working in groups is that it is more sociable, but it might be easier to concentrate on material, particularly where there is an imperative to keep it in order, in isolation. If salvage decisions about individual items are to be documented as they are made, a separate person should do this, as documenting and simultaneously completing forms with wet gloves becomes impractical. However, the time implications of this constant documentation must be borne in mind and the question raised: could these personnel not be put to better use assessing and treating damaged material? If there is a surplus of staff in relation to the availability of space, then this pressure on the documentation process is less of an issue.

Remove wet items from crates and examine them, dividing them into the following categories:

- dry
- wet – suitable for air-drying, subgroups for different object types or drying speeds
- wet – requires stabilization (kept wet or freezing)
- wet – requires professional assessment (e.g. adhesions, significant staining, soiling).

Some items will be found to be in wet enclosures such as a wet box or sleeve, which are dry inside. These items must be removed from their secondary housing immediately to avert the risk of any water penetration. Most archival quality boxes will keep most water out except for the bottom-most items in the box, but the longer dry documents are left in a wet box, the more seepage and wicking of moisture there will be. These items should be removed from the original box immediately, overturned and placed in a new temporary container, with the original box information placed in a polypocket and kept with the contents. If time permits, separate the damp material from the dry with a polypocket or plastic bag. The documents on the bottom of the original box will now be exposed and can dry.

Dry items in wet sleeves, files or envelopes should generally be cut out of enclosures rather than pulled. Any information on the sleeve needs to be retained and kept with the original items. This technique is even more important for removing wet items from sleeves. No drying will occur if these items remain in a microclimate, in fact deterioration will be more rapid, and if damp or wet material is pulled from sleeves, there is a risk of tearing or other physical damage. Items can be transferred more sensitively if they are cut out of sleeves. The same principle applies for framed paintings and pictures. In order for the painting to be dried fully, it may be necessary to remove it from its frame (although never from its stretcher).

Air-drying techniques

All materials found in heritage and information services collections can be successfully treated through air-drying, where water vaporizes from a liquid into the air in the form of water vapour. Water evaporation can be increased by increasing heat and velocity of air movement – but as the application of heat is not appropriate for drying typical collections, only air movement can be used to increase the drying rate.

The process can be completed at three speeds. The fast process will be to create a wind tunnel, by placing polythene sheeting over a table and taping down the bottom. Place blotting paper in the space underneath, so that wet objects can be put on it. A fan at either end of the wind tunnel on oscillating mode will increase the air movement and thus the rate of drying. String or tape can also be hung around the legs of tables, which can be useful to dry photographic material or pamphlets. Tables can be joined together to create a very long wind tunnel if fans or power points are in short supply. This technique is useful for drying modern hard-bound materials, as well as 3D non-porous objects (metal, high-fired ceramics, glass). Apply caution and place breakable items on their side if necessary.

The alternative technique is to dry at a slower pace, through laying material out on tables and on blotting paper on the floor to dry, rather than in the concentration of the wind tunnel. This is generally where moisture will have penetrated the surface of items, and it is desirable that this moisture is not drawn out too rapidly. Fans should still be blowing, but not directly at objects, with a view to increasing the air circulation in the room generally. Introduce dehumidifiers on a low setting to remove the moisture from the air and maintain drying. These are the types of items that respond best to this technique:

- leather
- textiles (best dried flat, so wind tunnel not very effective)
- basketware
- soft-bound items
- film and audiovisual materials
- bone or ivory
- 2D material (photographic collections and single-leaf documents, parchment)
- paintings
- anything suitable for wind-tunnel drying when the wind-tunnel space is exhausted.

In wind-tunnel and ambient drying, washing lines can be constructed to hang damp and wet items that are sufficiently robust to be draped over either string or cotton tape, or items such as negatives with emulsions on both sides. This can be used for drying thin files, pamphlets, photographic material and microfiche. Potentially it can be used for drying small textile items, but only with the approval of a conservator. Where there may be a concern about the stress point of being hung over a line and the risk of tearing, a sheet of Melinex can be rolled around the string to create a tube, secured with a paper clip and the items draped over a softer line.

The third technique is careful, slow dehumidification. It is used where moisture has penetrated the surface and if it dries too quickly, serious physical distortion through cracking and splitting can occur. This is the technique usually used for drying buildings, but it also applies to composite wooden objects such as furniture. In these circumstances manage and balance the dehumidification process to ensure slow desorption of moisture and desorption of water from the core of the item outwards, which will reduce the risk of cracking and splitting. Although there may be superficial mould growth on the exterior of the item, this is relatively straightforward to remove and a lesser evil than leaving a severely physically damaged and weakened structure.

Mixed formats

In a museum setting, often there will be objects comprising mixed formats, each of which may require different speeds of drying. Where possible, differing elements may be separated to be dried independently and then put back together when dried (e.g. when drying an upholstered chair, cushions may be separated from the wooden frame). In these cases shrinkage may be a problem so take care when selecting the drying methods. When the different elements cannot be separated, for example a wooden tool with a metal bit, there may be two preferred drying speeds to decide between. There are few hard and fast rules here unfortunately, and each combination needs to be assessed. As general guidance, it is worth considering what the implications of a particular speed of drying might entail for a particular format. So while fast drying would be good for a metal tool, the wooden handle may split, but slow drying, which is better for the wooden element, may be so slow as to result in corrosion forming on the metal part. Therefore a decision must be made by conservators taking into account which form of secondary damage is easier to remedy: which is the lesser evil. In this example the corrosion would be easier to treat than split wood.

General principles of air-drying

Air-drying is a straightforward process. Key principles include:

- Increase the surface area as much as possible without causing physical stress.

- Maintain shape of items through stuffing them with absorbent materials and change regularly.
- Do not interleave or stuff items (especially books) if this will radically alter the shape.
- Remove materials from enclosures if water has penetrated inside (including frames).
- Maintain order meticulously.
- Dry items flat or horizontally unless a conservator states that hanging or standing up to dry is advisable.
- Keep material wet-side down initially (except photographs, paintings and decorative surfaces) and keep moving it onto a dry blotter until liquid water is removed, then overturn and dry it damp-side up (if possible).
- Focus on getting material dry; try to overlook other issues such as curling or cockling until all items to be treated have been dealt with in the first instance.
- Never rub items dry. Patting dry is permissible for solid surfaces.
- Dry items with a loose surface face up and don't put anything on top of them.
- If time permits, wash off mud or sediment before drying (but not objects with water-soluble media, such as unstable inks).
- Ignore smoke or soot till items are dry: drying takes precedence.
- Do not air-dry mouldy material except in a fume cabinet or negative-pressure area.
- If the source of the water was foul, seek professional guidance.
- Isolate any items with leaching dyes.
- Stabilize items that may not be able physically to withstand drying where possible.

The principles listed above apply for the vast majority of items, although detailed notes on dealing with particular object types are given below. Evaporation will speed up if the surface area of an item can be increased, but care should be taken not to cause physical damage in the process. A closed book will dry very slowly but if the pages are splayed the drying rate will increase. However, although the book could be opened to almost 180 degrees and stand up, this would cause physical damage to the item, so is not appropriate.

Unprinted newsprint and uncoloured paper towels can be used as absorbent materials within an item (e.g. a basket or shoe) to help preserve shape and increase the drying rate. This needs to be changed frequently or may become a source of rewetting. Take care not to overstuff an item, radically altering the shape, even if it will expedite drying. For example, interleaving books can lead to the volumes drying in a triangular V-shape. Additionally, interleaving is time-consuming and arguably does not reduce the overall drying time significantly, and its benefits are negligible if many hundreds of items are still untreated in crates. Materials with loose or decorative surfaces, or any surface where there is a risk of adhesion, such as paintings or photographic material, should be dried with nothing covering the surface and in as dust-free an environment as possible.

Consider time constraints in general. Aim to lay materials all out to dry first, and then go back and finesse the process if time permits. In a situation where thousands of photographs are being dried, sometimes the emulsion side of the photograph may dry more quickly than the base, which may result in curling. This can be limited by gently weighting the corners. However, all the curling can be remedied after drying through pressing. If finessing the process and limiting the curling is at the expense of first-order drying for wet photographs that have yet to be even assessed and may deteriorate pending treatment, the ultimate outcome is not desirable.

Stabilization was discussed above as a way of deferring treatment in situations where drying cannot be completed within 72 hours because of the volume of material affected, level of saturation or lack of resource. There are further considerations as well where stabilization may be appropriate to defer treatment even in manageable incidents. If it is not possible to fan items out to increase the surface area, drying may not be at all effective. Fanning out saturated items may cause stress to the bindings through the weight of the text-block suddenly hanging off the bindings. Large format bindings and newsprint are difficult to air-dry for this reason, and are often more successfully treated through professional drying. Similarly, an item with a weak or damaged binding may suffer serious damage if left fanned open; if drying flat proves ineffective, freezing and professional treatment may be necessary.

In archival contexts, consider the need to maintain order and keep material together. Spreading material out and interleaving documents is crucial if it is to be air-dried effectively, but heightens the risk of collections becoming mixed up. Alternative processes such as vacuum drying may be preferable as these involve the drying of material in order, in their original boxes.

Materials that have been involved in a foul flood may be not merely wet but also dirty. If facilities exist for these items to be sprayed or rinsed clean, this can be attempted before drying. However, cleaning of dried sediment can be effective once the drying is complete, and may be more sensible if the washing process proves a bottle-neck. Seek advice from a conservator on the day where this applies. Materials damaged by foul water may also require sanitization as well as drying if the items are to be reliably and safely handled by the public. Processes such as gamma-irradiation and biocidal washing can be used. For museum objects rarely handled without gloves, this sanitization stage may not be necessary, and it can always be arranged after drying if necessary. Modern records and public library materials should always be sanitized, though, via a professional contractor. Items that are wet and affected by fire residues should be dried in the first instance and then smoke residues cleaned thereafter in a dry process using smoke sponges. Attempting to wipe off smoke residues when the item is still wet will only exacerbate the damage.

Air-drying techniques for library and archival collections

Specific information about dealing with individual object types is given below. As a general rule, if there is a library or archival major incident, nearly all material can be stabilized, mostly through freezing. Exceptions include gilded manuscript and glass plate negatives where freezing brings the risk of lifting gilding and physical fracture respectively. Usually materials being packed for freezing need not be bagged or wrapped but can be if time permits. This is only important if there is leaching dye or the surface feels tacky and there may be a risk of sticking. Freezing most paper-based items and bindings packed together in a crate is like freezing a loaf of sliced bread. Before freezing, the slices separate, but when frozen, the loaf is a mass where it is difficult to separate individual slices. When the loaf is defrosted, though, the slices separate. The same is true for the vast majority of library or archive holdings to be frozen. Although they may appear to be stuck together when frozen, they are not physically adhered and when thawed will separate just as they did before freezing. Materials are best packed flat usually, with heavier larger items at the bottom. The exceptions are clay-coated paper or items where there is a concern about the weight of the wet text-block hanging from the spine. In these cases, vertical packing, spine down is best.

Bound material

In order to dry effectively and increase the rate of water vaporizing, it is important to maximize the surface area as much as possible without physically damaging the items. Usually this means to fan them open to approximately 60–90 degrees although some bindings may resist being fanned if they are tightly sewn. Remove and dry dust jackets separately. Cut unprinted newsprint to size to place inside the endpapers to absorb more water, and change it frequently. Interleaving within the text-block can be attempted but may be very time-consuming and can result in the volume drying in a V-shape. Place bound items wet-side down to begin with on blotting paper and move regularly when the blotter is saturated so water will seep out quickly. When liquid moisture stops moving into the blotting paper, the books can be turned upside down so they are wet-side up and continue drying this way.

Leather and vellum bindings

The same principles apply for drying antiquarian bindings as for modern bindings, although in all likelihood it will not be possible to fan the pages open to a very wide angle. Take great care in judging whether the volume is able to withstand being dried upright. Keeping the area cool is important. Although it is preferable to avoid freezing if possible, freezing is definitely the lesser evil if the alternative is large volumes of items becoming physically weaker from prolonged wetting, and developing substantial mould growth as there is no space yet to dry them.

Leather and bindings can be successfully treated through controlled vacuum drying and processes such as vacuum packing, though the processes require high supervision to prevent over-drying. Vellum is typically more difficult to deal with than leather bindings. It may be necessary to rewet the binding through spraying to prevent over-drying or shrinkage, which may cause damage to the text block. Consultation with conservators and professionals is preferable.

Clay-coated paper or photograph albums

Bound material with clay-coated paper and photograph albums are at high risk of adhesions as they dry. Place them upright on a blotter to dry, and if pages cannot be kept separate by being dried directly by a fan, interleave each page with silicone release paper. This is a very time-consuming process and if the quantity is large, it may be easier to freeze the items immediately, stacking them vertically in crates, and treating through freeze drying or individual thawing and treatment at a later stage.

Soft-bound material

Soft-bound material often absorbs the most water in a flood. Attempts can be made to fan soft-bound items open although this may not be possible without resulting in physical damage as they are not as robust as hard-bound items. If pages do not easily splay and are clumped together it often indicates that the item is so wet that its rate of drying will be slower than the rate of mould growth, and these items may benefit from stabilization and professional treatment. If unsure about the drying rate of partially wet items, it is possible to mark the water level on a fixed page with a soft pencil (on the dry part of the paper) and then monitor the rate of drying with that benchmark: if drying is slow, the items may need to be frozen to stabilize them as they will not dry effectively. The bindings of some modern library materials are coated in plastic. This may result in the front and back covers drying more quickly and curling in on themselves as they dry. This can be rectified through pressing or even merely reshelving after drying.

Large formats or thick text blocks

Air-drying of very large volumes, or text blocks that are very thick, may also cause problems, as fanning open may cause physical damage to the binding owing to the bodily stress. These items should either be treated by a conservator immediately, or passed for freezing and then treated professionally. Bound newspapers are often very large, and absorb a great deal of water, rendering the text-block very heavy. These items may be a candidate for immediate freezing and then professional treatment.

Photographic prints, x-rays, negatives and microfiche

Some photographic types are very prone to rapid deterioration, including carbon prints, deteriorated nitrates, cased photographs and glass plate negatives. Others are a little more resilient but nevertheless prone to adhesions and should also be prioritized for drying.

Most photographic prints and microfiche can either be hung to dry or laid flat on blotting paper, emulsion-side up. Drying flat may result in some water staining on the image, but hanging may result in crimping or grazing of the very edges of the image. Usually hanging the images to dry is the best option in the circumstances, although the image should be clipped in the least invasive way possible. Hang negatives and transparencies to dry, rather than lay them on a blotter, as there is a risk of adhesion to the blotter.

Partially wet items may benefit from being rinsed in cold clean water before drying so the image is fully wet. Keep the environment clean and dust free. Certain photographic formats may require specialist drying so refer them to a conservator or other professional if you have any concerns. Place adhered photographs in shallow trays of cold clean water for ten minutes and attempt to separate them while they are still underwater (not carbon types). It may be necessary to separate a little, stop, rewet, separate a little, repeating the process iteratively if the images are stuck fast. If drying photographs flat, they must be dried face up, with nothing touching the surface. Shallow bread crates can be used to create makeshift drying racks to make maximum use of the floor space in a room.

Microfiche and most photographic prints can be frozen in bulk if there is a major incident, then treated through professional drying or batch thawing and air-drying. If being frozen, items can be kept in their sleeves and transferred directly to freezer facilities. An alternative stabilization process is to fill solid crates with cold water and submerge these items in water pending available time and space to treat them. This defers the need for treatment but it is not advisable to keep materials in this condition for longer than a week. Paper enclosures need to be removed and sticky labels may detach if the items are kept wet, which may render freezing a preferable option if it will result in the collection's identifiers being lost or muddled.

Further detailed information about techniques for dealing with specific photographic types is available in Betty Walsh's paper *Salvage Operations for Water Damaged Archival Collections* (2003).

Glass plate negatives and cased photographs

Glass plate negatives and cased photographs should ideally also be dried at an incline (resting on something so there is an air flow underneath and above the item). It is not usually recommended that wet glass plate negatives are frozen (because of the risk of physical fracture through impact in a large freezer and the reactions of the emulsion) and so immediate drying is necessary. Research on glass plates and the possibility of freezing to stabilize is ongoing, particularly for archives that retain thousands of glass plates, where space restrictions would not allow immediate air-drying. Cased photographs are not recommended for freezing either. Dry them immediately, disassembling the parts and drying separately.

Film (microfilm, motion picture film)

Often water does not extensively penetrate inside the reel because the tape is tightly wound and encased. Dry plastic or metal containers with paper towels before opening to prevent moisture ingress inside. If water penetration has occurred, film may be rolled off and dried, but this may be impractical given the length of the film. Rinsing in distilled water before unreeling may be beneficial if the water was dirty or carried contaminants.

If there is a major incident, submerge film in buckets or containers of cold clean water to stabilize it. However, such action is only advisable if the tape is definitely wet and should not endure longer than a week. Professional drying can be applied, or professional reprocessing of the tape. Names and contact details for film labs should be in your plan.

Audiovisual tape, reel to reel tape

As with film, water penetration of audiovisual or reel-to-reel tape may be minimal, so take care when opening boxes. If tape is damaged, conduct checks to see how far into the reel it progresses; it may be restricted to outer layers, making drying more straightforward. If drying occurs while the tape is wound, contaminants can dry onto the tape. Tape should be first rinsed or sprayed, still on the reel if the entire tape is wet, in distilled or deionized water, then dismantled and air-dried, with reels supported vertically or laid flat on a blotter. Dry tape should be rewound and test played. Tape can be stabilized by keeping it wet, although only if the tape is saturated and for a period no longer than a week. Tapes may be copied by specialists in large quantities and professionally reprocessed or dried.

Documents and files

Lay files and paper documents flat, face up, on blotting paper to dry. A file of documents which is secured by a fixing such as a treasury tag, may be hung to dry if only slightly damp, if all documents within are secure and it is not very heavy. Archivists have to decide whether to remove fixings or not: generally items are easier to dry if the fixings are removed, and they may corrode or degrade as a result of the water damage anyway. Documents can be sandwiched between blotting paper up to ten levels high in order to maximize the footprint of the drying area. Wet folders can be removed if they have no information on them. Usually the constraint with loose material and files is the space it takes up to dry, and often freezing and professional treatment is the most sensible course of action. No interleaving is required if the items are to be professionally dried.

Parchment

Lay parchment flat to dry, face up. Blotter or bondina can be placed over the surface, and the edges weighed down to prevent curling and over-drying. This is unlikely to result in sticking unless the parchment has been wet for a long time, so check it regularly. Pinning may be necessary to prevent shrinkage and to ensure the retention of shape, but only attempt this under the guidance of a conservator who will want to check tension regularly.

Support pendant seals and do not leave them to hang. In the event of a major incident, freezing is sensible to defer treatment. Professional vacuum drying techniques are rarely successful with parchment, but it can be defrosted in manageable batches and dried in conservation facilities. Avoid freezing illuminated manuscripts as it causes gilding to lift from the substrate.

Maps and plans

Maps and plans can be treated similarly to documents. Gradually unroll rolled plans to increase the drying rate. Take care when lifting large horizontally stored maps because of the risk of tearing. Melinex may be used to support the transfer of these items. Freezing is possible for all maps and plans if there is an emergency, and they can be professionally dried. Transfer of the maps can be awkward. Maps and plans can be placed into crates, wet side up, and the crate filled so that movement is limited. Otherwise they can be laid on the floor of a vehicle. Some specialist (e.g. wax-coated) types of paper may require test treatment before drying.

CDs

Ideally dry CDs at an incline (resting on something so there is an air flow underneath and above the item). Rinse the CD with distilled water, and take care not to scratch surfaces. String can be fed through the centre of CDs and they can be hung to dry. Paper enclosures may be air-dried or vacuum-dried, but the difficulty will be marrying all items together if they are separated, so keeping material together and air-drying is preferable where possible. It is not possible to apply professional drying to the disc itself.

Albums (vinyl and shellac)

Hold albums by their edges and pack them vertically. At the assessment area, remove any sleeves and jackets and dry them separately. Rinsing in deionized or distilled water will be helpful if the items are dirty but minimize contact with water. Dry discs upright or at an incline with good ventilation. Sleeves should be kept as close as possible to avoid confusion, at an incline and not in contact with blotter, given the risk of adhesion. Freezing or chilling have been successful methods of stabilizing these items but are not widely used. Jackets are often highly glossy and if immediate treatment is impossible, there is a high risk of adhesion. The temperature should not be as low as for paper, but −5°C to 0°C. Pack discs vertically in foam-lined crates to avoid physical damage if possible. If they are being frozen there is no need to separate discs from sleeves, although placing a polythene bag between sleeves may limit the risk of adhesion. Batch thaw and dry items as above.

Air-drying techniques for museum or historic-house collections

Dealing with major incidents in museums and historic houses is extremely challenging. Not only do you have many different formats and object types to consider, but unlike working with library and archival collections exclusively, the majority of items cannot be stabilized, and treatment cannot be deferred. Damaged items must be dealt with as quickly as possible to avoid secondary damage but with a finite capacity and human resource.

Salvage work in large museums can potentially be compounded by people from different curatorial departments all trying to compete to gain access to the finite air-drying capacity, each of whom is likely to consider their own collections the most important to save. There needs to be an overarching salvage strategy, made by a senior manager responsible for the collections in general, on how to allocate space and collections/conservation expertise amongst the different curatorial departments.

Generally speaking, when there is a museum emergency which involves archival and textile collections together with leather, the best option is to defer treatment by stabilizing items if possible, thus freeing up time and space for salvage staff to concentrate on those items where there is no option for stabilization. Advice from conservators is always desirable. Usually only a few items are affected when there are emergencies affecting museum gallery spaces and historic houses, as items are on display. This affords the opportunity to consider the needs of items individually much more easily than if a store with bulk storage is affected, and rather than two or three items, 200 or 300 items are involved.

Paintings

Identify any specialist equipment (wire cutters, security screwdrivers, crowbars) required to move paintings from fixings as part of the process of identifying salvage priorities and drawing up snatch lists (see Chapter 4). Where ladders may be required to remove the items, a section in your plan should list the locations of these ladders so they can be found quickly in an emergency, and the process of removal rehearsed. Usually paintings can be removed from fixings with an upward movement. Webbing may be required to lower heavy items to the ground. Support the frame during the moving process by holding underneath and to a height of two-thirds on the vertical sections of the frame, or, for larger paintings, place on straps or dollies and move with sufficient numbers of people. If a frame is held by the top member there is a risk of the frame being severely damaged as mitres may be weak.

Mouldings of frames are also fragile and may be equally valuable to the canvas in some cases so take care to handle them smoothly. Salvage personnel should avoid holding the frames where the mouldings are particularly elaborate, with the painting facing towards the body. Collect and document any pieces that detach so that a conservator can ultimately repair and reattach them. Never touch the surface of the painting directly or indirectly. A major concern is the risk of abrasion or tearing to the canvas. If paintings need to be stacked before assessment because of space restrictions, stack them upright front to front, back to back, taking care to ensure protruding wires or screws cannot cause damage.

When in a safe area, deframe canvases if the items are wet and damaged. Preferably this process will be conducted by a conservator. The canvas should remain on its stretcher for drying. It is best to dry frames all together in a separate area under controlled humidity conditions, and tag and identify them before separation. Place the canvas on wooden blocks, image side up, so that an adequate air-flow is maintained. Blotting paper may be slid underneath stretchers and replaced frequently to increase the drying rate in that microclimate. There may be issues such as the varnish to the painting becoming opaque. This is reversible via conservation processes after initial drying. The priority must be to dry all paintings in the first instance and to attend to secondary damage afterwards. Similarly fragments of paint and tears to the canvas can be repaired after drying has occurred.

Art on paper or photos in frames with glass

Similar principles, of removing from wall hangings and moving, apply to art on paper or photos in frames with glass, but bear in mind that the glass will add significant additional weight. If the glass is fractured in any way take great care to avoid scratching of the surface of the image by tilting the glass away from the surface.

Remove the frames and glass in the decant area. Take nails out from the back of the frame with pliers and then lift the backboard. Air-dry and retain the labels. Air-dry the image slowly, face up. If any resistance is evident and the image is stuck to the glass, halt the process immediately, consult a conservator and place the item glass side down.

Sculptures and plasterwork

Sculptures and plasterwork are likely to be too heavy to move and may be most effectively treated in situ. Small pieces may be strapped to lined sack-barrows. To protect these items in the midst of a flood, polythene sheeting can be used, or wooden blocks wrapped in polythene can be placed under plinths to raise the item from ground level, provided this is not considered to heighten the risk of the items falling over. Such items should not be lifted from a projecting member.

These types of objects are extremely vulnerable to the impact of fire and flood. They are porous, and absorbed water can corrode fixings, which may render the items unstable. Make them a priority for treatment. Remove excess moisture using paper towels, or if very wet by covering the sculpture in cotton wool, and change it regularly. Don't wipe or rub the surface. Dry and label damaged pieces that have become detached so it is clear where they came from. Keep the area for drying cool and use fans to increase air movement in the room. If there are any noticeable deposits, note and photograph them, collect a sample if possible, and contact a specialist conservator. Any images of the pieces before damage may be useful to conservators.

Textiles

Carry textiles to the salvage area on sheets of polythene, rolled if necessary. They may be very heavy and require many people to move them. As with paintings, these items when on display may be difficult to remove quickly without information on the fixings, so rehearse the process. When the item has been removed from its fixings salvage volunteers should take the weight at the bottom and lower the item carefully. Polythene sheeting may need to be placed over the surface if dyes are running to prevent leaching.

Spread textiles out in a well ventilated cool room to dry on either towels or a blotter. Don't place anything on top of items with a pile (e.g. rugs, carpeting) to prevent the pile from flattening. Otherwise press the items with towels or blotter, and replace them as soon as they are wet. Unfold delicate fabrics under a conservator's supervision. Encapsulated costume and textiles in sleeves should have been protected, but inspect them for any water penetration. If water has affected the objects, cut them out of sleeves and carefully transfer them onto a blotter to dry flat.

Textiles should not be hung to dry, or stacked. They can be gently pressed and gently reshaped while damp. If items cannot be dried within 48–72 hours they can be frozen. To prevent leaching of dyes while packed, wrap them in release paper or plastic, pack them flat, and stack them in crates, carefully labelled.

Furniture or wood

Weight may prove a major problem when attempting to remove furniture, as might the fact that individual pieces cannot be removed from a particular space without being dismantled. Prior planning and foreknowledge of such items will avoid wasting time and energy in the salvage operation. Moving aids such as trolleys and dollies can be used to move furniture. It may be possible to rock and lift items that cannot be moved onto polythene-covered wooden blocks if there is a fear of the items sitting in surface water. Remove any items in drawers before they are transported, but close drawers after removal. Lift from the lowest load-bearing member, fully supporting items from underneath.

To attempt drying, blot-dry all accessible surfaces with towels or a blotter, excluding decorative or painted or gilded surfaces, which should not be touched even if they are dirty, as cleaning them while they are wet may remove more than the surface debris. Dry items by gradually dehumidifying them so the moisture can be drawn out slowly, as speed may result in cracking or splitting. Attempt to dry wooden materials in a separate or tented area to ensure drying is not too rapid. A furniture restoration expert may be consulted. Hold veneers in place while drying by means of a clamp, with a protective layer in between the weight and the veneer. Any lacquered or finished surfaces that form a white haze can be treated or repolished after drying.

Ceramics and glass

In emergencies, the main initial problem will be breakage, either from falling debris, surface or falling water, or rushed removal or handling. Remove items to a decant area carefully, although it may be best to leave large pieces in situ for drying. Pack items into containers, bubble-wrapped, with heavy, larger items at the bottom of the container, lighter items on the top. Take great care when lifting items as old repairs using glues may have become weakened in the water or heat and may fracture on contact.

To remedy water damage, minimize handling to reduce the risk of breakage, chipping broken edges and engraining any surface debris such as soot and dirt. Lay pieces on a blotter to dry and dry them slowly using fans. Give priority to unglazed surfaces that are porous and likely to deteriorate more quickly than glazed surfaces and glass. Consult ceramics conservators where possible. Keep broken pieces from one original item together so they can ultimately be repaired.

Don't wash porous ceramics, even if they are dirty. Dry them first then surface-clean them with brushes. It is safe to wash glazed ceramics and glass in clean water as they will not absorb the water. Then dry them with paper towels and leave them in a cool room with fans. Refer any ceramic items with obvious old repairs or surface mineral deposits to a conservator immediately: do not wash them.

Stone

Stone is relatively resilient after water and fire damage and can be treated after other more vulnerable items. Smooth surfaced stone can be blotted gently and air-dried; stone with a rough or applied finish should not be blotted but air-dried on a blotter.

Metal

Metal is a vulnerable format in fires and floods, given the risk of corrosion, either through acid (fires) or presence of water. Give priority to moving and treating already corroded metals. Blot the surface and then air-dry the item in a well ventilated area. Use trolleys and dollies to carry heavy items. Metal objects are less susceptible to additional effects through being dried in a warm area so may be moved to a separate drying area, which may otherwise have been dismissed as unsuitable. Metal workings of clocks are highly specialized, so keep intervention to a minimum and seek the assistance of specialist horologists if necessary.

Leather

If surface deposits (excluding smoke) are present on leather items rinse them while they are still wet if feasible. Blot items and leave them to air-dry, padded internally where possible with blotter or paper towels, taking care not to alter their shape. Leather items can be frozen to stabilize them if drying is impractical, but to a temperature no lower than −10ºC.

Basketry

Lift basketry items from underneath and handle them with care as they can be fragile. Rinse surface deposits (excluding smoke) then blot and air-dry items slowly with fans. The shape may be retained by using paper towels or other blotting materials; change them regularly.

Bone, shell and ivory

Items made of bone, shell or ivory may be fragile and so handle them with care. Water and fire damage can cause staining, dimension changes and cracking, and it may be necessary to bubble-wrap them before removal. It is possible to remove surface debris through rinsing and patting items dry then leaving them to air-dry on a blotter. Treat human bone sensitively and religious artefacts of all kinds and ethnographic collections respectfully.

Natural history collections

Handle geological specimens with care as they may be fragile. Some items may have disintegrated if they got wet and so disregard them for urgent treatment as restoration is not likely to be possible. Transfer items to a drying area with good support, rinse and blot them dry, then air-dry them with good ventilation, provided they are not porous. Address any concerns to a conservator. If there are any items requiring specialist handling they should have be clearly signed in situ as part of the planning process and general housekeeping.

Treat animal skins and taxidermy mounts as a matter of priority to prevent the risk of rapid mould growth and deterioration. Handle them as little as possible as many stuffed mounts can contain dangerous compounds such as arsenic. Air-dry items, preferably in a separate area, but if this is not possible within 24 hours it might be preferable to freeze them so they can be treated in batches in the future. Freeze-drying may be possible but requires a specialist approach and methodology to be determined. Prioritize herbarium specimens for treatment to reduce the risk of mould growth. Minimize handling, removing specimens in their original drawers rather than transferring them to new containers for transport. Air-dry them with good ventilation in a cool area, with specimen boxes opened.

Treat fluid-preserved collections as a priority and do not handle them directly. Place specimens in sealed plastic boxes together with their labels. Rinse them with distilled water or a preservative and store them in a new jar with fresh preservative. Consult specialist curatorial staff in the planning phase about the potential for chemicals and whether specialist lab or fume cabinet areas may be required. Treat pinned insects within 24 hours to prevent mould growth. They require gentle and careful handling because of their fragility, preferably in their existing trays or boxes for transport. Air-dry them with any lids open.

When is material dry?

Instrumentation can be used to determine the moisture content of an item, but for library and archival items a touch-test usually suffices. Additional tests may be required for items where the moisture moved beyond the surface. However it is advisable to quarantine dry material for four to six weeks after it is considered to be dry, to ensure there is no pocket of moisture which could trigger an outbreak of mould. Also the affected area must be thoroughly dry before items are reshelved. This may require a professional examination of the moisture in the building fabric (see Chapter 8).

Large-scale drying

For large-scale incidents of flooding, immediate air-drying usually proves to be impractical because of the volume of material affected. In these incidents, techniques such as vacuum freezing or freeze-drying are often used, when materials are placed into drying chambers while still frozen, and dried at reduced chamber pressure. At low pressure, water vaporizes at ambient temperatures without exposing the materials to any excess heat. This process works very effectively for drying paper, including archival documents and bound volumes, both antiquarian and modern. Modified techniques can also be applied to drying photographic material and clay-coated papers. Specialist professional companies exist with large-scale drying plant, which can dry damaged material, particularly books and documents, in large quantities.

Figure 6.3 shows a library salvage operation with library staff working alongside professional document recovery contractors. Promptly contacting key contractors after an emergency ensures libraries, archives and museums are the first to receive help.

Figure 6.3 *Working with contractors*   © *Harwell Document Restoration Services*

The drying processes are techniques widely used in drying food and pharmaceutical products, including vacuum freeze-drying and freeze-drying. The Federal Emergency Management Agency (National Taskforce on Emergency Response, 1997) defines vacuum freeze-drying in the following way:

> Items are dried in a vacuum chamber at below-freezing temperatures to minimize swelling and distortion. Generally provides the most satisfactory results; recommended for historic collecting materials and glossy papers.

It defines vacuum drying as a process where:

> Items are dried in a vacuum chamber, often at temperatures above 100°F. Caution: this method accelerates aging and causes damage to many materials: animal skins (leather, vellum), film media. Widely available; slower than vacuum freeze-drying, but less expensive.

Ken McKenzie, Technical Director of Harwell Document Restoration Services, has managed a company which has been drying library and archival materials for over 25 years and comes from a chemical engineering background. He commented:

> In strictly chemical engineering terms, you are either freeze drying, below the triple-point of water where moisture sublimates, or you are vacuum drying which is above the triple point, and where moisture melts, then vaporizes. The term of freeze-vacuum or vacuum-freeze drying is widely referred to but technically is shorthand for drying of frozen materials in a vacuum chamber. High temperatures can accelerate ageing of material, but vacuum drying can be conducted at temperatures as low as 1°C. At Harwell we have developed both the vacuum drying and freeze drying processes (known as vacuum-freeze drying) to optimize on the drying of water-damaged materials to maintain the quality of the item.

In selecting a contractor for restoring damaged material, take care to ensure their technical competence, experience and capability of drying both modern and antiquarian material.

Figure 6.4 shows a purpose-built drying chamber for dealing with water-damaged materials.

These processes are always an option for dealing with most water-damaged library and archival collections and usually prove the most effective way of dealing with medium to large scale incidents, given the ability to dry large volumes of material to a high quality, in a compact and cost-effective way, without being labour-intensive.

Figure 6.4 *Purpose-built drying chamber for dealing with water-damaged materials*
© *Harwell Document Restoration Services*

Tokuda Seiko commented on her experiences in working with large-scale water damage:

> In the summer, I had an opportunity to participate in a project of salvaging wet mud-covered documents damaged by the post-earthquake tsunami on March 11. The project was led by Professor Isamu Sakamoto, a freelance paper conservator. The project completed the recovery of about 5,000 volumes of land register documents of two Legal Affairs Bureaus (under jurisdiction of the Ministry of Justice) in Tohoku within six months with the process of freezing and vacuum-freeze drying.
>
> In this case, damage to transportation infrastructure and radiation leakage

prevented immediate rescue of mud-covered documents within 72 hours. Rescue operations were delayed for a month, thus the outbreak of mould was inevitable. Documents were dried via vacuum-freeze drying and then required cleaning.

Professor Sakamoto casts doubt on the once-prevailing document salvage practice in Japan which depends on non-professional volunteers and library professionals themselves. He advocates a response involving external professionals in restoration for serious situations of water-damage rather than relying on library professionals alone. Of course, several non-profit professional bodies, such as the Nara National Research Institute of Cultural Properties, have been supporting rescue and recovery processes under the nationwide framework established after the earthquake. But it is not common in Japan that disaster response companies come to deal with the damaged collections.

In cases of mass damage, vacuum-freeze drying is a more appropriate technique because of the condition and amount of items requiring treatment. The air-drying technique is appropriate in smaller-scale incidents but professional treatment may be more appropriate than using library staff due to other demands on their time.

Even in this case when documents were restored through vacuum-freeze drying method, it was apparent that a lot of labour was required after the documents were completely dried to get rid of dried mud and sludge, and to have some of them rebound. However, this case also showed that vacuum-freeze drying successfully recovered more than 99 percent of these tsunami-damaged land registers without any dimensional distortion of the drawings, which enabled them to be returned to the bureaus for immediate use for local reconstruction.

Fire and smoke damage

Once a fire is out and access is permitted by fire services, damage is likely to be worst to items which were on display and thus more exposed. Usually a large proportion of items will be salvageable after a fire and can be restored. Those closest to the seat of the fire will usually have suffered the most severe damage and may have come into contact with flames, leading to charring and scorching, which may not be restorable. However, from an archival perspective, as paper burns from the periphery inwards, usually a large proportion of the information in a file or on a document will survive. In a library context, the worst of the damage will be to the binding and the cost-effectiveness and viability of restoration will depend on the nature of the collection and its value and possibility of replacement.

Figure 6.5 shows the damage heavy smoke can cause to archives.

Unlike water damage, fire damage does not require urgent treatment to avoid secondary damage, unless the items affected are wet and smoke damaged, in which case the items will still need to be dried or stabilized within 72 hours if possible. Exceptions to this rule include electronic equipment, plastics and metals, which can corrode as the residues are acidic.

Nearly all damage in fires is caused by smoke. Where dampers are not fitted, or in open-plan areas, smoke can travel significant distances through voids and defunct air shafts, and spread throughout a building. Damage will be worst closest to the seat of the fire or by windows, which might have broken and fed the fire. Smoke concentrations are likely to be at their worst on the highest shelves.

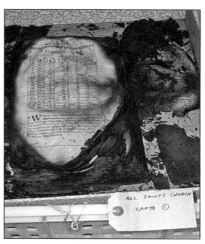

Figure 6.5 *Heavy smoke damage, but bulk of information still legible*
© *Harwell Document Restoration Services*

Figure 6.6 shows fire and smoke damaged books, with concentrations of damage closest to seat of fire (out of shot to the right) and at height, and the undamaged areas where books have been tilted off the shelf post-fire.

Figure 6.6 *Fire and smoke damaged books*
© *Harwell Document Restoration Services*

The situation may be more positive in storage areas, however, where the density of the storage buffers the extremes of heat and keeps out water and flames. Boxes and cupboards keep out much of the smoke, although there is usually some smoke penetration. Most of the smoke is likely to settle on horizontal surfaces, with some deposits on vertical surfaces such as the spines of bindings, and can often easily be removed through cleaning with smoke sponges made of vulcanized rubber. Sponges are more effective than brushes to remove fire damage. Take care with decorative surfaces as the smoke removal process usually involves careful lifting of the residues from the surface.

Figure 6.7 (overleaf) shows smoke damage being removed from the substrate with a vulcanized rubber sponge.

Figure 6.7 *Smoke damage removed from substrate with vulcanized rubber sponge*
© *Harwell Document Restoration Services*

The main challenge of dealing with fire damage may be the volume of material affected by smoke, albeit to a low level. Smoke-contaminated items cannot be used by the public and need to be cleaned, but potentially every item in a library may need to be cleaned. Even in a very serious flood, it is rare for absolutely everything to be affected. Plastics can compound the damage by melting or bubbling in the heat of a fire, which complicates damage, particularly in modern collections where books are covered in plastic rather than hard bound and audiovisual collections are encased in plastic boxes.

Generally smoke residue is relatively easy to remove but usually, as such a large proportion of the collection is likely to be affected, insurers pay for disaster recovery companies to clean items. Where both water and smoke have affected items, the water damage must be treated first as a priority, and then cleaning completed afterwards. The wetting of the smoke residues may result in residual staining which cannot be removed except for trimming of the edges of the paper, which can be costly. Only attempt to clean items once they are dry.

Odour may be difficult to remove as this may have permeated the object and be trapped inside. Dismantling and cleaning may be effective. Otherwise, consult damage management companies that deal with cleaning processes to see if any processes adopted for modern materials can be applied to heritage objects.

CHAPTER 7
Supplementary content

This chapter will provide guidance on what additional information may be required as a reference tool for an effective emergency response. In most plans, such information is usually located in appendices, and a list of suggested appendices was given in Chapter 1. They are discussed in order, although some are merely listed and the cross-reference given to where their content and design is explained in other chapters. Others are discussed in more detail. Although this section undoubtedly adds to the workload of plan composition and the overall size of the disaster plan, the appendices (sometimes referred to as annexes) are potentially invaluable if your plan is ever implemented.

Although you may have floor plans, supplier account numbers and contact details for depositors and stakeholders in your filing cabinet, this is not very helpful if you are denied access to your office in an emergency for safety reasons. The appendices function as a backup so that if the situation is too big for you to manage internally, or if the scale of the incident is causing an element of panic, which makes you question things you would ordinarily recall without question (e.g. the location of and process for isolating stop-valves), your appendices will be there as a bespoke emergency reference tool. In most small-scale incidents, for example involving a small leak and not much damage, the appendices will only receive cursory attention as the incident and its consequences should be relatively manageable. However, appendices are of immense importance when dealing with incidents that are bigger in scale and cannot obviously be managed without going to external agencies.

Personnel contact lists

When a large volume of material has been damaged, particularly when the nature of damage is water, the salvage operation will be enhanced significantly by involving large numbers of staff or volunteers to assist the recovery efforts to move quickly. Ability to corral large numbers of people to assist in this process is therefore crucial. Consider a task that takes a team of two people 100 hours to complete, or 10–12 days. This same activity, presuming the same work rate and no constraints in terms of access or resources, can be tackled in just 50 hours by four people, or 25 hours by eight people or 12.5 hours by sixteen individuals. The requirement for additional labour usually becomes apparent very quickly in major recovery situations but the lead-time will be accelerated by pre-incident human resource planning in this section of your plan and therefore reduce the amount of secondary damage affecting damaged items.

In some organizations, particularly archives and special collections libraries, there is a willingness among staff to participate in emergency response and an understanding that should damage to collections occur, their presence will be required wherever possible to assist with salvage. In other organizations, where the collections are more modern and replaceable, the urgency for disaster recovery may not be appreciated immediately and volunteers for emergency salvage may need to be specifically recruited. A useful tool for recruiting members to your salvage team could include a short seminar, which includes a salvage exercise with discarded stock and either a speaker from a similar organization relating their experiences of fire or flood damage, or at the very least showing photographs of incidents.

In some organizations there is a financial reward and a formal rota for being on call, together with a duty mobile telephone and a set of rules, which could involve abstaining from alcohol and distant travel for the period that the individual is on call. Such a formal system is comparatively rare, however, and most organizations arrange emergency callout on the assumption that staff will do their best to help, domestic arrangements permitting. It is always worthwhile seeking clarification with your human resources department or insurance officer or broker about how time spent by staff in the recovery effort will be recompensed. If individuals attend over the weekend, will they be paid, and at what rate, or will they be given time off in lieu? It is naive to assume that these questions will not be asked by at least someone in the organization (although possibly not on the first day of the recovery, but it could be an issue by the third day) so the organizational policy needs to be set out at the point of recruitment to avoid unnecessary delays and confusion. Individuals volunteering will appreciate this confirmation and feel that the salvage task is valuable and worthwhile.

Information to include on contact lists

Include:

- name
- job title
- work phone number (internal and external number)
- mobile phone number
- home landline number.

This additional information may be helpful:

- home address
- special skills (e.g. conservator or first aider)
- travelling method to site and time to get there
- additional relevant information.

When asked to attend a site, ask personnel to bring in some cash, a change of clothes (and wear layers), a charged mobile phone, a flask and snack if catering has not yet been provided, and their work ID so that they can get on-site. Any items in short supply such as torches may be beneficial too. Give them clear instructions about where to report to so that they are briefed before work on salvage begins. In some organizations, salvage volunteers are given a special identification badge that will signify to anyone staffing a cordon after a major incident that the individual should be allowed in to assist with the salvage operation. In order to be robust, the existence of this system must be communicated at an early stage to the police, contract security staff or other people who may perform this role in a major incident.

There are requirements under data protection legislation such as the UK Data Protection Act for information recorded to be circulated responsibly and with the permission of the individual. Indeed the need to provide this personal information may deter individuals from volunteering in the first place, so it is important to emphasize that this section of the plan will be restricted to Emergency Management Team members and kept securely.

Figure 7.1 demonstrates a sample format for a staff emergency contact list.

Name	Job title	Work tel.	Home tel.	Mobile tel.	Travel time and method	Home address	Additional information
Catherine Jenkins, Emergency Response Manager	Library Manager				30 minutes by car		First aider, collections handling

Figure 7.1 *Sample format for staff emergency contact list*

Selecting appropriate volunteers

When recruiting and compiling this list, bear in mind the aptitudes that are likely to be helpful in a disaster recovery situation. Although collections-handling experience is undoubtedly an advantage, with appropriate supervision those without collections-handling experience may make excellent team members in disaster recovery, particularly if they are industrious, good listeners, pragmatic and willing to work hard. Physical strength is also beneficial as much of the work is arduous.

Richard Nichols of Staffordshire Record Office described his experience of selecting volunteers in the following way:

> The call-out tree was found to be totally ineffective, being based on a hierarchy of seniority which was not at all practical. This has been replaced by a simple list of staff contact numbers. We learned to be flexible. We have since carried out training for all staff irrespective of their primary role so that if called on everyone can make a useful contribution to the salvage process. We update this training on a regular basis.

Give some thought to the balance of emergency volunteers, bearing in mind the challenging nature of fire and flood recovery scenes and the hazards that they present. Those with back problems, respiratory conditions such as asthma, the elderly and the pregnant are particularly at risk from working in this sort of environment, not least from potential mould spores and possible injury from manual handling lifting. These people can be involved in disaster recovery but the Emergency Management Team should assign them to tasks that are suitable for them.

Reciprocal networks

Institutions that lack adequate numbers of staff and volunteers to assist with the more physically challenging aspects of salvage should explore the possibility of setting up a regional network of volunteers. Reciprocal regional networks have existed for many years either informally or more formally (for example the REDS team (Regional Emergencies and Disaster Service) in the East Midlands Museums Service). Their number is multiplying rapidly as events such as the 2007 floods in the UK showed how critical it is to provide expertise and labour to recovery efforts in the immediate aftermath of a major incident to avoid damage escalating rapidly. This has led to the Yorkshire Fed and North West Emergency Response Team being formed.

Figure 7.2 shows a training session for volunteer museum professionals.

Figure 7.2 *Training session for North West Emergency Response Team, volunteer museum professionals from across the region*

© Harwell Document Restoration Services

In these networks, professionals agree to assist other institutions for a period (usually no more than 48 hours) free of charge in an emergency, but presuming the reimbursement of expenses. Contact information is retained securely so details can be provided to a site where necessary. In some cases (e.g. REDS) this involves a group co-ordinator who takes responsibility for managing callout; in others such as the North West Emergency Response Team the contact information is held on a spreadsheet on a restricted access website. Employers agree to release their employee(s) and cover their wages for the time. Many also hold useful equipment from blotting paper to generators and pumps. Most of the networks are happy to provide emergency assistance to all local institutions with damaged collections. Sometimes this involves paying a small annual subscription to ensure network volunteers receive training updates, and equipment with a shelf-life (e.g. safety helmets) is replaced.

The clear advantage of these systems is that people who are trained in disaster recovery and handling of damaged items can quickly be called to the scene of the disaster, so the efficiency of the valuable first 72 hours of disaster recovery can be maximized. The main disadvantage is that such networks require funding to maintain training, and the more formal a network becomes, the more involved its administration. Furthermore, sometimes without an enthusiastic and dynamic figurehead to manage the network the attention can shift and it disbands.

Informal networks also operate whereby through networking individuals get to know colleagues at counterpart institutions and their contact information is written into their emergency plan; there is an unwritten understanding that staff and equipment, wherever possible, will be loaned. Write these contact details into plans with permission. In addition to formal or informal networks, options include using temporary employment agencies, former members of staff, and friends of the institution. In historic houses, often gardeners and catering staff are willing to help in urgent situations. In higher education libraries, there are sometimes plans to recruit students temporarily to assist with disaster recovery. Insurance companies may also be an avenue to consider if you are concerned about the potential for increased levels of damage and about who would ultimately foot the bill for temporary staff. Loss adjusters understand the basic principle that it is much cheaper to spend money preventing secondary damage by providing labour, freezer storage and so on than it is to pay the escalated costs of restoration that would otherwise occur.

In all these cases, it is worth checking with your insurer or insurance officer that any 'volunteers' are covered by your liability insurance if the work is disaster-recovery related. Any such work ought to be appropriately risk-assessed, but it is better to ask the question in advance rather than for the question to be justifiably raised in a recovery scenario and salvage work halted while awaiting an answer from insurers.

In the event of having to use a callout list, strategic operational decisions will be required. In most cases, it makes little sense to call out all your volunteer staff before you know the scale of the problem or whether access is possible. It is usually better to assess the scale of the situation, control the source of the damage and only call in staff when the situation is properly risk-assessed. It is rarely advantageous to call out staff in unsociable hours unless it will prevent primary damage. Situations where this might be useful include removing items to higher levels from a predicted flood surge, or from the path of a fire, although safety must always be the highest priority in these circumstances. If the incident has already occurred and the source of the damage stopped, the worst of the damage has happened and it may be more effective to wait until early morning to call on staff so they have at least had a full night's sleep before the intense recovery work is begun.

Consider also the long-term impact of a major incident on staff. Counselling may be necessary in severe situations, and there should be an opportunity for staff to wind down and absorb what has happened in others.

Priority lists
Deciding priorities

This section covers possibly the most time-consuming and contentious element of the planning process. Value can be qualified and quantified in a variety of ways – monetary, cultural significance, historical, rarity among others. Different stakeholders will have different views on what should be retained. In one desk-top exercise observed by the author there was a heated debate on the fate of the card-catalogue: finding aids or acquisition records ought to be a priority, but in the case of the card catalogue the information existed predominately electronically, although a few individuals argued that the electronic catalogue was not complete and the card catalogue was essential.

It is not an easy process to decide priorities for salvage as part of the planning process. So imagine how much more difficult it would be if you were having to make such decisions on the spur of the moment at the behest of the fire service, who won't let you into the building but are happy to commence salvage for you while structural checks are conducted, which will perhaps take two days. What would you choose? Would your decision-making be as strategically sound in those circumstances? Clearly this issue must be considered seriously in advance. Composing snatch lists is part of this process for top-tier priorities (see Chapter 4).

Consider the format of items that need to be rescued. Some formats (unglazed paintings, illuminated manuscript, coated papers, photographs, parchment and porous ceramics) are particularly vulnerable to prompt deterioration, while others (glass, microfiche, high-fired ceramics) are more robust. It is a perversity of this process that often the higher value items are already relatively well protected through boxing or being in a strongroom, and so arguably the more vulnerable items should be recovered sooner, even though they have less cultural or monetary value. Decisions must be made about other items within the collection that present less risk of accelerated deterioration but will nevertheless deteriorate (albeit more slowly and not irretrievably), and are perhaps of higher financial value. How does an organization decide how to allocate priority?

Is a collection a priority for salvage if it is available digitally or is on microfilm or microfiche? Is an item a priority if it has yet to be digitized? Such questions must be answered by curators well in advance of any emergency and their priorities frequently reviewed. In practice a sensible strategy must be adopted. It may not be possible to salvage everything immediately, so pragmatic decisions are required. Where there is a duplicate, either electronically or on microfilm or microfiche, curatorial decisions must be taken about prioritization. Always be cautious when making decisions about disposing of collections. Items considered beyond restoration or replaceable, and which you intend to discard, may need to be stabilized pending disposal authority from your insurers if you hope to be recompensed for their loss, and permission may not be immediate (see the case study on the University of Sussex in Chapter 2). Salvage and stabilize first items you are sure should be kept, but it may be prudent at least to stabilize those items you would prefer to see replaced. At the very least, keep an inventory of any items you discard for documentation and insurance purposes, and take some general photographs where feasible. Bear in mind that it can sometimes be very difficult to be absolutely sure if something is duplicated so be cautious.

It may also be relevant for managers in higher education libraries to consider the collections in other institutions in their area. For example, if there are higher education institutions within 45 minutes' travelling distance, and each of them has material on chemistry but none has much on the history of art as that subject is not taught there, the chemistry collections should potentially fall down the priority lists whereas the history of art material be promoted up the list.

Ownership is another concern. Collections on deposit or on loan to you are your responsibility but how do you balance these with your own, equally valuable collections? How would a depositor feel if they found out their material was consciously ignored for two days while other items were recovered following an emergency? Although this might be the correct curatorial decision, justification and careful handling of the owner may be required.

Although some elements of disaster planning can easily be copied from other plans, priority lists need to be tailored to your institution. Drawing them up requires consultation and discussion but ultimately a decision may need to be taken by someone senior, perhaps the archivist, records manager, head of collections or a curator. A similar tactic to the business continuity exercise discussed in Chapter 9 can be adopted by surveying staff, users and stakeholders about priorities, and the information obtained can inform the decisions the collections manager makes.

In archives some people find it difficult to identify priorities given the irreplaceable nature of all archival collections; they may feel that any prioritization is impossible or presents a security risk. If this is the institutional position, it still needs to be stated in the plan with the intention for the strategy on salvage to be decided as and when necessary depending on the nature and severity of damage. Nevertheless, it is still possible in most cases to identify vulnerable types of collection according to their substrate (e.g. coated paper, parchment). Furthermore, materials such as finding aids and acquisition records could be classified as priority because of the disruption to service caused if they were damaged or inaccessible. Objects not directly owned by the repository, such as short- or long-term loans, could be classified as a priority to avert potential reputational damage if they were damaged and not recovered at an early stage. It is furthermore possible to state what is *not* a priority for salvage if it is backed up in some other format, thus ensuring salvage time can be targeted at unique material, which may save time. Training is essential to ensure that a cross-section of staff could make dynamic salvage decisions in an emergency without a predefined priority list.

Presenting priorities

Having considered and canvassed opinion about what the priorities are, this information needs to be transferred into your plan in a compact and user-friendly way so that collections can be promptly recovered and restoration commence if damaged. It complicates the logistics of recovery significantly if the salvage operation has too many levels of categorization. The more prescriptive the priority list, the less efficient the logistics of removing collections can be and the more complex documentation becomes, if, for example, you need to recover first five linear metres of shelving from one end of the store and the next priority is at the other end. Time can be lost simply moving from one area to another rather than working sequentially, which overall could lead to additional damage if the delay increases the total timescale for recovery.

Having reviewed disaster plans, the best techniques seem to be a tripartite categorization (high priority, low priority and then everything in the middle by default), or simply to identify high priority material and then state that strategic decisions on prioritization will be made on the day by the Collections Salvage Manager based on the levels of damage, type of collection affected and so on. Either system can work successfully. In both, the most important items are clearly identified. In the tripartite system there is a distinction made in advance between the items of moderate importance and those of lower importance (e.g. duplicates, items available electronically, or easily or cheaply replaceable). In the other system, where there is no such pre-incident distinction, decision-making on the day will be required, thus making the process of writing this section quicker but disaster recovery potentially slower.

Having identified priorities, there is a further advantage in labelling the items you consider to be of high priority in such a way that they can be quickly located in an emergency, particularly if external agencies are involved such as the emergency services or salvage companies, who will have much less familiarity with your building. You can do this by putting fluorescent photo-luminescent stickers on items, or the shelf or bay end they sit on, and include them on floor plans. Coloured stickers work as well, although these show up less effectively in dim lighting. Stickers can be obtained from providers such as specialist cycle shops, either as dots or as tape that you can cut to size.

Salvage is made even easier if all priority items are located together, for example in a secure cage or strongroom. However, should the worst of the damage be centred in that location, your highest priority materials will suffer the worst primary damage, so a calculation of risk is required. This is usually obviated if better protection (e.g. fire suppression) is provided for this area. Snatch lists are discussed in Chapter 4 in the procedures for dealing with fires.

Floor plans

Although you may feel you know your building exceedingly well and could locate stop-valves and priority objects on any floor, whatever the obstacles, inclusion of floor plans in your disaster plan is helpful for many reasons. First, there will be an initial period where you may be denied access to your building but specialist contractors or the emergency services can enter. Any visual aid for them may speed up the process of recovery significantly. Second, when meeting colleagues to discuss salvage strategy, floor plans can trigger discussion and enable potential stumbling blocks to be identified much earlier, through showing where collections are housed, access routes, locations of stop-valves, possible paths of damage, and fire containment.

Formal building plans can be useful although they can sometimes be awkward to find in a usable and adaptable format. Additionally sometimes they can be very complicated to read unless in an A0 print size, and without specialist computer-aided design (CAD) software, you may not be able to superimpose your own key (an architect will not include 'emergency equipment store' or 'CO2 extinguisher' but you may want to). If possible, source the building floor plans but use this outline and redraw in a program that you and colleagues have readily available. Using this base you can produce information for different audiences. They will also be simpler to keep updated in a more accessible piece of software.

The main interest of fire service personnel will be in fire compartments or fire doors, fire hoses, wet risers, fire extinguishers within the building, sources of water, drainage points, voids, stop-valves (gas, electricity, sprinklers) and high priority areas. For the purposes of planning salvage, you will be more interested perhaps in priority locations, potential sorting areas, loading bays, power points and emergency equipment locations. There is some cross-over (emergency equipment location, high priority areas) but the interests are to some extent separate. Therefore it makes sense either to have separate versions, or possibly a fire service overlay on a transparency that shows the site information that they are most likely to be interested in.

Fire service personnel will usually be happy to take information on floor plans or site plans in hard copy, or increasingly as electronic documents that can be uploaded to fire tenders en route to site. To establish the best way to supply this information, contact the chief fire officer's department for the correct person to contact. Nevertheless, have hard copies of these plans to hand to the fire service on their arrival.

Depending on the size of your building and the complexity of your areas within the building, it may be worth including plans at many levels of detail – site plans (showing drainage points, access and so on), building elevation (showing location of strongrooms, priority collections, plant rooms and so on), floor plans and individual room plans. This is excessive if your collections are all housed within a single storey industrial unit, where just one plan will suffice, but if your layout is more complex, the more user-friendly the better. It is advisable to ensure that information is clear and there are a couple more pages to the plan than that too much information is crammed onto the floor plan in order to prevent increasing the bulk of your plan, only to render the floor plans essentially impossible to read. It is important also not to feel confined to A4. You can print floor plans onto A3 pages and fold A3 poly-pockets into a standard A4 ring binder, and also produce larger A1 or A0 plans, which can be rolled and stowed in your emergency equipment cupboard.

For reference purposes, it may be useful to have known locations of asbestos in the building noted on your plan, if relevant, as this could be a cause for concern. If your building is asbestos free, it may also be worth clearly stating that on floor plans for the avoidance of delays caused by doubt. In addition, keeping a log of locations of hazardous materials such as radioactive objects, chemicals and mercury, some of which can be found in museum collections, could be extremely useful if access to offices and catalogues is not possible.

Emergency equipment

A disaster kit is an essential investment to maximize the speed and success of the disaster response. Sometimes known as emergency kit or a battle box, it should perform three main functions:

- contain an incident such as an escape of water by providing quick access to the equipment needed, without having to dash out to the local DIY store or builders' merchant, or rely on facilities staff to come and do this for you
- provide basic equipment to begin dealing with damage to collections where prompt intervention will prevent the damage from escalating and secondary problems from occurring (e.g. mould growth, adhesions); space and budgetary constraints might prevent you housing all the blotting paper you would potentially need, but the cache should see you through the first day of salvage, by which time either all the materials damaged will be drying or stable, or, in bigger emergencies, you will have had time to obtain emergency stocks from other institutions or specialist suppliers
- enable this to happen safely, by providing personal protective and general safety equipment.

Before the potential cost of supplying a disaster kit becomes alarming, it is important to mention that many of the most helpful materials can be purchased relatively cheaply. Furthermore, expensive pieces of kit (such as submersible pumps and generators) can usually be hired in emergencies, although there is a risk that if you require a pump because of very heavy rainfall in your town, many other domestic and commercial properties will want to access the same equipment as you, so you will either need to respond quickly, or travel further afield to hire plant from adjacent towns or cities. Even in the best circumstances it will delay your response. Restricted availability of storage space is also a constraint for many organizations. A balance needs to be struck between what is practical, storable and affordable. You can also justifiably ask whether you need an *emergency* mop if a mop is generally available and accessible in a cleaner's cupboard.

Many of the items included in the lists below can be obtained from national suppliers for a next day delivery even if ordered on a Sunday or from DIY shops. Therefore, although there will be a lead time, you can obtain most items reasonably quickly if you do not retain pre-incident stock, except in a situation of mass damage such as an urban flood. Buying-in on an ad hoc basis will result in an initially slower response, as you will need to await delivery, and there will be certain times of year such as Christmas and New Year where most businesses will be closed and you will not be able to access any external supplies for a number of days.

Items which are more difficult to source in an emergency include the specialist items for collections handling and air-drying. Although there is some scope for improvization in an emergency (outlined below), blotting paper is not easy to source quickly and there is no viable alternative to it, so a sizeable stock in your disaster kit will be vital if your salvage operation is to be effective and appropriately resourced. It makes sense to ensure that you have enough blotter to cover at least double the floor space of all your likely sites for air-drying.

It may be tempting to opt for an off-the-shelf all-in-one kit, which claims to contain the basic materials for salvage. However, experience of their use in disaster recovery situations varies as they often do not include the right quantities of the materials that you will need in greatest volume (e.g. blotting paper) and often the personal protective equipment (e.g. masks) is not the appropriate grade for disaster recovery. They can be competitively priced, however. Although it involves a bit more shopping around and time, it is worth thinking through carefully what your organization needs and spending the same amount of money as you would spend on an all-in-one kit on items that you choose.

What to include
Immediate response kit

This cache will enable you to contain leaks and spills promptly and serves to minimize the total number of items that get damaged and the level of saturation that they suffer.

These are the basic materials to include in an immediate response kit:

- polythene sheeting
- absorbent cushions or pillows (if you have collections at risk from drains backing up or fluvial floods)
- gaffer tape on a tape gun
- a Stanley knife
- appropriate safety signage (e.g. wet floor signs, although these can often be commandeered from cleaners' stores)
- appropriate personal protective equipment (chemical gloves and Tyvek® suits)
- a wet vacuum and safety extension lead
- a submersible pump and hosing
- a generator
- security screwdrivers, foam blocks, etc. for artwork.

Polythene sheeting is inexpensive yet extremely useful to shroud shelves and objects thus preventing them from coming into contact with water. Even items that are already wet can be covered up to prevent them getting even wetter. This is sometimes known as builders' sheeting and is often available in 2-metre or 4-metre widths folded to 1 metre to make it easier to deploy and handle. Ideally it should be cut to go up and over and down the other side of shelving in advance so that in an emergency you don't waste too much time and materials cutting lengths in the midst of a leak, putting them up and finding they are too short. Gaffer tape can be used to fix it where possible to the floor, and this being on a tape gun is much easier than having just a reel of tape and some scissors. Where shelving is fixed to the wall, sometimes staple guns can be used. A Stanley knife can be used to cut more sheeting (against the example length of the pre-cut sheet). Where possible include one cache of this equipment on each floor of your collections, or as close to them as possible.

Figure 7.3 shows shelves sheeted to protect them from water.

Absorbent cushions or soakage pads are also very helpful. Various kinds are available but ensure you verify their overall absorbency and note this may vary for seawater. One type widely available is designed to be the length of a standard doorway or long edge of a standard drain cover, and so once its 17-litres' absorbency is used, it also acts as a physical barrier to the water, like a sandbag. Leak diverters are also available and have been successfully deployed to contain leaks from sprinkler heads and water pipes.

Christine Willoughby, Head of Planning, University of Northumbria Library, has some practical advice:

We prefer sheets of plastic ready cut up to plastic on rolls which are unwieldy and difficult to cut to size in an emergency. Our other top tip is 'door nappies' which are absorbent cushions to contain floods – so good when the toilets overflow! They have been so useful we now keep them next to the at risk doors – which of course we have identified in our plan.

Figure 7.3 *Sheeting of objects on shelves protecting them from further seepage of water*
© Northumbria University

Equipment to deal with damaged items

Before investing in any supplies to handle and air-dry damaged material, it is important to give some consideration to the points in chapters 5 and 6 on salvage tactics, which prompts an assessment of your capacity for restoration in-house, taking into account your space and staff. If you are so restricted for space that you would always outsource restoration, there is no need to retain much of the equipment discussed below, aside perhaps from documentation kits. If you would have a great deal of capacity for air-drying damaged items, you will need plenty of these materials, particularly those items which are sourced directly from conservation suppliers.

These are the basic materials you need to deal with damaged items:

- blotting paper (base for drying)
- unprinted newsprint (for interleaving or padding out)
- silicone or release paper (for interleaving coated papers or photographs)

- Melinex (for picking up individual documents from a flat surface with the minimal direct physical contact to prevent tearing, and to support fragile items in transit)
- cotton bandaging (to prevent swelling of bound items; see Chapter 6 for caveat)
- cotton tape or string (washing line)
- grip seal polythene bags (various sizes – to isolate items to prevent leaching, mould or disintegration)
- kitchen roll (interleaving, patting dry and cleaning up puddles)
- polythene sheets (to create wind tunnels)
- bulldog clips or brass or plastic clips (to hang items on washing line)
- spray bottles (for washing off debris)
- scissors
- bubble wrap (for wrapping large items, or lining crates)
- roll polyurethane (for labelling or isolating items quickly)
- documentation kit (pens, labels, clipboards, tags, pre-printed cataloguing sheets)
- fans and extension leads.

Safety equipment

The safety of those participating in the salvage operation is of the utmost importance. The required personal protective equipment will be determined as part of the risk assessment before salvage starts (see Chapter 5), but to some extent the potential hazards can be predicted and appropriate safety equipment sourced and retained in advance to facilitate the prompt initiation of salvage.

A list of basic protective equipment is given in Chapter 5. The inclusion of materials should not be seen as a green light to enter a building that is not properly assessed for its safety. For example, safety helmets are frequently included in disaster kits but safety boots and wellingtons are not, or individuals are instructed to bring their own. It is a basic tenet of health and safety that if one is required to wear a safety helmet, one should also wear safety boots. The reason that safety helmets are provided and safety footwear is not is probably because safety helmets are a universal size, and boots are not, and safety footwear is more expensive. Furthermore, if safety helmets are required as part of the risk assessment, it may be decided that professional disaster recovery specialists should conduct the recovery within the building, and ferry damaged items to a safe area for staff to sort, or for the professionals to remove them from the site and treat them.

Staff most likely to be involved in a salvage operation may be provided with a size-specific set of this material that they keep in a rucksack and are responsible for, while also having a set of back-up materials in various sizes, if funds permit. A reasonable rule of thumb that has worked in surveys to equip a large number of staff is to have a distribution of sizes – 15% small, 30% medium, 40% large, 15% extra large – although it is always worth asking volunteers to try on sample sizes and to order them individually. Local safety standards such as British Standards will apply to these items.

These are the basic safety materials to include for each member of staff involved:

- safety helmet (check expiry)
- headlamp (advantage that it will leave the individual's hands free; provide batteries but don't install)
- safety masks (disposable masks or higher specification if possible, to FFP3 (filtering face piece))
- safety goggles (including some that can be worn over glasses)
- Tyvek® suits for the disaster scene
- catering aprons for the salvage area (although Tyvek-style suits are preferable if possible)
- waterproof coveralls (advisable if fluvial flooding risk is high or you have a basement store)
- safety footwear (ideally wellingtons; steel sole an option but only if walking through standing water, which is not advisable)
- gloves – chemical gloves with long gauntlet for disaster scene; surgical gloves for salvage area (nitrile usually best – bear in mind latex allergies; these decay)
- a hi-visibility vest.

Advise salvage volunteers to bring in layers of clothes to wear. If funds permit it is useful to have hi-visibility pre-printed with 'Salvage Team'.

Additional equipment

There are many other items that can potentially be helpful to the recovery operation. Many of these can be hired in, or sourced through a facilities department. Any institution that does not have its own direct supplies of these items should know where they can obtain these items in an emergency, even if they have an in-house facilities department. In the event of that provider being required to assist multiple sites, there is no guarantee that your needs will be deemed the most critical and a risk that you will have to wait so long that increasing quantities and grades of damage will occur. It is therefore sensible to ensure you have your own separate emergency supply to ensure that your salvage operation is not stalled.

These are additional items to consider:

- a tool kit (pliers, screwdriver, crowbar, etc.)
- a spare set of keys (to be kept in a secure off-site location, well labelled)
- a mop and bucket
- a dust pan and brush
- an extension lead with circuit breaker
- floor wet signs and safety signage (e.g. PPE (personal protective equipment) must be worn in this area)
- black and clear refuse sacks (two colours in case of need for two types of categories of waste)
- buckets
- lighting (torches and emergency tripod light)
- a first aid kit
- barricade tape
- a broom
- a padlock and chain
- solid sided shallow trays or crates (for keeping material wet where necessary, fragile items and separating adhered items)
- air movers or blowers
- an analogue phone (in case your digital phone system not functioning)
- spare mobile phone chargers
- spare polythene sheeting
- trestle tables
- packing crates
- generators
- sandbags
- dehumidifiers
- submersible pump
- trolleys, sack barrows and other manual handling equipment
- heaters (for any rest areas, not for the building unless a restoration professional advises)
- badging system for contractors (see below)
- walkie-talkies
- a flip chart and pens.

Making the most of your kit

The main stores of personal protective equipment and equipment to deal with damage can be stored in a single location rather than small caches being dispersed throughout your building like your incident containment stocks. Make sure that it is easily portable. Hotel-style laundry bins, which are shallower than wheelie bins but also on wheels, are helpful. Lidded crates (wheeled if possible) are useful but be careful not to overfill them to the point that they cannot be easily lifted. Label containers and load them sensibly so the items most heavily used are not at the very bottom: 'The deep bins we found to be completely impractical – they had to be tipped over and everything emptied on the floor to see what was there' (Andrea Lydon, National Gallery of Ireland).

Keeping the supplies secure is also important: a balance needs to be struck between the materials being readily accessible but also secure, to avoid the situation when the day you need the torch and polythene from your kit you realize they have been borrowed and not replaced, and your response is therefore delayed. In extreme cases, kit can be placed in a locked cupboard with access restricted, or with a break-glass by the entrance to the cupboard. In other cases, cable ties are used to secure crates (with a pair of scissors also taped to the side of the container so that they can be quickly opened) or a length of barricade tape is stuck over the opening and clear signage placed on the lid that the equipment is only to be used in an emergency. Conduct periodic checks on the kit to ensure that their contents are present and operational. If you have multiple containers put an inventory into each one to save time. Put the kit somewhere that is accessible and unlikely to be moved. Ideally an outhouse would be useful but otherwise somewhere on the ground floor which is easily accessible.

Make sure that the kit is assembled and ready to use. A desk fan in an unopened box may require assembly, which could be incredibly fiddly in the midst of a disaster recovery situation. To avoid the risk of batteries leaking in torches, it can be useful to tape the batteries to the outside of the torches, or have a policy of replacing batteries every 12 months. It may also be helpful to label items with their name and purpose. For example, an individual may be sent off to fetch Melinex with no clear idea what it looks like and what its function is, so the statement e.g. 'Melinex – for picking wet documents from the floor' might be helpful. Pre-cutting unprinted newsprint to standard page sizes may also save time.

When determining your requirements, consider your budget, risk levels and impact of damage. You could spend thousands on this material, which you hope you will never need to deploy. Clearly the more staff you have, the more personal protective equipment you will require and so the costs will go up. If costs are prohibitive, at the very least make sure you have the basic incident containment equipment, some blotting paper and personal protective equipment such as masks and gloves. There is often the possibility of improvising: Melinex is the most appropriate material to use in an emergency, but old-fashioned acetates or the clear covers of presentation folders essentially perform the same function. You can also elect to build up your supplies over several financial years, on the understanding that you will need to make an emergency purchase if you do have a fire or flood before they are complete.

Figure 7.4 shows emergency equipment located close to known problem areas for quick deployment in an emergency.

External suppliers and utility companies

Beyond the specialist equipment, it is useful to list in your plan potential sources of professional assistance for complex disaster recovery situations because of the scale or nature of the damage. Most organizations can deal with incidents to some extent themselves, but there is usually a tipping point where the involvement of external companies can ultimately save money and reduce damage.

The usual online sources are very useful in shortlisting emergency suppliers but it is dangerous simply to take someone from their Google advert without making contact and ensuring that they fit your need. An internet search on disaster recovery will bring up not only companies that help with the physical restoration of your building and contents, but also a number of companies that provide temporary offices and data recovery. These services are important but not much use to you if you are trying to source a service provider to help you pump out a flooded basement and install dehumidifiers. Make telephone contact with the companies you intend to list, and verify their out-of-hours capabilities. For critical functions (disaster recovery, emergency trades, tool hire) it is usually possible to obtain an out-of-hours contact number. Some companies operate a retainer system providing priority access to their services. Assess the risks of delay balance with the cost of the retainer; if these are unacceptable, establish a contract and set up an account.

Some of the suppliers listed are obviously highly likely to be required in emergency situations, others less so (e.g. those loaning portable restrooms). Consider each supplier one by one. If you cannot imagine a single scenario where you would need the service described, it would be superfluous to list the supplier of it. However, if in a worst case scenario there could be a potential need for a supplier's services, it is much easier to have a number in your plan than to be trying to search the internet in the middle of the night for something you need, wearing down your valuable mobile battery and rueing the fact that you elected not to include the supplier's contact

Figure 7.4 *Location of emergency equipment close to known problem areas for quick deployment in a museum setting*

© *Harwell Document Restoration Services*

information. Again, it is risky to rely on assurances that your facilities section will provide some of these services. If you have absolute confidence in their emergency and surge plans you may not wish to list some services, for example, a separate drain clearance company, but if you have any shred of doubt, it is better to list one than be disappointed at the critical moment.

Making the most of your list of suppliers

Setting up a credit account in advance for at least some of these services may be advantageous. The required paperwork is done in advance and it eliminates some of the questions that could crop up on the day you need the service. Alternatively, establish whether suppliers will accept credit card payments over the phone. Ensure that the organizational policy for engaging emergency contractors is clear and known to all those who might be involved in the salvage and recovery efforts. Increasingly organizations are becoming very fastidious about procurement, but unfortunately emergency situations are not conducive to being able to obtain purchase orders and two signatures and establishing a cost code in a fast timeframe.

In one salvage situation I encountered, 40 linear metres of special collections library stock was affected by a flash flood. The flooding occurred during the absence of the library manager, who had written the plan. Her deputy filled in, as planned, and realized quickly the incident could not be treated by air-drying because of lack of space and the saturation levels, so the invocation of a pre-existing salvage contract with a professional disaster recovery company was necessary to remove and stabilize the damage. In the initial phone call, an estimate was required by the deputy librarian for the cost of the crating, removal and freezing process. This was given at £200, which would be invoiced at a later stage. However, the deputy requested we stand down until she had authorization as she did not have budgetary control. The request had to be escalated and ultimately it took five days for a decision to be made to authorize the removal of the damaged material. In that five-day period, responsibility for the cost was tossed between library services and the insurance officer. Unfortunately by the time salvage was authorized, wet material had become mouldy and the costs of restoration increased significantly.

This situation could have been avoided in various ways. A statement on each supplier's page of the plan about circumstances when they can be contacted and permissible costs, and an escalation procedure for any costs higher than expected, should have been provided. Increased resilience would have been provided had training and familiarization sessions on the plan been conducted between the library manager and her deputies. Obviously some individuals would have taken the cavalier approach and decided to risk spending the money on the assumption that the manager would sign it off on her return, but the individual concerned was fastidious, although in wanting to avoid unauthorized costs, additional costs were incurred.

Although it would obviously be a mistake to waste money, in emergency situations spending a comparatively small amount, for example £150, on the delivery and hire of some air-movers could prevent an enormous bill for sanitization of the building and workspace as a result of mould that would have been prevented by the hire. Remember that depending on your policy and excess level, insurance companies usually reimburse legitimate expenses, providing receipts are kept. If it is not clear that individuals have the freedom to engage the services of contractors, they may try to get permission from the finance section and this can cause lengthy delays for the initiation of salvage.

A simple statement at the top of the suppliers list should state who is authorized to spend up to what figure, and where the next point of call is should the sum involved escalate beyond it. How do you go about increasing the limit on your corporate credit card in an emergency? What if it is a weekend? Consider all the contingencies and ensure in the text of your plan and through training exercises that all decision-makers are clear about what actions they are permitted to take. In major local emergencies where phone lines are down, credit card machines will not be working so cash may be the only acceptable form of payment. Some organizations have a contingency emergency cost code established in advance so that should there be a sudden requirement, purchase orders can easily be generated and budgets adjusted to provide funds.

Make sure that your supply-chain risk is balanced. If all your suppliers are known to you and local, that is very helpful for an isolated emergency, but those suppliers are likely to be inundated if there is a major local emergency. So also have contingencies for regional or even national suppliers where necessary. Dr Mary Clarke, Dublin City Archivist, recalls sourcing problems to prepare to deal with a major city-wide event: 'We planned to order dehumidifiers from a hire firm during the flooding. As flooding was city-wide, there was huge demand for dehumidifiers the following day; we eventually sourced them from Northern Ireland.'

These are the sort of suppliers whose services you might need:

- disaster recovery firms for buildings
- disaster recovery specialists for collections
- conservators (all objects that you house in your collections)
- specialist moving contractors (e.g. artwork, large museum objects)
- removals firms or packers
- temporary storage companies (which offer warehouse space, ambient storage, e.g. removals or archives firms, freezer storage)
- skips and waste removal companies

- suppliers of racking and all specialist storage equipment (in case of failure)
- event hire companies (for marquee hire, event tables, portable toilets, etc.); they will have large quantities of covered space and tables on which to air-dry material; insurers often prefer customers to hire rather than purchase outright as it is not acceptable to benefit materially from an incident)
- specialist IT services
- crate and pallet hire companies
- specialist moving equipment companies (cherry pickers, etc.)
- all trades (plumber, drain clearance, carpenter, electrical contractor, gas technician, locksmith, glazing contractor, roofers)
- commercial building contractors
- lift engineers
- alarm engineers
- structural engineers
- specialist stationers (in case your pre-printed boxes, files, etc. are damaged by the incident).

You may also wish to list here the suppliers for all the items in your disaster kit.

Additional appendices

The appendices discussed above are the most time-consuming to produce and demand the most independent work in the process of writing an emergency plan, as, whilst criteria for selection and layout can be borrowed, the content must be self-generated. The remaining suggested appendices listed below are vital for inclusion but take the form of either blank forms or information that is not so site-specific. Many of these have been discussed in more detail in other chapters, and so this content is not repeated here:

- Salvage and treatment guidance by object (Chapter 6)
- Risk assessment forms (Chapter 5)
- Prepared press statements (Chapter 9)
- Damage record forms (Figure 6.2, Chapter 6).

Incident log form

Several of the authors of the case studies for this book commented that it was important to record what decisions had been made in an emergency for the purpose of insurance claims. It is also helpful when reviewing the performance of the plan and learning from any mistakes made. Figure 7.5 shows an example of an incident log form, which notes this information. It is the responsibility of the Emergency Response Manager to complete an incident log form after an emergency has occurred.

Date	Time	Person responsible	Notes
15/4	10.31	Simon Blackstone	Water ingress in library reported to Simon Blackstone at the issue desk. Simon contacted Facilities and Jenny Ferguson (Head of Collections).
15/4	10.34	SB	Asked users to clear the area and work in the other reading room. Restricts access to the area, then goes to look for leak source.
15/4	10.43	Jenny Ferguson	Jenny Ferguson arrived, bringing emergency equipment with her. Inspects area from a distance and decides not to enter as water falling across light.
15/4	10.57	Facilities	Facilities staff arrive and isolate electricity; turn off stop-cock.
15/4	10.59	SB/JF	Risk assess, then put polythene up to protect collections. Start as soon as electricity isolated.

Figure 7.5 *Sample incident log sheet*

Accommodation and sites for salvage

It is helpful to consider in advance potential locations that could be used or commandeered to assist with emergency response, including:

- an Emergency Management Team meeting room (in the building, and an external site if possible. The room should have IT and telephones on site/campus; a hotel meeting room may be necessary)
- a back-up Emergency Management Team meeting point for an out-of-hours emergency (which may need to be further away from the building than your main meeting room, outside the perimeter of a potential cordon); consider personal security if staff might need to meet at night
- staff and visitor evacuation points (will already be identified in fire

procedures, but consider if you are evacuating to an area along with other organizations in your area – see Chapter 9)
- treatment areas (cool, with loading bay, no steps, securable)
- decant areas for unaffected but removed materials
- temporary staff workspaces or study spaces (libraries)
- rest and refreshment areas for salvage staff
- a first aid point
- emergency freezer locations (e.g. if there is a lab on the university campus, or a quarantine freezer at a local museum you might be able to access).

Include the contact details of those required to activate these arrangements in your plan. Some organizations have informal arrangements to use a freezer in a local museum to store small quantities of water-damaged items, but it is important to be able to contact someone within that museum to authorize this out of hours or over the weekend and to provide access. Similarly it may be possible to identify ingenious additional spaces that could be made available, such as church halls, community centres, exhibition spaces and schools during vacations, but contact should be possible outside the standard working day. Some of these spaces may be seasonally unavailable, but include their details nevertheless.

Sarah Stauderman, Collections Care Manager, Smithsonian Institution Archives, described how she commandeered a freezer after a construction accident:

> Our most recent emergency resulted from a construction accident where a sprinkler head was knocked off by equipment. Because we have a freezer on site we bagged the 30+ boxes and put them in the freezer while we waited for insurance to pay for a freeze drying contract. The freezer (a walk-in box of about 5 square meters) is an excellent tool for our collections and others that get water damaged. We also use it for integrated pest management, and have cabinets within that we use for permanent storage of cellulose acetate film based collections.

Instructions for isolating utilities

Provide guidance on isolating the utilities. Even when this will be conducted by the facilities department, it helps to have a copy of the guidance to give to them on the day to speed up the response. After all it could be a new member of their team who does not know your building at all who is tasked with this job. If you can, insert photographs of mains switches for electricity, water and gas, and instructions for fire suppression systems, for example, with a superimposed arrow to show how to turn it off, and whether to pull the lever clockwise or anti-clockwise, 90 degrees or 180 degrees. It may just remove doubt and hesitation from the mind of the salvage staff.

Label the lever clearly in situ, too, and provide instructions locally. Make sure that staff can make sense of the numbering of circuits on distribution board panels and how they refer to rooms or galleries: labelling must be clear so it is universally understandable. Post any caveats or checks that should be conducted before turning off the utility (e.g. 'tell security staff' or 'check lift is empty') clearly by the valves.

Plant rooms can be confusing places (Figure 7.6). If the location of levers and instructions for isolating them (e.g. by superimposing an arrow onto the image, showing to turn anticlockwise by 90 degrees) are shown clearly it will eliminate doubt and reduce the time it takes staff to use them in an emergency.

There are likely to be internal and external switches for water supply and power. Know where the external ones are as well as the internal ones. It may also be an advantage to mark their location on a wall, or measure the distance from a particular point so that they can be found if covered in snow (for a situation such as a burst pipe in the middle of the winter, as detailed in the

Figure 7.6 *A plant room*

quotation from The Wordsworth Trust in Chapter 2). Provide documented systems for rebooting telephones, systems and IT. Utility company contact details can either be included there, or in the contacts directory.

Insurance cover details

Give a summary of insurance cover, exclusions, excess or deductible levels for all collections, business services (many policies cover increased costs of working and business interruption), public or employers liability and any building policies, including any specific policies for collections on loan. The situations in which it might be advisable to involve insurers are discussed in Chapter 5.

Contacts directory

In the contacts directory include contact numbers for people and organizations that are not suppliers, contractors or staff but might be useful in an emergency, for example utility providers, depositors, local media outlets, neighbours, people who share your building, stakeholders, trustees, key people within your wider organization, and colleagues at other institutions from whom assistance could be sought.

   For a discussion about business continuity, business impact analysis and targets see Chapter 9.

Incident report forms

It is useful to include a standard-format incident report form to be completed by a member of the Emergency Management Team to determine:
• what happened
• how the emergency plan performed
• what worked well
• what should be revised or learning points
• the cause of the incident
• remedial actions taken.

This can be a very useful tool in the reporting of incidents afterwards and in gaining funding or support for building renovation or additional investment, particularly if there are repeated incidents and a pattern of problems emerges.

CHAPTER 8
Dealing with the building

This chapter explains some key issues in dealing with damage to buildings after physical damage through water or fire. Restoration of buildings is a specialist area and ideally requires professional input, therefore these notes are intended as a reference tool rather than as content that should be inserted into the plan. The notes for the Building Recovery Manager suggest that air-movers and dehumidifiers should be introduced immediately, and that a specialist contractor should then be appointed to advise on how to use them.

In the aftermath of an incident involving damage to collections, such is the focus on the salvage and recovery operation for these items that often the impact on the room and building is forgotten. This can be a very costly error, however. Even after the smallest leak, failure to consider the impact on the storage environment can lead to long-term problems with humidity, which may ultimately cause mould growth on items due to poor environmental conditions perhaps weeks or months in the future.

Katie Sambrook, Special Collections Librarian, King's College London, described an emergency resulting from an overflowing drain:

> Heavy rain over a weekend caused an inadequate drain to overflow and water to enter a lower ground floor corridor and collection store. No collection items were damaged but the water ran under the false floor supporting the mobile shelving units. The response from the estates department was prompt once notified and they arranged thorough drying, cleaning and disinfection of affected areas. Fortunately authorisation of expenditure to contract the mobile shelving company was prompt. They were asked to move the shelving units and lift the false floor so that it could be dried and disinfected where water had been trapped.
>
> Investigation of cause was conducted and steps have been implemented to minimize risk of a similar flood in the future:
>
> • installation of a water detection alarm system

- construction of a concrete 'dam' next to drain
- introduction of regular checks of areas during heavy rain.

Incident happened over the weekend but was not detected until Monday morning, despite presence of security staff and porters on site (no system of checking then in place, but one was subsequently introduced).

In this case, although no collections were directly damaged, the trapped water underneath the false floor of the shelving could have caused major environmental damage, raising the humidity and triggering widespread mould growth, thus creating significant safety problems for access to this entire store. Although a cost was incurred in moving the mobile shelving, this dwarfed the potential costs of the mould remediation clean-up that would otherwise have been required.

As with objects, damage can be categorized as primary damage (directly related to the flooding or fire, such as wet building fabric, expansion and shrinking of wood, or burning and charring to walls) and secondary damage, resulting from prolonged presence of the primary damage, particularly associated with moisture. Failure to take action to remedy issues associated with water in particular may trigger long-term and costly problems.

Structural problems may need attention after fires or serious natural disasters such as hurricanes or earthquakes. Refer any such concerns to a structural engineer. In these cases salvage can only begin after professional building contractors have made the structure safe to enter. This may involve propping walls and ceilings with supports. Water rarely leads to structural damage, although there are issues with floods of depths over 1 metre, particularly if water is pumped out too quickly (discussed below). If the ground around the property has been washed away or large items (e.g. cars) have been carried in the water there may be structural impacts. Classic signs of structural damage include bulging masonry, cracks greater than 6 mm above doors and windows and at ends of buildings, and major tilting or leaning.

Water damage

In flooding, the level of primary damage and potential for secondary damage is related to the severity of the incident and the path of the water on entry. Key factors determining the severity of building damage include the depth of the flood water, the length of time within the building before retreating or being removed, and the time drying takes. These factors combined will determine the rate of absorption into the building fabric and increase the volume of water that will need to be removed before the space can be considered dry. Physical and structural damage may be present as a result of the water, its flow, and the reaction of wood in particular, and factors such as black water contamination will complicate the restoration process. It is important to remember that flooding incidents that do not result in standing water (shallow flooding incidents) and clear quickly may result in significant damage to the building if water is trapped in voids.

There is the potential for mould growth in rooms unaffected by the original problem through the natural movement of water vapour from areas of high concentration (the flood area) to an area of lower concentration. Items that were not wetted by the original flood may develop surface mould growth in the aftermath of a flood because of their hygroscopic nature and susceptibility to even slight rises in humidity. Take prompt action to avert these problems and stabilize the environment as quickly as possible. Even if the bulk of water vapour in the air has been reduced and humidity has dropped substantially from the immediate aftermath of the flood, this will not necessarily mean the building is dry.

Drying buildings effectively is a specialist process. Seek technical expertise from damage management companies after any substantial flood, particularly if this resulted in standing water. Damage management contractors will have experience of where water may be trapped and could lead to microbial growth if unattended, as well as a range of techniques to dry buildings. They carry high-specification moisture meters and have access to technically superior drying equipment. The process of building restoration is perhaps more straightforward for storage areas and modern buildings. Older buildings and historic interiors require a careful and cautious approach, with frequent monitoring, as rapid drying may be harmful and techniques sometimes appropriate in modern buildings such as removal of skirting and door frames and plaster may be wholly inappropriate in historic buildings.

Figure 8.1 (overleaf) shows water damage after a major flood.

It may be sensible to ask the contractor for a written method statement to confirm that all relevant and vulnerable aspects of your building are being appropriately considered when the drying method is being selected. It may be important to consult local conservation officers and organizations such as English Heritage and equivalents. Older buildings that were constructed without cavity walls or damp-proof courses present challenges for drying as their pre-incident equilibrium moisture content is so different from buildings of modern construction. It is important to ensure that any contractor has the experience and competency to deal with your building. Even commercial public buildings of modern construction may be challenging because of their size. If you are not satisfied, seek a different, qualified contractor through local

Figure 8.1 *Level of water damage after a major flood, showing water penetration to building fabric*

© *Waterford County Council*

agencies, or if your insurance company or loss adjuster has appointed the contractor then raise your concerns robustly.

In cases of water damage, once visible surface moisture has been removed, further water may be trapped in other locations. It may be necessary to confirm this by inspecting the damage using moisture measuring equipment or boroscopes (a sort of keyhole camera). Typical locations for trapped water include panelling, plinths for racking, building voids and tiled areas. In floods where the water has entered via ground level or from drains, tracing the water is straightforward. In vertical floods, where there has been a leak on a higher floor, the water may take an unpredictable path down through the building, and careful investigation will be necessary. Water takes the path of least resistance and potentially runs through ducting and voids, moving horizontally on some floors before it ultimately finds its path downwards. Vertical floods are likely to affect electrical systems, which should be isolated until they can be checked by a qualified electrician.

After water damage mains services need to be reconnected after being checked by a qualified person. Structural issues may have caused problems with gas pipes, which require investigation. Drying requires power and so while pumping can be carried out with generators and temporary power sources, checking, stripping and reconnecting the mains electricity supply enables a faster and adequately resourced start to the drying process, which will avert secondary damage. If there is any evidence of blockages to foul-water drains (e.g. foul water returning from the u-bend) report it to the water utility immediately.

These are the initial actions that are needed to control the environment and limit further building damage after a flood:

- Remove standing water with submersible pumps or wet vacuums.
- Release water held in plasterboard ceilings (vertical floods) by puncturing 10 mm holes and collecting water in a suitable receptacle such as a bucket.
- Turn heating systems down or off initially while the salvage operation is under way (ideally the temperature should be below 18°C) and while wet collections are still in the area, as heating in areas with wet materials will cause severe additional damage and accelerate mould growth. Heat can be used with care to assist with drying the building when the wet collections have been removed. Drying can soak up ambient heat energy as water evaporates, which cools the area and further slows the drying process. Topical heaters and other methods may be used, but monitor the temperature and obtain professional expertise. Although heat can be an agent in speeding drying, it can also help mould growth to develop rapidly and cause shrinkage and warping of wooden building materials if ventilation or dehumidification is not also used. Apply heat to drying buildings under professional supervision and with consideration of its impact on initially undamaged collections in the area that was water damaged (e.g. on higher shelves), which may still be in the building. These may need to be removed.
- Inspect voids under floors and pump or vacuum water out if necessary.
- Check lift wells.
- Clear all furniture in front of walls.
- In the event of major flooding (above 1 metre in height) to a basement, rapid removal of water may cause structural problems if adjacent basements are not being pumped at the same rate. This is because of hydrostatic pressure difference. Generally water should not be reduced by more than 1 metre per day.
- Remove all wet objects (even those you may not consider worth restoring), carpets and empty boxes as they increase the wet loading in the room and any dehumidification will remove the moisture from those items, rather than the building fabric. Remove and replace plinths for racking if necessary.

- Increase ventilation by opening doors to effect drying before dehumidifiers are installed.
- Refer clean-up and sanitization of the building after black water flooding to a professional damage management company where possible. Staff will advise if porous and absorbent items (e.g. plasterboard, MDF, hardboard, upholstered fabrics on functional chairs which are not part of the collection) need to be removed as they cannot be effectively sanitized. Some absorbent materials can be sanitized but require specialist conservation treatment off-site.
- Clean and sanitize all surfaces affected. This may involve flushing and rinsing of the flooring with an alkaline detergent, with care taken to clean all surfaces and into all crevices. It may be necessary to remove door frames and skirting for non-historic interiors, though it may be possible to flush skirting with a water spray without removing it (but avoid using high-pressure sprays).
- Conduct tests to ensure that common bacteria resulting from flooding have been removed. Results from these tests may not be immediate as cultures will need to be taken.
- If floorboards are dry, it may be necessary to lift some to provide ventilation to the damp area underneath. If floorboards are saturated they can be damaged very easily so lift, dry and rotate them frequently.

After the removal of standing water and wet loading, drying can start. Take care to select a method appropriate to the building structure and internal fittings. Remember that drying tactics must be adapted to historic interiors, and to stores where items vulnerable to rapid alteration in humidity (e.g. wooden objects) are housed. Take decisive action to prevent mould growth on items not initially affected caused by high levels of moisture. Be prepared for drying out to be a long process. Drying moisture from the surface of building materials (the second phase of drying) can be relatively quick, but there may still be moisture trapped in the pores of the building fabric. Moisture may need to move through the building fabric as a liquid to the surface, where it will vaporize into the air and ultimately be removed through ventilation or dehumidification. This can take months but is preferable to forcing the pace, resulting in damage to the building fabric or interior.

These are some drying methods:

- Simple ventilation – just opening windows and doors – can work but it will depend on external conditions and vapour pressure. It will not work if the humidity or vapour pressure outside is higher than that inside. Ventilation is most effective in the first few hours after a flood and in winter. In summer, when there is external high humidity, the ventilation will not serve to dry the affected room out.

- Dehumidifiers can work to reduce the moisture in the air and ultimately to dry the building fabric, too, as they force sub-surface moisture in walls to move to the surface where it will vaporize. They work by extracting moisture from the air either by condensing it onto a cold surface (refrigerant dehumidifier) or by absorbing moisture into an absorbent material (a desiccant dehumidifier). Desiccant dehumidifiers are often more effective and can be used to target drying with hoses into cavities and so on. Fit the dehumidifiers with a humidistat, which will allow some control over the rate of drying. The ideal is to maintain the air-moisture content at 40–50%rH (relative humidity). The selection of the dehumidifier will depend on the temperature in the affected area, and dehumidifiers will not work effectively with windows and external doors open. Dehumidification may not be appropriate in buildings with lime plaster.
- Create a tent over the wet surface and use forced hot air and dehumidifiers in combination to dry spaces very quickly, focusing the effort on the wet parts of the room only. This may be a suitable method to restore a public space quickly.
- Air movers or blowers should not be used without humidity control as they can rapidly increase the airborne water vapour leading to mould problems and condensation. However, they are effective at moving damp air from the boundary layer (by the wet surface) to speed up the drying process; when used in conjunction with dehumidifiers they are very effective.
- Specialist processes are available to dry behind voids and under flooring without having to remove building fabric, akin to keyhole surgery. Professional expertise is required.
- In order to keep the air free of fungal spores, air scrubbers may be used which are fitted with a high efficiency particulate air (HEPA) filter. Although mould growth may be minimized by ongoing dehumidification and air moving, it remains a risk.

Pickles (2010) described the importance of creating a balanced drying system:

> The objective should be to create a balanced drying system, i.e. one where the rate of water evaporation is equal to the rate of water-vapour removal by either ventilation or dehumidification. If drying is unbalanced, for example if fans are used to speed evaporation but with inadequate removal of water [from the air], then two problems can arise; the rate of drying will progress more slowly as the relative humidity rises, or high concentrations of water vapour will move from

where the drying is taking place to other rooms where the concentration is lower. This can result in humidity change such as mould growth in rooms that were previously undamaged.

Moisture meters can be used on wet surfaces to measure the moisture content and monitor the rate of drying, and take readings regularly. All building materials will contain a degree of water before flooding, and the drying process should return the item to its equilibrium moisture content where water is present, but no rot or mould growth or physical distortion will occur. It can be difficult to know when a surface is dry without knowing its pre-incident moisture content as a benchmark, although taking readings from similar rooms in unaffected areas after the flood may be informative, although these may have also been affected by the high moisture content of the air so could give a false indication. It may be helpful to take readings of the moisture content of your building as part of your building threat assessment process so you at least have a point of reference if you ever have to dry out after a flood. Ultimately it should be possible for surveyors or contractors to certify buildings of modern construction as dry. This is potentially not possible with an older building where a judgement call may be required in light of the data from moisture readings and when moisture removal appears to have become stable.

If redecoration work begins too early, the result is likely to be that paint flakes on the wall as sub-surface moisture is still slowly moving out of the building fabric. Facilities departments of large institutions sometimes take on drying work themselves, hiring equipment. This approach can be successful but only when coupled with professional expertise as to declaring the building dry and close monitoring. It is not recommended where substantial water is trapped or after significant fluvial flooding.

Fire damage

In the aftermath of fire damage, action is necessary to limit the risk of further secondary damage. Undertake a triage assessment to prioritize action for the building. Prompt removal and cleaning of certain items will be essential, as prolonged exposure to a post-fire environment can result in problems which may not be immediately apparent but which develop in time. This will serve many purposes, not least facilitating faster reopening of the service.

These are some of the problems that result from fire damage:

• Electrics and electrical equipment can be damaged through corrosion of internal components, and reaction from residues that conduct electricity, which cause short circuits.

- Metals become corroded and discoloured.
- Plastics (including UPVC windows and doors and laminated surfaces) melt.
- There is a risk of mould growth and physical changes to wet items.

Removing items from the room or at least introducing dehumidifiers to reduce the relative humidity to below 60%rH should help prevent damage, although care should be taken with dehumidifiers and historic buildings. Cleaning metals and plastics as a priority will prevent corrosion and irremovable staining.

It should also be remembered that fire activity can result in chemical reactions. Formation of hydrochloric acid, for example, can occur after fires. When PVC is burned, hydrogen chloride can form, which then combines with water (even moisture in the air in the form of water vapour) to form hydrochloric acid. Formation of hydrochloric acid is limited at lower relative humidity. Wear appropriate equipment including chemically protective gloves. All fire residues are hazardous to health so take appropriate measures to limit inhalation and contact with the skin.

Surfaces of the building need to be cleaned. Fast-burning and oxygen-rich fires generate a lot of smoke but the particles are often small and easy to clean, even with just dry sponge cleaning, and leave minimal staining. Slow-burning or oxygen starved fires (such as in electrical cupboards) generate residues that are often difficult to clean and can leave residual staining. Loose dry contamination can be removed using vacuum cleaners with specialist filters, and sponges, but specialist detergents may be necessary for some residues. Seek professional advice when cleaning and removing smoke residues; it is worth test-cleaning before undertaking major cleaning work. Take care to select a competent contractor for large and/or historic buildings. Observe Control of Substances Hazardous to Health (COSHH) regulations and local equivalents when using chemicals to treat fire damage.

It is likely that the worst staining and contamination from smoke is evident in the upper areas of rooms as smoke, like other hot gases, rises within a room. Smoke may also move through ducting into other areas. Gases move from high to lower pressure areas in order to reach an equilibrium, which may result in a spread of smoke far away from the source of the fire. These areas will also be contaminated and require cleaning, although the contamination will be to a lower level. The ducting itself will require cleaning.

Residual odour may require professional treatment also. Odour is subjective and there are no objective techniques to measure whether an item has a residual odour, or its degree of severity. Initially odours will be strong but they dissipate quickly afterwards. Persistent odours, even after surfaces have been cleaned and fire residues removed, can be treated. It may be that there is an area in a void or ducting that is still contaminated with smoke that has not been seen. This residual odour source must be located and removed. This is usually the most effective means of removing odour.

Other techniques include processed fogging, which 'air-washes' particulates of smoke and deposits them on the floor to be vacuumed. They can use deodorant chemicals to mask scents, which dissipate. Fogging must be applied by a trained and competent person using proper personal protective equipment and engineering controls. Remove accessioned collections and objects before such treatment. Do not reoccupy the building for many hours after fogging, by which time the fine particles produced by fogging will have fallen. As with all techniques, the suitability of these processes for historic interiors must be determined individually for each case, although they have been used extensively for residential dwellings and commercial premises globally.

Preventative measures

Although the focus of this book is on responding to emergencies, as part of the emergency planning process, it is worth conducting a fresh review of threats to the building and its staff and contents and identifying opportunities for improvement as part of the continuing emergency planning process. Some preventative measures involve building repairs or improvements or enhanced monitoring, which may prove to be a budgetary matter. However, sometimes increased vigilance, simple seasonal maintenance and improved housekeeping may reduce risk, and the impact of an incident should a fire or flood occur.

Many organizations monitor for pests, relative humidity and other problems such as leaks; carry out these checks regularly otherwise the monitoring is futile. Encourage all staff in the building to report anything out of the ordinary to the Building Recovery Manager so it can be investigated fully, as it may be the sign of an incipient problem. All sites should fall under this process, not just the main sites.

Table 8.1 lists the actions to take when carrying out a building risk assessment.

Thermal imaging equipment can be used to show areas where items are overheating or leaking and may be a useful tool for flat roofs and gutters in particular. Leak detection via a sensitive cable can be installed if risk of leaks is high but must be integrated into a building management system, otherwise it may bleep to indicate a leak but nobody is aware unless they enter the area affected and hear it in person.

Table 8.1 *Building risk assessment guidance*

Item	Actions
Roof	Inspect visually regularly. Flat roofs – look out for puddles of water and plant growth. No evidence of flashing damage, slipped tiles, bowing. Lightning conductor fitted if necessary.
Drains	Proactive checking and flushing of system if collections could be affected by back-up. Fit non-return valves. Drainage at bottoms of downpipes free?
Gutters, downpipes, gulleys	Proactive checking and cleaning of blockages, particularly in autumn and spring (nesting, leaves). Fit tops of downpipes with wire guards.
Building fabric and damp-proof course	Visual inspection to check for evidence of damp, structural defects (bowing).
Flood protection	If building is in a high-risk flood area (1 in 100 year), then flood protection products can be purchased, such as door protectors and air-brick covers. Tactics for minimizing flood risk are discussed in Chapter 4 in the section on preparing for flood.
Fenestration (windows, skylights)	Check regularly for breakage, condensation, rotting wood, sealant intact.
HVAC system	Regular maintenance and plan for failure (back-up dehumidifiers). Service the boiler professionally annually. Double-check the rH and temperature levels achieved periodically by using standalone loggers at varying points in the store, with particular efforts to monitor the conditions on hot days and in the night. System should shut down automatically if a fire is detected. Check for evidence of mould around outlets.
Fire prevention	Are sockets for portable appliances and extension cables used appropriately? Are electrical systems and appliances regularly checked? Is a no-smoking policy rigorously signed and observed by all building users, including tenants and contractors? Are combustible materials (insulation, packaging) stored away from high-risk areas such as boiler rooms? Are kitchens and catering services fitted with fire suppression systems or additional forms of protection? Is hot-work with contractors monitored and permits issued? Is fire-retardant polythene used where possible for sheeting (especially where it may come into contact with light fittings)?

(continued on next page)

Table 8.1 *continued*	
Fire detection	Check that all rooms are fitted with detectors, and alarms audible. New smoke sampling and very early detection (VESDA) being developed. Can your system be improved? Alarms should automatically route to fire service.
Fire suppression	Consider carefully. Sprinklers have a very low failure rate and are extremely effective. Most wet items can be restored; charred and fully combusted items may not be restorable. Modern systems have dry pipes and can dispense as a mist. Sprinkler head distribution needs to be confirmed as fit for purpose (particularly in racked stores) to detect a fire early enough and their height sufficient to minimize accidental knocks but maximize fire suppression. Gaseous suppression also an option though the space needs to be completely sealed for the gas to work – regular integrity testing is important. Anoxic environments now being installed in some institutions to completely eliminate fire risk but is more suitable to new-build facilities.
Fire stopping	What is the fire resistance of doors – can this be improved? Are holes drilled for network cables in the building sealed up properly? Do HVAC systems automatically turn off if a fire is detected?
Fire-fighting equipment	Ensure extinguishers are available and regularly checked. Dry risers and hydrants should also be regularly inspected by appropriate contractors. An annual inspection by the fire service is desirable.
Fire evacuation	Are all routes kept accessible and unblocked, and signs visible? How often do fire marshals rehearse the evacuation process?
Chemical cupboards	Store chemicals in an appropriate container or cupboard and keep lists of chemicals in the building with your floor plans.
Walls and ceilings	Monitor closely for evidence of leaks or salting. It is better to encourage redecoration and replacement of stained tiles so that new problems are more easily spotted.

In addition to risk reduction, there are several options institutions have to manage residual risk better. These will serve to ensure faster response to an emergency and minimize the impact on collections. A substantial element of

Table 8.1 *continued*	
Electrical systems and appliances	Ask a professional to check these systems and appliances annually. Conduct portable appliance testing on all items and remove any item with a damaged flex from service. Unplug appliances overnight. Labelling in distribution should make sense to staff and electrical engineers and use the same terminology for zones.
Plumbing	Lag and label plumbing, and ensure that stop-cocks are easy to find. Inspect hidden piping regularly (hidden behind ceiling tiles, etc.). Fit non-return valves where possible.
Basements	Tanking may be fitted to reduce water ingress. Sumps and associated pumps may also serve to reduce water ingress. For areas of high flood risk, seek specially engineered solutions if collections are kept underground via an architect.
Security	Review periodically to minimize risk of arson. Monitored response 24 hours required. CCTV can be used. Ensure external bins and toolsheds are kept in a locked compound away from the building.
Pest activity	Properly dispose of all waste, especially food waste, daily in a wheelie bin. Contact rodent control. Check all voids regularly. Monitor insect pest traps regularly and operate a quarantine process.
Smoking	Enforce a no-smoking policy for all staff, visitors and contractors. Preferably there should be no smoking on-site.

this is improved emergency planning and training but the following additional activities may help:

- Check extreme weather reports for known problem areas.
- Find out what is stored directly underneath known problem areas or high-risk locations. Is it high-priority material? If so, move it.
- Never keep material on the floor. Place large items on blocks or pallets.
- Never keep empty boxes on the tops of racking as they exacerbate fires.
- Close racking fully at night, with the position of the open aisle rotated. If a fire or flood occurs then damage will be limited.
- Remember that boxing and secondary housing such as encapsulation keeps water and fire damage out.

- Place fire-retardant polythene in position under known escape of water risk areas or use it to protect objects on shelving during building work.
- Limit collections at ground level (do not use bottom row if possible).
- Maintain enhanced supervision of contractors working on plumbing, drilling or undertaking hot-work. External power-washing can also cause major problems. Prevent work during weekends if there would not be enough hands to contain an escape of water quickly. Essentially the institution needs to be informed when any work outside the normal maintenance and checks is being conducted.
- Ensure facilities staff are familiar with the building. Can signage be improved to ensure that response to any leaks is as fast as possible? (For example, put a sign on the door of your strongroom: 'The distribution board for this area is located in room x. Stop-cocks are in these locations.')
- Make keys easy to access and use.
- Check strongrooms visually daily even if no retrievals operate to spot any problems early.
- Conduct a check of the building and storage areas over prolonged closed periods such as holiday weekends.

Proactive checking of known problem areas during incidents of heavy rain will ensure incipient problems are detected quickly (Figure 8.2).

Figure 8.2 *Checking problem areas during incidents of heavy rain to detect incipient problems*
© Harwell Document Restoration Services

CHAPTER 9
Business continuity

In the aftermath of any major incident, the business or service that the organization provides will be affected and it is essential to consider strategies that might be adopted to mitigate the impact of any incident on service as part of the emergency planning process. Indeed the planning process may provide an opportunity to assess vulnerabilities and improve resilience. The case study of the Brisbane flood affecting the State Library in Queensland in Chapter 2 demonstrated how crucial this can be.

In the commercial sector, this process is known as business continuity, which can be defined as the ability of an organization to respond to incidents so that any disruption caused is minimized to a predetermined acceptable level. The Business Continuity Institute's (BCI's) Good Practice Guidelines define business continuity management as a 'holistic process that identifies threats to an organisation and the impacts to business operations that those threats, if realized, might cause. It provides a framework for building organisational resilience with the capability for an effective response that safeguards the interests of key stakeholders, reputation, brand and value-creating activities.'

So does this apply to organizations in the heritage and information services sectors under the definition provided? Clearly a major incident has the capability to impact on brand and reputation and the core mission of an organization. If a higher education library contends with a major incident poorly, consider what reputational damage could be created when stories are published about students unable to complete PhDs and examinations being disrupted. Given internet access and social media, reputational damage could be international. Affected library stock must be treated, but the core mission of the library in a higher education institution is to provide learning support and research facilities for students and academics. Customers and users are also stakeholders and their interests and expectations of continued good quality service must be protected. The international reputation of prominent institutions could be affected, possibly affecting loans programmes and other services. Trustees and wider parent organizations have a responsibility to ensure that the service is maintained, to avoid breaching statutory obligations and regulatory requirements, such as freedom of information legislation, for example, and the ultimate responsibility as custodian of the collection.

Value creation also applies: many organizations generate a revenue stream through public services or opening to visitors, and must question the impact of the removal or reduction of expected cash flow to their short and long-term financial situation.

Thomas Croall, former Business Continuity Manager for Manchester City Council, and Chair of the Emergency Planning Society Business Continuity subgroup, described business continuity planning in the following way:

> In business continuity planning, we accept that we may not be able to provide a full service in a time of crisis and scarce resource, however what we should be doing is considering what's important to our customers and ultimate stakeholders and having backups and contingencies in place, such as alternative facilities, innovative use of IT and technology, and importantly robust communications strategies to ensure we can communicate with our wider stakeholders. Business continuity is underpinned by legislative requirements, but it is also good practice to have robust procedures in place and showcase to public officials and insurers that you strive to deliver an excellence in your service.

Collections salvage must co-exist with business continuity protocols. Clearly the weighting of business continuity in the recovery process varies depending on the nature of the organization. The weighting for organizations such as higher education libraries, public libraries and records management services, which house some irreplaceable collections but are mostly concerned with public service, may be in favour of business continuity rather than prioritizing salvage of print collections. In these organizations it is not uncommon for collections salvage to be outsourced completely, leaving institution staff free to focus on minimizing and managing the disruption to service. Salvage of collections remains crucial but expert in-house staff must be used in the most appropriate way. In organizations such as museums and archives, where collections are irreplaceable and the collections form the backbone of the service offered, the approach may be more balanced but business continuity will remain an important consideration.

Sara Cunningham, Business Continuity Manager of the Victoria and Albert Museum, described continuity planning and emergency planning at the V&A:

> Since 9/11 the Trustees and Department for Culture, Media and Sport requested that the national museums took a more robust view of emergency and business

continuity planning. From 2005 we started looking at approaching it in a more holistic way, partly because there were so many high profile disasters, such as Buncefield, hurricane Katrina affecting New Orleans and the London bombs.

The V&A is a 7-day-a-week operation, with an international presence. If our business was interrupted for more than 24 hours, reputation would suffer and we would lose money. Very soon things would grind to a halt. Our timetables are such that we just can't afford to stop: loans, exhibitions, touring shows, in and out all the time, corporate events, school visits, a licensing business not to mention our own collections. For us, a national collection, avoidance of reputational damage is a key issue.

Collections staff have been surprised that in exercises we've held that they have taken second place. Collections are a low priority in a major incident for the first 12 hours. It's the people and the building and communications that take precedence: accounting for people, accounting for staff and making sure that visitors are evacuated safely. Then making sure that the building is managed and secure and we have telecoms, utilities and IT.

The IT department have back-up systems to minimise the period of outage and we can update our website remotely. We have a recovery suite at our off-site store, with a small office facility that's available for the business continuity team to start recovery. PR, HR and other individuals that the Business Continuity Manager would choose to be available would attend that site, including estates, a health and safety representative, a collections representative, Visitor Services Manager, a Welfare advisor, the finance department and someone from the V&A's trading company. Each of those would then alert their own sub-teams. The office suite has an independent seven landlines and 12 computers, a rest area and a dedicated room for HR and Press. The computers are not dependent on the V&A network. If there is a London wide problem then we would have a problem but there is only so much that you can control.

Communication with staff is crucial as we have hundreds of staff and volunteers. Cascade systems operate, but in addition there is a separate staff website and a staff emergency helpline which we can add a recorded message to. We have a contract in place with a company to deal with staff queries as the HR department would otherwise be overwhelmed. We can also update our website remotely and divert our public numbers so that systems are not overwhelmed. Finance has mechanisms for paying suppliers if we weren't able to occupy buildings, operating payroll, and we have mechanisms for emergency expenditure.

We also have a local business resilience forum working with the Royal Albert Hall, Imperial College and the other South Kensington Museums, with a centralised control room so response can be coordinated.

Practical experiences from incidents in public libraries also demonstrate that provision of continued service is important after major incidents. Jackie Taylor-Smith, District Manager, Kent County Libraries, has experience of this:

> The fire happened in August 2004 and the portakabin opened for service delivery the following April. The time in between was mostly taken up with locating a suitable site and agreeing it with the district council. Once a site had been found quite a lot of ground work had to be done to enable installation of utilities into the unit. Buildings continuity insurance paid for extra mobile library services that were in place until the temporary facility was ready. This insurance paid for the complete fit out. Staff were deployed at other libraries within the district as well as working on the mobile library and then at the portakabin. Local residents were most anxious to have a library built on the original site and to preserve as much as possible of the Carnegie building that had virtually been destroyed.

How to write a business continuity plan

The process for business continuity planning is laid out in documents such as the BCI's Good Practice Guidelines and British Standards such as BS25999, the Business Continuity Management (BCM) standard. In order to determine how best to minimize disruption, there are crucial steps to follow, known as the BCM lifecycle, with an emphasis on the need continuously to review and maintain plans and obtain executive buy-in from the start. This involves:

• understanding the organization
• determining the business continuity management strategy
• developing and implementing a business continuity response plan
• exercising, maintaining and reviewing.

Understanding the organization – business impact analysis

The first step is to understand the organization, and determine what areas of service provision are most important. This is known as business impact analysis, which highlights the business functions that are most critical and then shapes the strategy in the plan, by showing what will need to be reinstated first. The process of business impact analysis first requires the identification of all services and functions that the organization provides and performs, then for each of these determines potential impacts that would result from disruption.

Having acknowledged the potential impacts, an assessment is required to identify the maximum tolerable period of disruption, which is the duration of disruption that could be borne before unacceptable damage occurred that affected staff, reputation, financial operations, service quality and adherence to regulatory requirements. Seasonal variations may affect the maximum tolerable period of disruption. The tolerable period of disruption for a higher education library during exam periods and start of academic year would be shorter than perhaps during the middle of the long summer vacation. The maximum tolerable period of disruption is not a guarantee that it will certainly be possible to recover in the time stipulated, particularly if there are external factors that are out of your control, although contingencies should be as resilient as possible.

This process of business impact analysis also needs to identify the dependencies that are required so that the area can operate effectively. This may involve IT, power and essential building services such as lighting, lifts and workspace, as well as human resources and access to catalogues and information.

In order to complete the business impact analysis, business activities must be identified, the maximum tolerable period of disruption assessed and a view formed as to how these business activities might be prioritized. This can be done through workshops or questionnaires directed to staff and potentially also users groups. There must be a cross-section of opinions canvassed to avoid bias of one particular department skewing the business impact analysis. Thereafter, a senior management decision will be required to take all views into consideration to produce a definitive version.

Figure 9.1 (overleaf) shows a business impact analysis sample form showing the functions involved in delivering services in an organization.

The prioritization is often defined as having four levels:

- Level 1 must be restored with 1 day.
- Level 2 must be restored within 3 days.
- Level 3 must be restored within 7 days.
- Level 4 can be restored progressively after 7 days.

There is no reason why further levels cannot be added if more appropriate. The timescales applied above can be amended to suit an organization – so Level 1 could be 'must be restored within 4 hours'.

With the prioritization established, identify the recovery time objective, and the resources required to achieve it. It is important to be realistic. After a major incident, it may not be possible to recover full service within a day. It may be more realistic to aim for a phased recovery, so if your library services pre-

Function	When would disruption cause a serious impact? Select 1 hour, 4 hours, 1 day, 3 days, 1 week and give any reasons for your choice.	Are there periods when this function is more important?	Priority rating 1–4 (1 = most critical, 4 = least critical)
Provision of study space	1 day – lack of other facilities	Exam times	2
Provision of electronic resources	4 hours	Exam times	1
Provision of ICT study space	1 week – ICT capability within individual departments. Not all reliant on library.		4
Circulation of short loan stock	4 hours	Exam times	2
Reception or registering new users	1 day	Start of academic year	3
Enquiry services	1 day		1

Figure 9.1 *Business impact analysis sample form*

incident require 40 computer terminals, perhaps the recovery time objective could be to have 4 terminals working within 24 hours, 16 within 3 days and so on.

Figure 9.2 shows a sample recovery time objective form.

Dependencies and resources

Resources are required to restore business functions. It is helpful for an institution to have a plan of its normal provision, and thus plan for a timely reintroduction of services, working up to full capacity. If the resource is affected by the incident itself, you will need to hire, borrow or purchase new equipment, for which there will be a lead time. Staffing may be affected if lots

Function	Recovery time objective	Comments
Provision of study space	*3 days*	*Liaise with university estate on alternative site* *Regional collaboration with other HE libraries*
Circulation of short loan stock	*3 days*	*Liaise with salvage team and contractors over prioritization for recovery* *Liaise with insurers over purchase of new stock* *Negotiate access with other HE libraries*
Enquiry service	*1 day*	*Staff who cannot participate with salvage of print materials can work from home using PCs and log into server*

Figure 9.2 *Sample recovery time objective form*

of individuals are engaged with salvage work, and it may be necessary to outsource this work if this cannot be tolerated to assure business continuity. Dependencies can include staff, work or study stations, shelving, specialist IT and software, specialist equipment for audiovisual equipment, PCs, loading bay, radio-frequency identification (RFID) scanners, parking, telephony and internet access. List external suppliers for these services or equipment in your emergency plan suppliers' directory or even as a separate list for business continuity issues.

Space is a major requirement for most library and archive services (storage and working) and pre-incident planning about possible sites may shorten the service resumption period after a real incident. These can be listed in your appendix on alternative sites. It may be possible to revert to manual working processes for some activities such as loans if power is cut for a protracted period. Defunct equipment may exist buried in a basement somewhere. Place it in an accessible location in case it is ever needed.

Figure 9.3 (overleaf) shows a sample dependencies log.

Resource	Normal	Time period for recovery			
		1 day	3 days	1–2 weeks	3–4 weeks
Networked PCs	50	0	10	20	50
Microfilm reader	2			1	2

Figure 9.3 *Sample dependencies log*

IT and data recovery

For IT functions, a similar process must be undertaken. Here the terminology used is 'maximum data loss allowable' and the 'recovery point objective'. This relates to a sudden loss or corruption of data on your systems and servers. Would one day's loss of data be tolerable, so one day's e-mail and digitization would need to be recovered? What about loans, accessions, work completed and saved that day? Would this be an acceptable loss? Various back-up systems are available and, unsurprisingly, those that provide the minimal loss are often the most expensive. This comes down to a policy discussion and risk assessment. Some of the data could be rebuilt, other data could not be. Would a loss of a day's work be a frustration or potentially involve significant reputational damage?

Generally, data can be backed up to:

- the last key stroke (real-time)
- intraday, i.e. during the working day
- the last full back-up (usually the previous day close of business).

A recovery point objective is the point in time to which data must be restored to be acceptable. If the business impact analysis indicates that your maximum acceptable data loss is not supported by current systems, further investment may be required. In addition to having a back-up, it is important to detail the operational procedure to follow to access the back-up and reinstate it. Any software that may also have been lost should have back-up discs and passwords stored off-site. Store administrator passwords for any web services such as e-books off-site too.

Business continuity is full of acronyms and terminology, which can be confusing. However, an advantage to those working in services embedded within a local authority or higher education context is that increasingly business continuity planning is being adopted within public sector organizations at a high level and libraries or archives are being required to write plans, but they are supported and provided with templates. The Head of Collections describes how this has operated in a major university research library in central London:

> The focus of our disaster planning has shifted markedly over the last five years or so, from an approach based largely on protection and salvage of collections, to one focused far more directly on business and service continuity. Although special and rare collections still deserve attention as valuable assets, the real value of the library as far as the university is concerned is in the service it is able to provide to staff and students, and the collections are only a part of that service. Any catastrophic event that hinders the library from providing a service is likely in turn to impact on the student's or the researcher's experience, and therefore becomes a matter of institution-wide interest.
>
> The library is a member of the M25 Consortium of Academic Libraries [www.m25lib.ac.uk/m25dcp/], who have built up a wealth of best practice information and a recommended template for library disaster plans, and under this guidance we formulated our first approach to disaster planning. However, a real shift of emphasis in our own institution came in the mid-2000s, when the directorate created a post of Director of Business Continuity (DBC). The DBC had a remit to coordinate business continuity planning across the university, ensuring that individual departments and units had robust and up-to-date plans, to set up an emergency command and control framework, and to ensure that appropriate staff in each department were trained in emergency response procedures. The university also put in place a governance structure to oversee this activity, forming a Business Continuity Steering Group that reports up to the directorate.
>
> From the library's point of view we found working with the DBC highly beneficial. Firstly, because it enabled us to bring our plans into line with a common university-wide standard, and on a wider level to ensure our plans were compliant with external and statutory obligations, e.g. HEFCE recommended best practice and the local authority's civil contingency plan. Secondly, and probably more important for the library, it gave us institutional approval of, and buy-in to, our own local plan; it enabled us to highlight the main risks faced by the library service, and flag up where central resources might be needed to be given in an emergency, the most obvious example being the need to find hundreds of study spaces for students elsewhere on campus, should the library building become unavailable!
>
> Using the university-wide template our business recovery plan now focuses squarely on service continuity. The plan singles out three priority areas for service recovery: 1) access to study space, 2) access to networked resources, and 3) condition assessment and salvage of print collections. Under each of these areas a detailed plan is set out, covering aspects such as: minimum recovery

times; critical times of the year; contingencies in place to resolve the situation; how communications will be managed; and 'back to normal' restoration procedures. A critical part of the planning process has been to ensure that staff roles are clearly identified in the plan, i.e. who would be responsible for each part of the process, and ensuring back-ups are in place if key staff are not available.

We have also worked with the DBC on defining the roles our key staff would play if the university's major emergency response procedure is invoked (this involves a Gold/Silver/Bronze command chain with which we would interact at various levels). We have also taken part in disaster scenario modelling exercises, facilitated by the DBC, which have helped us test and revise our plans.

Apart from our contact with the DBC we continue to work at a local library level through our own business continuity planning team. This group focuses on more local matters such as resilience of our local IT systems, fire evacuation procedures and training of fire marshals, ensuring staff (especially those on evening and weekend duty) are trained in basic emergency response, and maintaining staff skills in physical salvage procedures.

In general, our link with the university's central business continuity planning gives us confidence that our plans conform to an agreed standard, and are validated at a senior level; it also gives us confidence that should a disastrous event occur, that we will have the backing of the university to help us continue providing as good a service as we can.

There may be a question as to how emergency plans and business continuity plans co-exist. Business continuity plans are usually not invoked in small-scale incidents, which can be met through normal working practices, whereas emergency plans can apply to a large range of situations. There is a potential conflict for large high-profile institutions that run corporate events. For example, a wedding is taking place later today, and as a result of a flood in the basement, power is cut to the site. A single generator is available to run emergency lighting either for salvage of valuable objects, or for the event: who gets it? These issues need to be considered fully well in advance of a real problem occurring. Write contracts in a way that conveys to clients that salvage issues may take precedence over their event, if indeed that is the corporate position.

With the business impact analysis complete and the recovery points identified, write the processes for reinstatement of services in the same vein as the response to water damage (described in Chapter 4). Insert all reference material required, and suppliers, passwords, contacts at other institutions who may be able to accommodate extra users, into the plan as you cannot guarantee you will have access on the day of a real emergency. Integrate training and testing of these procedures into the wider emergency plan rehearsal schemes in place.

Effective communications

When high-profile heritage institutions are affected by major events such as fires and floods, the media is bound to be interested in what has happened. The only exception may be when there are other bigger stories at the time, as Deborah Shorley described in her case study in Chapter 2, but this cannot be planned for. Anything that involves the fire services will be in the public arena, often because those in newsgathering monitor emergency services' radio frequencies. Anything that happens in a public area may also become public knowledge very quickly as a result of social networking sites. If an organization is well prepared to manage communications, it can be much more in control of the information that is circulating and limit any potential hyperbole that may lead to unnecessary concerns among stakeholders and staff, and wider reputational damage that can be difficult to eradicate. If there is an emergency, communication will need to be managed with employees, users and clients, visitors, owners or donors of objects in the custody of the institution, and potentially the media.

Dealing with the media

As the message needs to be controlled, it is crucial that only authorized people speak to the press, and that any staff assisting with salvage are asked to direct reporters to the nominated person to deal with communications. Staff should be mindful about what is being said in public areas and what can be overheard. It can be tempting to be drawn into speculation about the cause of the incident, but this is unhelpful. Even if the damage to the collection is upsetting, this information needs to be controlled to avoid reputational damage.

The manager of a national museum with a significant collection described anonymously her experience of dealing with the media after a major incident:

> A major incident occurred on a large site which brought the emergency services on-site and initiated their site emergency plan. As a major employer such an incident brought media attention and, fortunately, staff were wise enough to refer all requests for information and comment to the organisation's spokespeople who would issue a statement. In the real world the media are hungry for information and while waiting for the official statement journalists went to a local pub – which also happened to be the local pub for a number of

members of staff who were discussing the incident, the reaction to it, problems with the reaction and how the response could be improved.

All of this was overheard and duly reported as a non-attributed comment but so accurate as to spark a review on who was speaking directly to the press with all of the members of one department immediately suspended and removed from site pending the result of the enquiry. All were exonerated.

The lessons – while in wartime 'careless talk costs lives' careless talk today costs reputations and never underestimate the need for the media to have accurate information quickly. Be first to capture their attention. Be aware of the ability of new technology in relation to news gathering. All media outlets will encourage and use photographs and video captured by the public and consequently we do need to be aware of the need to have accurate information available quickly. The ready availability of technology has led to the creation of a huge number of 'citizen journalists' encouraged by the mainstream media with constant requests for information and photographs from their readers and viewers.

On a slow news day a minor incident can be elevated to prominence. Photographs, on social networking sites, of water being swept out of a gallery following a minor leak take on greater significance when aired in the media and you have no spokesperson to comment on the damage or lack of it. Media organisations, particularly 24 hour rolling news programmes, are so news hungry that they will have no problems in finding an 'expert' to establish what happened and what you should have done. Particularly inconvenient if you had not felt that the issue was an emergency in the first place and being on the back foot does make it look as if you didn't care, couldn't or wouldn't react and are generally incapable of any effective response. After all, the media were able to find an 'expert' in no time at all [so] why couldn't you?

Some preparation can be done in advance to deal with the media, which can later be tailored to the specifics of the situation. General background information about your institution, which would be used for other press releases, can be kept, together with a basic outline press statement to help save time in the immediate hours of the emergency response, which should provide:

• information on what has happened, when and where
• confirmation about the status of staff and visitors (if anyone is unaccounted for do not release names until family members have been notified)
• confirmation that emergency services are in control
• confirmation that your emergency plans have been activated.

Reassurance is key. Use simple and matter of fact language. It is better not to be drawn into speculation about the nature and severity of damage to specific objects and the cause of the incident. It is impossible to know what the value or quantity of items damaged is, so it is best to state that specialist staff are examining the damage if anyone asks about it.

For high-profile institutions such as national collections, rehearsal and specialist media training may be beneficial given the national and possibly international interest. The organization may have a central public relations section whose staff may be able to provide assistance in the preparation and execution of these communications, although members of the Emergency Management Team (especially the Emergency Response Manager) should approve any statement before release. The media will publicize the incident rapidly, perhaps before an institution's staff are aware or depositors have been informed of what has happened. When the Cutty Sark caught fire in 2007, the Chief Executive of the Cutty Sark Trust was interviewed by national radio at around 7 am, less than 3 hours after the fire was detected and the fire service contacted. Stories of heritage damage are of particular interest to the public and this must be given due prominence in the emergency response plan.

For this reason it is crucial that information about depositors, donors and lenders is accessible, in the plan or in a separate secure location, so notification of any major incident comes from the institution, rather than a rolling new channel. Although it may not be possible to provide any detailed information about their objects at this stage, it is better to establish lines of communication early and reassure interested parties that you are aware of their donations or collections and are dealing with the situation.

In some specialized situations such as pharmaceutical companies, damage to some critical records may need to be reported to regulatory authorities promptly, such as the Medicines and Healthcare products Regulatory Agency or Food and Drug Administration, for quality assurance purposes. Include contact information in plans for such communication. If public records are damaged, notification to national authorities may be required.

In major incidents affecting large organizations, there should be mechanisms for staff to be contacted to notify them whether they should remain at home, or report to work (and if so, where to report to). Some organizations have detailed telephone trees to contact people quickly, or text sweeps for staff with mobile phones. Alternatively a toll-free number can be set up as part of the emergency planning process at low-cost onto which a recorded message can be loaded if there is an emergency. Issue all staff with this in advance and locate it on their staff ID badge so it can be found quickly.

Dealing with users and clients

Notifying users is also critical. Interested parties could include members of the public, the wider community, students, researchers, and in records management services other staff in your wider organization. All these people use the service provided and may be concerned about how the incident will affect them. Be prepared for a surge in calls and website hits in the immediate aftermath of an incident; if websites cannot accommodate this it severely impairs communication. Speak with your hosting service or IT section to confirm capacity. Be aware that internal systems may be down as a result of the incident. It may be possible to update websites remotely if logins and passwords are retained elsewhere. If all internal systems are down and they are not immediately reparable use social media. Two of the case studies in Chapter 2 discussed using Twitter and Facebook when their e-mail system was not functioning.

The information provided when notifying users may need to be more detailed than that given to the media. Although it is important not to contradict any press statements, it is also important to be realistic about the impact on services. It can be highly disruptive if a press release is issued that downplays the incident, so that internal users' perceptions of the incident are affected and their tolerance of service disruption is lowered.

To some extent one can predict the level of service provision that can be offered or the extent of denial of access to the building in an emergency such as a power cut, as one can calculate what electronic resources can operate without users needing physical access to print collections and the building. Factsheets or web pages can be prepared in advance. Wherever possible mass circulation e-mails can be used to communicate quickly and effectively. Set up an information desk within a day of an emergency taking place to ensure that users can talk to someone from the library service. It may be worth posting notices too.

It may be useful for organizations open to the public that have corporate events and bookings to have a back-up calendar with contact information that is accessible remotely, so staff can notify clients about the impact of the emergency on their event. Activities such as school visits can be rearranged, but mismanagement of communications about booked weddings or filming in historic houses, which are increasingly common, can generate bad publicity, which will impact on future business.

CHAPTER 10
Ensuring the plan's efficacy

It is vital to write a plan determining your emergency procedures, but this is only the initial step in ensuring you can make an effective emergency response. However good an emergency plan is in theory, additional effort is required to make sure that the content is well presented and user-friendly, and that staff can confidently and competently implement it.

Making your plan user-friendly

Consider the potential circumstances of implementing an emergency plan. It could be dark, your workplace under the control of the fire services, with an unknown amount of damage to collections you've striven for years to preserve. Good procedures and content are critical, but so is the presentation of that information. Where possible, use bullet points, tables and flow-charts to communicate procedures rather than prose. The rationale behind the instructions should already be understood by the Emergency Management Team through pre-incident training and familiarization. It should not be necessary to justify your recommended procedure with explanatory padding. Such information merely adds to the girth of the plan, which can make it unwieldy.

It is very helpful to salvage volunteers if salvage information is presented in a table, with all relevant formats listed in the first column, followed by basic guidance on packing, air-drying and dealing with large incidents (as in Table 10.1 overleaf); this can act as an invaluable checklist. Instructions for individual formats on a single sheet can also be provided and included in kits in a larger font size, together with photographs of the techniques required. Laminate these if possible.

Try to use a large font size. Avoid jargon wherever possible and use simple and direct language. Some institutions prefer to use paragraph numbering systems rather than bullets so that particular paragraphs can be referred to with maximum speed. Use page numbers and provide a contents page.

Table 10.1 *Extract of salvage information*

Material	Moving and packing	If treating on-site	If large quantity
Books with coated papers and photo albums	Pack books upright in crate for transfer and prioritize for treatment. Danger of pages sticking together.	Stand volumes on blotter. Interleave with silicone paper if necessary to prevent pages touching on each page (this is very time-consuming). WIND TUNNEL SUITABLE – keeping in blast of air may stop adhesion without interleaving.	Freeze as quickly as possible, packing vertically in crates. Professional drying.
Paper documents and files	Paper is very weak and can tear. Use Melinex to lift and support individual documents. Prioritize records with water-soluble inks for treatment.	Lay flat on blotter, transferring with Melinex if necessary. Turn documents regularly to encourage drying on both sides, unless water-soluble ink, which should be kept face up at all times. If space restricted, create layers: blotter – records – blotter – records – blotter. Keep items fastidiously in order. WIND TUNNEL DRYING NOT BENEFICIAL.	Freeze. Place into crates, keeping flat. No need to interleave unless in folders with leaching dyes.

Diagrams and photographs are very useful to demonstrate techniques that are complex to explain in text. A photograph of a wind tunnel may be easier to follow than written instructions on how to construct one. Disaster kits should have contents of containers listed, and individual paper types labelled so salvage staff can be reminded what they are for, as outlined in Chapter 7. Try to avoid putting too much information onto one page, so it is easier to absorb it: it is far better to have a longer plan with lots of page breaks for each section so that information stands out clearly than to try to make the document shorter and thinner, but the information is too densely presented to be absorbed easily.

Do not hesitate to use colour to make important information stand out more clearly, even though it will be more costly to print. Certain parts of the plan such as salvage crib sheets can be laminated or placed in poly-pockets so they stay dry. Some sections may benefit from being printed in larger scales – floor plans on A3 for example and A1 or A0 plans can be made available for the fire service if they attend. Place the plan in a rigid A4 folder. The Museum of London has produced a neat A5 version of the elements of the plan pertinent to the collection, which is widely liked by the collection's care team.

The front cover of the plan should look serious. Although it may be amusing to emblazon the cover with the phrase DON'T PANIC, and indeed that instruction may be useful, the plan needs to be taken seriously and should be in the style of a corporate document. Include the institution logo, document title (in large font), the version number, the date and the endorsement from the head of your organization. The first section of the plan should also follow suit, stating the purpose of the plan, its application, its endorsement and the review period and process.

Information should also be cross-referenced and signposted wherever possible. In addition to saying 'microfilm can be reprocessed by a specialist lab', guidance should also be given: 'two contractors are listed in Appendix D on page 33', for example. These instances may seem small but help enormously in emergency situations.

Plan distribution

It is not necessary to regard your plan as one homogenous document. The plan with all annexes and supplementary information may be bulky and large, even though each section should be succinct and well designed, and the information included for a valid reason. In a major incident all of this information will be necessary, but not everyone will need every piece of information. Indeed, very wide circulation of the plan may present security issues given the content, and may also raise questions of data protection if personal and home contact information of staff is in there.

For the sake of continuity, Emergency Management Team staff should have the entire document, and should have a copy at home and a copy at work. Provide working laminated copies of checklists, together with other sections highly relevant to each person's role, for ease of reference and clip them to the front of the plan or place them on a special clipboard (for example, the Collections Salvage Manager would want their checklist, salvage priorities, salvage guidance notes, but not the utility shut-off instructions). If possible, lodge further copies in secure locations in external buildings that these staff could gain access to if evacuation occurred during the day and there was not time to get the plan, and close to the fire panel or at the main reception. It may be necessary to put the plan in a safe. Copies can also be lodged on the intranet, appropriately protected. Encourage Emergency Management Team staff to copy all key telephone numbers into their phone memory or give them a work handset with numbers preconfigured. Some organizations provide the plan on a password-protected USB stick, although this is considered by some to be a security risk.

A memory stick may be supplied to the fire service containing key information to upload to their fire tender on the day. Fire service staff also can hold electronic information about buildings centrally, which can then be downloaded to tenders when required. Contact the fire service headquarters to see where this information should be uploaded. A special secure box, such as a Gerda box (see Figure 4.2, page 79) or a wallet underneath the fire panel, may be made available on-site to house this information.

Emergency Management Team staff should carry with them a credit-card-sized crib sheet so they can start making calls wherever they are when an incident is reported. Post instructions about evacuation and how to deal with emergencies, including on doors to stores, with guidance on where the nearest landline is to report a leak, and the nearest disaster kit. List key Emergency Management Team and other emergency telephone numbers by all phones. Provide packs of abridged information for other staff as necessary, and salvage guidance for those assisting with the salvage effort, perhaps on a two-sided sheet.

Figure 10.1 shows emergency response and reporting instructions, posted strategically throughout a museum's sites.

Plan testing

When the Emergency Management Team considers the plan to be complete, scrutinize its content. There may be omissions, duplications, unclear or contradictory passages that only become obvious by checking the plan. This process is a vital step and the nit-picking that may take place will only serve to improve the plan.

Conduct real-time scenario testing as follows. One member of the Emergency Management Team does not participate in the exercise but

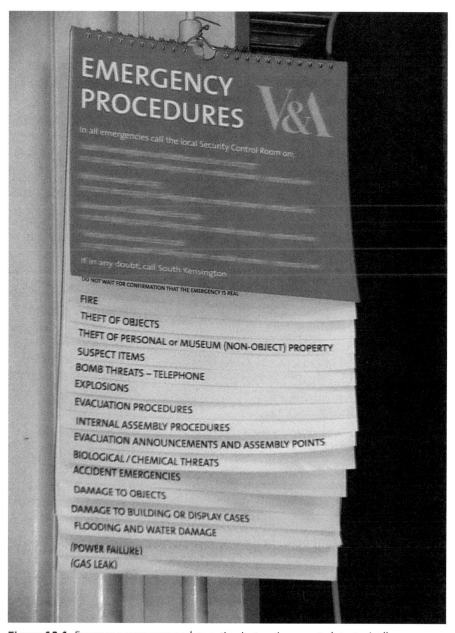

Figure 10.1 *Emergency response and reporting instructions, posted strategically throughout the Museum's sites (contact numbers blurred)*

© Harwell Document Restoration Services, with the permission of the V&A

provides a given scenario and at certain junctures gives information such as 'emergency crews hand over the building' or 'ten staff arrive to help with salvage'. This process doubles as plan training and familiarization and an opportunity to ensure that information is clear, consistent and comprehensive. Consider these scenarios:

- A flood is likely to hit in 48 hours, and affect your basement and ground floor. The head of service is away. What would be done; when would we close; how would roles and responsibilities work; what would we need in terms of resources?
- There is a power failure at 3.30 pm on a winter afternoon. What services would be kept running or would the decision be made to close?
- A fire has affected the building. The fire incident commander is asking what items you would like the fire service to evacuate for you. Areas affected include galleries, offices, stores.
- A burst pipe has flooded the bottom row in the basement when the archivist (Collections Salvage Manager) is on holiday and the head of the service (Emergency Recovery Manager) is at a conference. Public services are unaffected. How would this be managed?
- A key-holder has rung at 3 am to say an alarm has gone off and the system will not reset. There is a suspected flood. Should he go and investigate on his own?
- The flood is confirmed: what do you advise the key-holder to do? Who do you tell on the Emergency Management Team or do you wait until morning?

Another technique is to consider a moderate and a major sized scenario and ask Emergency Management Team staff to write down what they would consider necessary actions should they be managing them, and then compare their listed actions to the plan. Are all areas covered? Are there any services or contractors missing?

Training

With your plan agreed, train staff in its content and the procedures that would apply to them in reporting or responding to an incident. Training is essential if the content of the emergency plan is to be followed with any degree of confidence or competency should there be an emergency. Training enables individuals to function effectively under enormous pressure. Without training, individuals will not necessarily understand the rationale behind the procedures in the plan, which may result in time being wasted in a real incident with unnecessary questions.

Train all members of staff and long-term external contractors such as cleaning contractors and security guards who are based in your building in immediate incident response, and incorporate this into general induction training. Design the training to ensure that all staff can identify incidents that may threaten the building and collection, recognizing that they should report seemingly small-scale incidents and minor issues so action can be taken that may prevent damage. Make clear to staff whom they should contact on the Emergency Management Team and how to do so, emphasizing that it is better to be safe than sorry and to report any incident that concerns them. This is particularly important training for security personnel and staff who work a different shift pattern from the Emergency Management Team, as they may hesitate to contact senior staff when they are at home. Review and extend fire marshal, evacuation and extinguisher training where necessary.

Andrea Lydon from the National Gallery of Ireland described the importance of training:

> All staff have to feel a sense of ownership in relation to the disaster plan and disaster prevention. This goes without saying for staff who are directly responsible for collection management but those not working directly in this area should be briefed and provided with training also. You don't know when a disaster will happen, who will spot it, and who will be around to help with the response/recovery. After each disaster (no matter how minor) we always review plans and make any necessary changes.

A preservation manager from a national collection had experience of an emergency occurring out of hours and reflected on how policies in the organization have changed as a result:

> Estates didn't call salvage teams out because they didn't think that any damage had been done to the collections, whereas there was. It was agreed that from then on salvage would be called out if an incident is anywhere near the collections. We also found out in a recent test that 30% of trained volunteers on our salvage list were immediately available on a Sunday morning.

Provide targeted training for those who have volunteered to be on salvage callout lists in specific tasks in emergency situations. This may include using specialist equipment like leak-diverters and pumps so that the equipment in disaster kits can be used effectively without fumbling in a real incident. Wet vacuum cleaners, for example, can be awkward to assemble and techniques for emptying them baffling without practice. In one recent training event, when opening a leak-diverter from its pack to practise assembly, it became clear that the coupling provided did not fit the hose, and the participants were very glad that this had come to light in a training situation rather than during a real flood. Additionally, wherever possible, provide training on how to isolate electricity and turn off stop-cocks. As argued elsewhere, if staff know how to do this it could save them valuable time in responding to incidents and minimize the amount of damage that occurs as a result. Desktop exercises on dynamic risk assessment can be drafted.

Figure 10.2 shows salvage staff practising starting a generator.

A useful technique to embed the concepts of safety and incident containment may be to put the activities in your emergency response (as detailed in phases 1–3 in Chapter 4) on postcards, arrange them alphabetically and ask salvage volunteers to put them into sequence for particular scenarios, such as discovering a major incident as a key-holder through an alarm call, discovering an incident during the working day and so on. It may be necessary to hold these sessions at weekends so that staff who work on different rotas can also be involved. This practice embeds the principles of

Figure 10.2 *Salvage staff practise starting a generator in emergency training*
© Harwell Document Restoration Services

safety and focuses on the wider picture of control before individual damaged objects.

Provide training in handling and treating damaged items. Collect discarded stock before disposal or buy items from charity shops, and wet them in solid containers that act as buckets, so techniques documented in the plan can be more fully understood. Rehearse ergonomically awkward tasks such as moving paintings, rigging up polythene and so on. You can tailor events to concentrate on a particular type of material, or on the logistical constraints of salvage from particular stores. It is useful to practise the timings for moving a crate of material from locations such as a basement store or the top floor with no lift working, to get to a loading area. Use the information to project timings in a real emergency response and ensure the manual handling is properly resourced.

Helen Burton from Keele University Library Special Collections described how staff were trained in emergency procedures at the university:

> Prior to the new disaster plan, we were lucky that staff were on hand during library opening hours to help move and protect stock, but people needed a lot of instruction, not knowing what they needed to do. Luckily, it has always been on a very minor scale. The turning point has been the practical disaster training we rolled out in house for every member of staff, so everyone is now aware of the newly written procedures and the plan doesn't lie forgotten in the Library. It's been a real success – everyone knows where to go for the disaster kit and what to use. Nearby stacks are readily covered with polythene and I see effective air drying techniques being implemented without delay. I did a Christmas disaster quiz last year too – 20 quick questions that acted as a revision exercise, which people found really helpful.

Sharon Robinson, Collection Care Manager at the Museum of London, explains how the development of an e-learning tool has assisted in providing basic training for all staff, including staff who work weekend shifts:

> It sits on our intranet and all new staff are required to complete it as part of their induction. When we launched it last year all existing staff including the Directorate completed it. The front page shows the content of each section and learning outcomes. At the end of each section is a short quiz. It takes about 15 minutes to complete and we have had very positive feedback. Our aim was to raise awareness of emergency planning and what to do if anything untoward was spotted to all staff across the organization, not just those who were already relatively aware. The tool supports more detailed training sessions for collections staff with external trainers, and also short equipment demonstrations

for duty managers and security staff (like how to use a wet vac and how to put up a leak diverter). This combination of types of training and information has worked very well for us.

Figure 10.3 shows the Collections Emergency Planning e-learning portal used

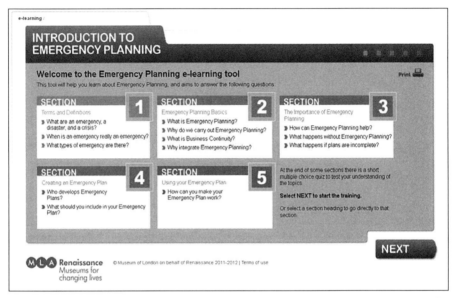

Figure 10.3 *The Collections Emergency Planning e-learning portal used at the Museum of London*

at the Museum of London.

There should be regular training for the Emergency Management Team itself, similar to the plan testing, with deputies filling in regularly and rehearsing different scenarios. Team building may also be helpful. Ultimately it is excellent if good relations can be established with local fire crews and major scenarios tested with them. Even inviting fire crews to conduct simple walk-arounds can be informative and their input can help you refine your plan. Full-scale exercises take a lot of organization but are extremely valuable learning experiences for all parties. Nicole Targett from Royal Berkshire Fire and Rescue Service describes how the fire service operates:

> All Fire and Rescue Services have similar plans with regard to dealing with incidents at heritage sites under their risk management planning process. This would be done at a service level rather than by contacting individual fire stations as an emergency response to a serious incident would be drawn from

many different parts of a FRS [Fire and Rescue Services] area.

There is national operational guidance and also shared command protocols which support collaborative working between Fire and Rescue Services as required. In Berkshire, we hold detailed plans and information relating to every heritage site in the county, plus information on valuable items, whereabouts on the site they are housed etc. together with risk information and contact details. This is available to all crews via the computers on the fire engines, plus crews train at various heritage locations and also use virtual training programmes based upon this type of scenario.

Fire crews and operational managers are also required to have detailed knowledge of all the specific risks within their area and this includes heritage sites. Some of these sites also have joint fire and emergency, site-specific tactical plans, covering detailed salvage considerations together with building plans. For all of these sites we regularly train for salvage scenarios to ensure we are aware of the site, contents and joint procedures.

It is worth contacting the headquarters of your local fire authority if the fire service is not aware of your collections.

It may also be useful to arrange seminars locally with colleagues from other institutions in similar situations and invite speakers from institutions who have suffered from incidents to find out the lessons they have learned as a result. Such events raise awareness and maintain the momentum behind the plan. Rehearse arrangements with key suppliers regularly and hold tests of callout procedures periodically to ensure numbers are up to date and monitor likely turnout.

Scheduling of such training obviously depends on resources and time constraints, but the training is very worthwhile. It keeps the plan fresh in people's minds. Short frequent training is preferable to longer training that is held annually, and helps people retain information. Attendance may be higher if shorter sessions are scheduled, whether for critical senior managers who may find the thought of a whole day away from their desks off-putting or for technical staff.

Working with other sections of your organization

Integration with your wider organization is critical for the effectiveness of any plan, most particularly those organizations where facilities, insurance, press and IT are handled by different departments, who also serve many other sub-departments in addition to the library, archive or museum. In such organizations, it is likely that emergency plans (perhaps known as business continuity, major incident or crisis management plans) already exist.

Kristie Short-Traxler, Preventive Conservation, Bodleian Libraries, Oxford University, discussed the importance of gaining staff support to the success or failure of a plan:

> The importance of engendering continual organisational support in your institution is integral to the success or failure of a plan. Codifying or publishing a written emergency plan is just part of the process. A written plan is useless or at worst even harmful without the procedure and training to back it up. Ownership and buy-in should take place from the top down and form part of the institution's main objectives.
>
>   Once you have buy-in – it is essential that the library remain committed to the plan and communicate with one another in order to continually improve procedures and response mechanisms. It can be difficult to maintain momentum for planning in a large organisation that has multiple large scale priorities but a consistent and effective series of training courses for staff will help achieve this goal. It is necessary that all staff know their own responsibilities and are aware of others'.

Failure to integrate your plan with the overarching plan for your organization may very well lead to the complete failure of your local plan in a major emergency. If the incident is so serious that it invokes the central plan for the organization, this will take precedence. The danger is that your plan will be overlooked or dismissed on the day as it is an unknown quantity. For those organizations where no liaison has occurred pre-incident, there may be no awareness of the particular requirements of your department and the urgent need to recover assets from the site. Salvage may be delayed for an extended period as the central plan may take no account of the urgency with which access may be necessary in order to avert mould growth and other forms of secondary damage.

Sometimes the sheer volume and value of material retained by a heritage and information services collection may not be appreciated by the central organization. One medical records store can house millions of individual documents. Such records can be impossible to replicate. An academic library housing even a modest 100,000 volumes could have a collection worth over £5,000,000 in outright replacement value, though replacement is not an option for archives and museums. The cumulative financial impact and asset loss, when considered, is potentially immense, even though the value of individual items may be low.

Service disruption to a library service can affect a very large number of people. In a higher education institution, although an incident affecting a single department has a significant impact on the staff, research groups and student body working within that department, researchers and students in other departments are unaffected. However, an emergency in the institution's main library has the potential to have an impact on everybody, disrupting the academic calendar immensely. When central organizations plan for crisis events, the focus is usually on incidents that affect people and IT first. It is crucial that those working in information services buildings ensure that their needs are high up on the agenda too. It may also come to light that in the event of a major local emergency, your building will be commandeered as a shelter – which would be useful to know in advance, so that appropriate arrangements can be made to secure collections in that event.

Seek the input of those responsible for central response plans into drafting your own. Their input may assist in providing you with pre-approved contractors and procedures that otherwise would have had to be generated anew. It is often helpful to format your document in a style close to the standard format of the central plan and your general corporate style, as it will thus appear more credible.

Inevitably in small-scale incidents where central incident plans are not invoked there is a reliance on facilities departments. As discussed elsewhere, the quality of the relationship with facilities staff can have a direct impact on the extent and quantity of damage that occurs. Persistence may be required to achieve the minimum response time to deal with incidents such as leaks. It is often helpful to involve facilities managers in your Emergency Management Team training as it fosters mutual understanding and builds a good relationship between all involved, which may lead to a better attitude to preventive work.

The conservator at a university library in the UK described a training session with facilities staff:

> In one particular training session, which had been cancelled twice as the facilities section had not turned up, there was a moment when the penny dropped and the two facilities officers realised that the contents of the entire five-storey building could not be replaced and would need to be removed and restored even after a fire. Their entire attitude to emergency response and prevention has been profoundly changed since that day.

Christine Willoughby, Head of Planning and Resources at the University Library at Northumbria University, has established excellent relationships with security services, who are pivotal to the effectiveness of the library staff's emergency response:

> We have a great set of security staff we've worked closely with over 24/7

opening and they now seem to appreciate the importance of the Library for students. We've recently had four drain blockages and they have worked really hard to get problems fixed, get the water board out and arrange alternative toilet facilities so that 24/7 opening could continue safely. This included bringing staff in to keep another building accessible overnight. I guess it's just talking to them and supporting them also, saying thank you. They are very focused on student services and very supportive, from their manager downwards.

In incidents of multiple damage sites, there will be a pecking order over how resources are allocated. It is critical that libraries, archives and museums lobby to be as high on that list as possible.

Another point of note is that if you share your building with another department or an external agency, you should consider how access routes, facilities and buildings management, and insurance will work if there is an incident. Naturally your neighbours will be concerned about their own business needs, and not yours. If this constrains the salvage operation, it is better to know in advance so that contingencies can be arranged. List the contact details for any people with whom you share your building in your contacts directory.

Continuous improvement

A plan should never be considered as final. Staff change, collection priorities may shift, business continuity objectives alter as the organization changes. Training and perhaps real incidents may throw up issues with the plan, which may necessitate alterations and tweaks to make information clearer or rectify glitches in the plan. Declan Kelly from the Church of England Record Centre recounts their learning points after a flood: 'The disaster kit was all stored at the back of the warehouse so was inaccessible, but [it] has now been moved, and improved, [so there are] torches by all warehouse entrances.'

Review your plan periodically, at least annually, given the potential for changes to personnel and contact information such as telephone numbers for staff and suppliers. Make clear in the plan who is to conduct the review and where suggestions should be addressed. When you review and reissue the plan impose a system of version control and document numbering, then recall previous copies and destroy them.

CHAPTER 11
Conclusion

The bizarre feature of emergency planning and its surrounding training is that an organization hopes never to have to implement its content in a real situation that threatens people, collections, the building or the business, despite all the hard work invested in the creation of the document. As threats to collections can never be minimized absolutely, a residual risk will always remain and so emergency planning is required. Effective emergency planning should ensure that the response to any such incident operates as efficiently as possible.

The book has demonstrated information that institutions globally have found useful when responding to heritage and information services collections under threat of damage, or wished that they had had in hindsight. If this emergency plan information is presented well, and colleagues are familiar with how to use and navigate the document, it should be extremely useful in a real incident. Having suggested formats for forms, content for salvage guidance notes and suggestions on how roles and responsibilities may be allocated, this should provide a useful point of comparison to any institution reviewing its existing plan or an institution starting from scratch. The most important aspects from practical disaster recovery experience are to ensure that staff are clear on their role and clear on what they are authorized to do if incident control is to operate smoothly.

Every library, archive and museum is different. A bespoke plan must be crafted for each institution, working on the basis of formats suggested within this book and templates from other comparable institutions, but developed into something fully reflecting the dynamics of the individual institution. It may be tempting to copy another institution's document but such plans rarely work effectively.

Training is key. A plan may have very good content, but if those implementing it lack familiarity or confidence in its content, the plan will not deliver operational effectiveness. Regular training will deliver real results if your plan has to be implemented in real situations. Dealing with real disasters is not easy. It involves compromise, dealing in least worst options, physically demanding work, difficult working environments, stress and the upset of seeing a collection in real peril. Emergency planning makes the process easier though, enabling timely and organized salvage so that the inevitable recovery operation is completed as quickly as possible, minimizing the impacts on people, the collection, the buildings and the service.

Bibliography and references

British Standards Institute (2006) BS 25999-1:2006 Part 1, *the Code of Practice*, The British Standards Institute.

British Standards Institute (2006) BS 25999-2:2007 Part 2, *the Specification*, The British Standards Institute.

Business Continuity Institute (2010) *Business Continuity Institute Good Practice Guidelines*, The Business Continuity Institute.

Child, R. E. (2011 [2004]) *Mould*, The Preservation Advisory Centre, British Library, www.bl.uk/blpac/pdf/mould.pdf.

Dadson, E. (2011) *Emergency Planning Template*, Harwell Document Restoration Services, www.hdrs.co.uk/templateplan.html.

Dorge, V. and Jones, S. L. (1999) *Building an Emergency Plan: a guide for museums and other cultural institutions*, The Getty Conservation Institute.

Health and Safety Executive (2011) *Five Steps to Risk Assessment*, The Health and Safety Executive, www.hse.gov.uk/pubns/indg163.pdf.

Health and Safety Executive (2011) *Getting to Grips with Manual Handling*, The Health and Safety Executive, www.hse.gov.uk/pubns/indg143.pdf.

Hiles, A. (2011) *The Definitive Handbook of Business Continuity*, Wiley.

Matthews, G. and Eden, P. (1996) *Disaster Management in British Libraries: project report with guidelines for library managers*, Library and Information Research Report 109, The British Library.

Matthews, G., Smith, Y. and Knowles, G. (2009) *Disaster Management in Archives, Libraries and Museums*, Ashgate.

Mitchell, L. (2006) *Mould & Fungi*, BDMA Information Sheet 131, The British Damage Management Association, www.bdma.org.uk/Technical/Papers/Mould.

National Taskforce on Emergency Response (1997) *The Emergency Response and Salvage Wheel*, Federal Emergency Management Agency.

National Trust (2006) *Manual of Housekeeping*, Elsevier.

Pachauri, R. K. and Reisinger, A. (eds) (2007) *Climate Change 2007: Synthesis Report. Contribution of Working Groups I, II and III to the Fourth Assessment*

Report of the Intergovernmental Panel on Climate Change,
www.ipcc.ch/publications_and_data/ar4/syr/en/spms3.html.

Pickles, D. (2010) *Flooding and Historic Buildings*, English Heritage,
www.english-heritage.org.uk/publications/flooding-and-historic-
buildings/flooding-and-historic-buildings-2nd-ed.pdf/.

Richford, S. (2008) *BDMA Official Training & Reference Manual: damage
management*, The British Damage Management Association.

UNESCO, The Radenci Declaration, adopted at the Blue Shield Seminar on
the Protection of Cultural Heritage, Radenci, Slovenia, 12–16 November
1998.

Walsh, B. (2003) *Salvage Operations for Water Damaged Archival Collections: a
second glance*, Canadian Council on Archives,
www.cdncouncilarchives.ca/salvage_en.pdf/.

Index